THE SAGA OF FRIDTJOF NANSEN

FRIDTJOF NANSEN

THE SAGA OF
FRIDTJOF NANSEN

BY JON SÖRENSEN

TRANSLATED FROM THE NORWEGIAN BY
J. B. C. WATKINS

NEW YORK
THE AMERICAN-SCANDINAVIAN FOUNDATION
W. W. NORTON & COMPANY, INC.
PUBLISHERS

PRINTED IN THE UNITED STATES OF AMERICA

CONTENTS

ILLUSTRATIONS

EDITORIAL NOTE

JON SÖRENSEN is a Norwegian educator whose personal acquaintance with Fridtjof Nansen came about through their mutual love of outdoor life and their faith in its educational value. His admiration for the achievements of the man, whose personality he thus came to know more intimately, inspired him with the desire to write the biography of his great countryman, and when Nansen's Norwegian publisher, Jacob Dybwad, planned to celebrate Nansen's seventieth birthday by issuing a biography of him, Jon Sörensen was entrusted with the task of writing it. The plan was submitted to Nansen, who gave his approval of the book at its inception.

When Fridtjof Nansen died without having attained the age of three score and ten, the scope of the projected biography was extended, and *The Saga of Fridtjof Nansen* now appears as a full and authoritative account and interpretation of his life and character. Mr. Sörensen has not only made diligent use of Nansen's voluminous printed works, but has had access to much material not before available. The family of Dr. Nansen have placed at his disposal unpublished diaries and letters from which he has been allowed to quote. In addition he has had the support and collaboration of the men most closely associated with Nansen in the several phases of his eventful life, among them the artist, Erik Werenskiold, his friend and neighbor for many years; Professor Björn Helland-Hansen, his collaborator in his scientific work; Professor Jacob Worm-Müller, an authority on the history of Norway in 1905; Minister J. Irgens, Secretary of the Legation in London while Nansen was Norwegian Minister to England; Consul General Wilhelm Morgenstierne, Secretary of the Nansen Commission in Washington; and Major Vidkun Quisling, his co-worker in the Russian Relief.

H. A. L.

THE SAGA OF
FRIDTJOF NANSEN

FRIDTJOF NANSEN

"IF ANYONE should be tempted to believe in a guiding Genius allotted to him by fate, I should," wrote Fridtjof Nansen in a letter of March 30, 1885. "So often, just at the critical moments of my life, such strange events have occurred, seeming to point out the way."

It was the will of this Genius that the rich gifts which were laid on his cradle should come to full fruition and application. When we survey his career, now that his life is ended, we cannot but see that his Genius held a protecting hand over the many daring steps of his active life right up to the moment when, gently and painlessly, it stilled his heart as he sat in the sun on a balcony of his home, looking down at the blossoms which lay like a fall of snow on the trees in the garden below.

This iron-willed man, whom one would obviously call the architect of his own fortunes, did not, as he looked back over his life, feel himself to be any such master builder. The proud self-confidence of his youth gave way to a humble feeling of gratitude to a Genius for the rich gifts that he had received and the deeds that he had been able to perform. Nevertheless he was no Aladdin. He had to win his victories by severe training and hard work, by an indomitable power of never giving up, which, according to Carlyle, is the mark and condition of genius.

He sometimes felt in his later years that there was a lack of unity in his career: he had advanced along so many paths. Yet he accomplished great things in every one of them—as zoologist, as oceanographer, as explorer of the polar regions and as such the greatest pathfinder of all time; in Norwegian politics at its most fateful hour, and finally in world politics as the Good Samaritan of the World War, the great apostle of reconciliation.

His Genius, more clear-sighted than he himself, did not grant him the repose and happiness of absorption and concentration within one sphere. It bore him off from field to field, thinking first and foremost not of him but of where the greatest need lay.

He finally came to realize that this same Genius had staked out his whole pathway through life, that however devious the road might seem to him, it nevertheless led him where necessity met and called forth his greatest, his noblest powers. He was chosen to lead a life filled with great deeds.

Just when it seemed to him that he was being torn away from his own particular field—the scientific research which was his life work—when Mr. Philip Noel Baker came as an envoy from the League of Nations to persuade him to reconsider his refusal, he was in reality being called to perform a greater service to humanity. It was something more than the mere lending of a world-renowned name from a neutral country to enable the League of Nations to carry out its work of international relief, something grander even than the saving of millions of human lives. Nansen lifted up the standard for a new age, an old standard, downtrodden and bloody, the standard of an army of a thousand defeats, a dauntless army; and the voice of Nansen raised its battle-cry:

"We must kindle our beacons till their light streams from every mountain-top. We must hoist our banner in all countries, must encircle the world with a chain of brotherhood; the governments must join hands with us in honest labor for the new era. Never has suffering and erring mankind longed more ardently for the Prince of Peace, for the men who hear His call, for the leaders of humanity who raise up the white banner on which the one word *Work* shines forth in golden letters. Each one of us can enlist in that army, and join its victorious progress through the world to inaugurate a new creation—to bring in brotherly love and an honest wish for peace, to restore to mankind the will to work and the joy in work; to give back to men their faith in the dawn of a better day."

Against the dawn of a new day the figure of Nansen looms larger and clearer as time passes.

THE FAMILY TREE

THE FAMILY tree's first hint of what is in store is the famous burgomaster of Copenhagen in the years 1658 and 1660, Hans Nansen, born in Flensborg. Not only is he the great ornament of the family tree, but he has been bodily resurrected in his great descendant whose disposition and career are strikingly similar to his.

At the age of sixteen we find Hans Nansen on his uncle's ship in the White Sea. This was, in those days, a really hazardous voyage, which might be the cause of anxiety enough to those at home as well. Scarce of maps, most probably entirely without them, the voyagers were not much better off for instruments. Cannon and broadswords had always to be kept in readiness. Twice they were overhauled and plundered by the English. The winter in Kola the boy turned to good account by learning Russian, and the next summer, when his uncle turned his bows in the direction of home, Hans did not go along. He wanted to travel farther. All alone, he set out across Russia and finally reached Copenhagen by sea in September. A restless boy was Hans, bold and eager for knowledge.

When only twenty years old, he was commissioned by King Christian IV to lead an expedition for furs to the regions about Petschora. The ice forced him to winter a second time in Kola. While here he received a message from the Czar of Russia asking him to explore the coast of the White Sea, and not until he had reached Archangel did he again board his own ship.

He remained in the service of the Icelandic Company for eighteen summers, and was director of the company for another ten years.

A born leader, Hans Nansen had the explorer's urge to investigate and observe, to make notes and to supplement them by reading. One day, as he was looking over his "extracts and registers," it occurred to him that others too might derive pleasure and profit from reading them, and so "for their use, I have had this short extract printed."

Hans Nansen's *Compendium Cosmographicum* (1633) contained physics, geography, chronology, directions for measuring the altitude, tables of flood and ebb tides, marine charts, the declination of the sun and stars, etc. An extremely useful book of reference, it became a regular institution, with edition after edition, and it has done service right down to comparatively recent times. A copy in the possession of the Nansen family has an inscription on the cover written by a skipper who sailed by it: "This book is of great use to seafarers.—*Ole Börgersen Aas.* 1841."

Hans Nansen was both a scholar and a man of affairs, and he had acquired his knowledge by his own efforts. He mastered German, English, Russian, Dutch, Swedish, and Icelandic and was an excellent speaker and writer. Determined in character, he was brusque and authoritative, a commanding figure; big and powerful, kind-hearted and true, and in good company the gayest of the gay.

At the age of forty the arctic skipper was given a bigger ship to steer—the citizenry of Copenhagen. He became alderman, then one of the four burgomasters, and during the critical years when the Fatherland's very existence was bound up with the fate of the capital, chief burgomaster.

This was the time when the Swedish King, Karl Gustav, broke his agreement and landed in Zealand. On that February night when his white-clad storming party descended upon Copenhagen, they met a transformed city, with new moats and new walls, against which the dreaded warrior king, with an army that had smelt powder in at least thirty battles, beat his head in vain.

Hans Nansen was the soul of the defence, on the walls and in the city. He provided for everything: supplying the city with food and weapons, quartering soldiers and thousands of fugitives, drilling and commanding the citizens. He transformed an open, defenceless, despairing town into a fortress. But its sturdiest wall was the will to victory which flowed out from the bold burgomaster through the whole defence from the royal pair down to the boys at the pitch cauldrons behind the walls.

Later, during the political revolution, he was again on the quarterdeck, the resourceful and intrepid leader of the burgesses in the struggle for their liberties and rights against the prepotent nobility. He succeeded in uniting the citizens and the clergy, and struck the decisive blow against the power of the aristocracy when he offered the King the hereditary sovereignty.

The famous meeting between nobleman and citizen on the castle bridge took place the next day. Otto Krag pointed furiously at Blaataarn, the sullen prison: "Do you know what that is?" Nansen raised his arm towards the tower of Frue Church: "Do you see what hangs there?" There hung the tocsin which called the citizens to arms. When the nobles, at the Riksdag which was convoked, were about to spoil the game completely for the citizens and the King by fleeing from the city by night, Nansen blocked all the gates with a strong watch.

He later became president in Copenhagen, royal councillor, and judge of the supreme court. Vigilant, resourceful, resolute, and inflexible, he was magnificently like his great-great-great-great-grandson.

From his mother Fridtjof Nansen inherited the blood of the Wedels.

The first Wedel came to Denmark just after the establishment of the absolute monarchy in 1660. A younger brother, General Gustav Wilhelm von Wedel, bought, in 1683, the earldom of the famous statesman Peter Griffenfeldt at Tönsberg in Norway, which was at that time united with Denmark. The old royal domain of Sem was called Jarlsberg; Gustav Wilhelm Wedel became Count of Jarlsberg and later commander-in-chief of the Norwegian army, when he directed the building of fortifications along the Swedish border. His father had been leader of a cavalry regiment in the Thirty Years' War under the Swedish general, Banér, and had won for himself the nickname of "Dare-devil."

The same name is eminently suitable for several members of the family. The Count of Jarlsberg's grandson followed the war-path in Italy, Spain, and Morocco. His great-grandson was the well-known statesman of 1814, Norway's Prime Minister and Viceroy, Count Herman Wedel Jarlsberg. A splendid specimen of a man, he was happiest when in danger of his life—at sea on black, stormy nights when, during the years of war and famine, he crossed over to Jutland in an open boat to buy corn for the starving Norwegians; or when, on his own responsibility, he steered Norway's finances through turbulent seas with daring strokes, staking his own life at the same time, and, summoned before the High Court of the realm to answer for his audacious conduct, was brilliantly acquitted. A fearless, reckless fellow, a man, a leader of men!

In 1814 we see him come hobbling in on his crutches to the hall at Eidsvoll on one of the Constituent Assembly's great days of battle. Early afflicted and finally broken by the gout, he died on a journey to a watering-place abroad. Norway brought her chieftain home on a battle ship.

A younger brother of this Count Herman Wedel Jarlsberg was Baron Christian Frederik Wilhelm of Fornebo, and his daughter was Fridtjof Nansen's mother, Adelaide Johanne Isidore Wedel Jarlsberg.

The male line of the Nansen family came to Norway with Ancher Antoni Nansen who in 1761 became district judge in Ytre Sogn. He married a Miss Leierdahl and their only son,

Hans Leierdahl Nansen, was a member of Norway's first extraordinary Storthing. He acquiesced in the union with Sweden, but with sharply defined reservations that in all cases where community was not absolutely essential, Norway's independence and autonomy should be established in clear and unequivocal language, and that anything which might give the Swedes the slightest shadow of authority should be excluded from the Constitution.

He is described as a clear-headed man, upright and courageous, an ardent patriot, bold with tongue and pen, urbanely ironical. In the course of a debate as to where the Bank of Norway should be located, Judge Nansen parried the other not entirely disinterested proposals with his sly suggestion: "Egersund is a pretty little town, and that's where *I* live."

His second marriage was with a daughter of Möller, court printer in Copenhagen. She is described as "a woman of uncommon ability, highly educated, with literary interests, a wide knowledge of languages, and no inconsiderable gift of style." The grandson's pronounced interest in and love of art and literature, and his artistic powers which are revealed in his sketches and drawings, may derive, among other and more hidden sources, from his grandmother.

FATHER AND MOTHER. CHILDHOOD

FRIDTJOF NANSEN'S father, Baldur Fridtjof Nansen, was born at Egersund in 1817. He was a worthy man, industrious and exemplary in every respect. He succeeded, under the influence and stimulus of his able mother, in taking all his examinations with honors and became a soundly trained lawyer. He had none of the vivacious cleverness and extravagant humor of his brilliant ancestors; but a thoroughly refined, supremely courteous, and complaisant manner was so peculiarly distinctive of him that it always appears in the foreground of any estimate of his character. His work consisted mainly in handling money transactions and transfers of property. He enjoyed unlimited confidence.

Small and slight of build, he took no part in sports of any kind, nor was he in the least tempted to seek adventure in woods and mountains. In this respect he was the very opposite of those big, sturdy, out-of-door enthusiasts, his sons. However, he was not like the hen with the brood of ducklings. He was a wise, sensible, and kind father who understood his children. He allowed them to indulge freely in games and sports, but in matters of discipline he was stern and unyielding, a gentleman of the old school; and his strictness, tempered as it was by a discriminating and lenient nature, was recognized as the fond severity of a beloved father.

Baldur Nansen's first wife was the daughter of Major-General Sörensen, and sister to the wife of the poet, Bishop Jörgen

Moe. His second wife was Adelaide Johanne Isidore Wedel-Jarlsberg. She was a tall, vigorous woman, resolute and firm of character. Her first marriage with the son of a baker had been made in defiance of her noble father's wishes. Sport was not considered seemly for women at that time, but she flouted public opinion and took great delight in skiing. She was not afraid of any kind of work, dug in her garden like a man, and acted as tailor for her own boys until they were eighteen years old. There was nothing she could not do with her hands, and she did not spare them. She was an extraordinarily capable housewife, but in the midst of all her housework she found time to add to her knowledge and keep up her intellectual interests. History was her favorite study.

After their marriage the Nansens settled down on her estate, Store Fröen, then three kilometers north of the capital, but now a part of the city of Oslo. Here Fridtjof Nansen was born, October 10, 1861. The only other child of this union was a son, Alexander, a year younger than Fridtjof, and these two, with the children of the two former marriages, made a large family.

At a meeting of the Pedagogical Society at Oslo in 1900, Nansen paid a tribute to his father. "Personally," he said, "I am of a weak nature, but what character I have has come from my strict bringing up in my youth. The will and the character are often strengthened by severe treatment. Education must be a training in self-discipline. In this respect the example of the parents as well as of the teachers may be of tremendous significance. My father exercised a powerful influence on me. I recall a particular instance in illustration of this. On account of his health my father was advised to drink a glass of wine with his sandwich at the office in the forenoon. He kept this up for some time, and it did him good. But one morning when I was in the office with him, I noticed that he was no longer drinking his glass of wine. I asked the reason, and my father answered: 'I always noticed that I was in particularly good humor after the wine. This would not have been the case if it had not had a stimulating effect on me. I do not approve of the use of stimulants, so I stopped the wine.' I remember what an indelible impression this made upon me."

His luminous intelligence Nansen could not have got from his father; but his father did give him character, will, self-control, the ability to persevere in training and in work, judgment and prudence, patience, a sense of duty in small things as well as great, and the integrity and sensitiveness that characterized his work as Good Samaritan in the wake of the World War.

Two letters, written after Fridtjof had left home, indicate clearly the relation between father and son and give a picture of the home life at Store Fröen. The first is dated September 4, 1882, when the son had become a curator in the Museum at Bergen, a month after his return from his first arctic trip in the *Viking:*

DEAR FRIDTJOF:

I am writing these lines to tell you something you certainly do not suspect. I miss you exceedingly, and the longing grows greater with every day. When you were away on the arctic trip I missed you, of course; but then I was always looking forward joyfully to our meeting again. I thought, the time will go quickly, God will be merciful and watch over him on his way, and once I have him back again, I can keep him with me so much longer. Then, too, my happiness and faith in the special value of the trip for your future bore me up. But now everything is so entirely different, now it is almost a separation for this life. It is going to be appallingly blank for your old father. But I must console myself just as I did during the arctic trip. People who really know about these things all insist that this position will be extremely helpful to you in getting ahead in the world and will ease the burden of your studies immensely.

The other letter is dated December 20, 1883.

MY DEAR OLD FATHER:

Christmas is drawing near, the first one that I shall not spend at home; that happy glorious Christmas time which to the childish soul seemed the culmination of all happiness, the summit of all earthly joy, and the inevitable emblem of eternal bliss whenever thought or tongue touched on the theme of the everlasting blessedness of immortality.

My thoughts fly silently homewards on their downy, melancholy wings towards all the bright Christmas memories surrounded by the peculiar glamour which always rests over a good and unspeakably dear childhood home where so many happy Christmases have been spent. How peaceful and solemn they always were! How softly and silently, Christmas, pure and white, snowed itself in! Great soft flakes fluttered gently down shedding a kind of seriousness over the childish soul even while it leaped and bounded in irrepressible glee.

At length the great day dawned—Christmas Eve. Now our impatience reached its height. We couldn't stay quietly in one place or sit still on our chairs for a single second. We had to be up and doing something to pass the time—to distract our thoughts. So off we would go tobogganing or skiing until dark. Sometimes it would happen that someone would have to make one last flying trip into town to do an errand or two before the candles were lighted. What fun it was to sit back in the cutter while it sped into town and back over roads that were perfect for sleighing, with the bells tinkling merrily and the stars sparkling in the dark sky!

At last the moment arrived. Father went in to light the tree. Our hearts thumped and leaped. Suddenly the doors were thrown open, and all the Christmas candles shone before our dazzled eyes. Ah, what a sight! We gasped for sheer joy. We were struck dumb and could not say a word for the first few minutes, only to burst out all the more wildly afterwards. No, indeed, I shall never forget those Christmas Eves as long as I live.

The reins of education in the Nansen home were held by firm and wary hands, which knew when to loose the bridle, take out the bit, and turn the young horse out to the woods in perfect freedom. Fridtjof soon became a hardy, self-reliant boy. His diet was plain and wholesome; bread and milk for breakfast, porridge and milk for supper. Sometimes the old servant Martha would give the boys a couple of sandwiches as a special treat.

Store Fröen at that time was a genuine farm with horses
and cows and pigs and chickens, with hills for skiing all around,
and just alongside it the Frogner river, then a fresh trout stream
with rapids and deep, secret pools. A more excellent home and
playground could hardly be imagined.

The house was beautifully situated, with the luxuriant Aker
valley stretching down in front towards the city and the fjord,
and best of all, the mighty forest of Nordmarka behind it.

The Nansen boys could thank their nearness to Nordmarka
for the fact that they became pioneers of outdoor life in woods
and mountains, just as the youth of Oslo today may thank this
stretch of deep forest so near the capital that they are deserving
in some measure of the reputation they have won as the boldest
and fittest young sportsmen in the world.

When Nansen was a growing boy, Nordmarka, now criss-
crossed with tracks in all directions, was virgin country, a wilderness with which the majority of city folk had no concern. Some
few had travelled vicariously in Asbjörnsen's *A Night in Nordmarka* and *The Haunt of the Capercailzie in Holleia*. Asbjörnsen made the scenery of Nordmarka the vivid setting of his fairy
tales and folk stories, and his and Bernard Herre's classical descriptions of natural scenery certainly did much to awaken the
feeling for nature in the growing generation. Two tow-headed
boys at Store Fröen sat many a winter evening with their noses
buried in Asbjörnsen until the forest seemed to surge right into
the very room with them.

But Fridtjof Nansen's relation to nature, right from his
boyhood days, was after all at first hand. For him, nature was the
arena for the training of his youth and for the exploits of his
manhood. It was the subject of his research, a rejuvenating foun-
tain for him all his life long, the sounding board of his soul, the
temple of his religion.

Besides its proximity to the wild forest, the Nansen home
had another advantage in that it was situated where the sons
could get their education at one of the best schools in Norway,

that of Aars and Voss in Christiania, now Oslo. A three kilo-
meter walk to school was not reckoned anything in this family
where excellent legs were inherited. In summertime an addi-
tional five kilometers to the fjord for the daily swim made a total
of sixteen a day all summer long; and usually there was a fight
with the Balkeby boys on the way home.

The customary wrangling before the battle, the exchange of
notes preliminary to the breach of peace, did not interest
Fridtjof, his brother tells us. He considered himself above that
sort of thing; but once the fight was on, he was in the thick of
it. Then, as later, he was somewhat curt and unceremonious
when he went into battle, and was not popular among diplomatists, and if he became really angry in his boyhood days he
was not to be trifled with. One time when the Balkeby boys,
using slings with stones in, struck his brother on the head, drawing blood, Fridtjof became furious and put the whole band to
flight. The Oslo boys' world of that day was like the European
states before war—always ready to settle differences with neighboring states by force of arms. They were not, however, actuated
by such ignoble motives as the desire for material gain, a place
in the sun, and so on, but by the sole and eternal and honorable
motive of boys at all times: the desire to fight and to win.

Out on the vacant lots between different sections of the city,
I have, as an Oslo boy of the eighties, seen grand battles between
troops of boys from the various neighborhoods, Rodelökka,
Sagene, Kampen, Enerhaugen, Vaalerenga, and the rest of those
suburbs that have sprung up sporadically on the outskirts and
gradually been included within the city limits. It might be quite
thrilling even in peace time for a boy to pass through a suburb in
which he was not at home. I have known what it was to be surrounded by twenty or thirty boys. It meant a good fight. The boy
who was a good fighter, skilful and tried, commanded respect
among the boys of Oslo. The battles of the Nansen boys with the
boys of Balkeby are, therefore, illustrative of a trend of contemporary history.

Those days are over now, owing less, I imagine, to the efforts of the strong arm of the law to keep the peace than to the sport movement, with all the new fields it has opened to the city boys, from the great Nordmarka and Östmarka to the many athletic fields within the city itself. The champion of peace from the League of Nations had, as the apostle of sport and its great example, a large part in the change.

There are many characteristic traits to recount from Nansen's childhood years. Some of these anecdotes he has told himself, some are from Alexander Nansen, his brother and closest companion, and some are from childhood friends and others.[1]

Fridtjof was, as might be expected, a precociously enterprising fellow; prudence was a later development. His Genius had its work cut out to hold a protecting hand over him.

At the age of three he was standing out in the yard in front of the kitchen window hammering on a wheel-barrow when Martha noticed that smoke was ascending from the boy. "The child's afire!" she shrieked and, running out, tore the clothes off his back. He had made a flying trip into the wash-house, where a spark from the open fireplace had lodged in his woolen petticoats, and he would certainly have been burned alive if the aforesaid Genius had not had Martha at hand.

As a little shaver of five Fridtjof had his first serious encounter with the ice. He struck his forehead on a rough sheet of ice in the yard, and the blood streamed down until there was not a white spot left on his face. He trotted quietly into the kitchen to Martha, but did not cry, and was anxious to avoid a scolding.

Once when he was fishing the hook caught in his lower lip. Without a murmur he allowed his mother to take the razor and resolutely cut it out.

When the period of hunting squirrels with bows and arrows gave way before the discovery of gun-powder, Fridtjof got hold

[1] Collected in Brögger and Rolfsen's book, *Fridtjof Nansen 1861-93*, long since out of print.

of a cannon and loaded it full of powder, but it missed fire. He then made a maroon and dug about in it until it went off in his face at the same time that the cannon flew into a hundred pieces. His mother had to come to the rescue again and pick out the grains of powder one by one.

Fridtjof's memory, which became so famous later, exhibited a characteristic weakness already in his boyhood; when a disagreement or quarrel was honestly and fairly settled, it was banished completely from his mind.

In the second class of the elementary school Fridtjof was the strongest boy in the class and went about as cock of the walk. Then a new boy, Karl, came. He was strong too. During recess he began hitting the other boys with a ball. "You mustn't do that!" said Fridtjof. "Oh, mustn't I?" answered Karl and hit him. Then they fought till they made the fur fly and the blood spurt. Mr. Aars, the head master, arrived on the scene and shut them both in an empty class-room. "Now, just sit here, you two, and look at each other, and feel ashamed of yourselves." Whether they felt ashamed is doubtful, but they looked at each other and began to talk. When Mr. Aars came back the two boys were sitting with their arms around each other's shoulders reading out of the same book. Henceforth Fridtjof and Karl [1] were inseparable.

When he was absorbed in anything, Fridtjof was oblivious to everything around him. He had a habit of falling into brown studies. There might be a prolonged interval between the first and the second stocking in the morning. Then the others would cry: "Look at old slow-poke again. You'll never amount to anything, boy, the way you dawdle along!"

He had to know all about everything. He would ask questions until his older friends were completely worn out with his eternal Why, Why, Why? When a sewing machine was brought to the house, it presented a problem which, of course, could only be solved by taking the whole machine to pieces. His mother re-

[1] Admiral K. Dawes.

turned from town just as he had finished, but the story goes that he did not give up until he had put the machine together again.

The Nansen boys got fifty öre a month pocket money, and it had to be strictly accounted for. Fridtjof was not more than eight years old when he and his brother were for the first time allowed to go alone to the fair.

Christiania Fair was in those days an event of such magnitude for the Christiania boy that when one of the city pastors asked a candidate for confirmation to name the church festivals, he replied: Christmas and Fair-day! It was held in the beginning of February, and crowds of people flocked into the city from the rural districts for all manner of trade and barter. At "Jongstörjet" were booths with merry-andrews and jugglers and strong men and there were counters full of toys and whole houses full of gingerbread.

Fridtjof and his brother were munificently supplied with money that day, provided by father and mother, grandmother, and aunt. They went right past all the jugglers and gingerbread and toys and laid all their money out in tools. This made such a good impression at home that they got the same appropriation a second time. They set out again and completed their collection of tools. With the four pennies that remained, they bought rye cakes at Hegdehaugen.

Fridtjof was clever at school; he took his intermediate school examination and his matriculation with high marks in history and science; in drawing and mathematics he had perfect. And still he had time to attend to his training in all sorts of sports, to take trips in Nordmarka, to use his tools, and to find answers to ever more difficult Whys.

In natural science, his favorite subject, it was necessary, of course, for him to perform experiments. He and Karl had, at the age of fifteen, got hold of a box containing pyrotechnical materials and a mortar. They were to be extremely careful with it. Consequently one evening they poured into the mortar the various liquids which they had in bottles and the nature of which they wanted to test by experiment. Their results were like those of the famous monk and his mortar. A spark fell into the mixture, the flames leapt to the ceiling. The investigators pitched the mortar out of the window, threw themselves flat down on the floor, and blackened their faces so that Fridtjof's brother, Alexander, would think they were dead when he arrived.

Like all half-grown boys, Fridtjof had his loves and fancies, and his faithful friend, Karl, likewise. They often joined in worshipping the same lady, on the same moonlight evenings, before the same windows in touching harmony. Healthy, unencumbered, and unspoiled, he passed through the years of adolescence.

His brother tells a story about his chivalry. One night as they were going home from a children's party in the city, they met a lady and her maid pursued by three men. "That's the girl for me," shouted one of the ruffians, and all three bolted after the women. "We'll have to help them," said Fridtjof, and with that the brothers attacked the superior force. Fridtjof got one of the roughs up against the fence, planted one fist on the chest of his antagonist, and with his other hand tore open his own coat. "Don't you know who I am?" he cried, pointing to the cotillion favors which sparkled in the moonlight. It worked. The two cavaliers were victorious, and the damsels in distress were rescued.

YOUTH AND OUTDOOR LIFE

NANSEN himself tells about his first ski and his first big jump: [1] "Of course I do not mean my very first ski. They were dreadfully poor, patched together from old ski that had belonged to my brothers and sisters. They were not even of the same length. But Mr. Fabritius, the printer, took pity on me. 'I'll get you a pair of ski,' he said. Then spring came and summer when even with the best will in the world one could not go skiing. But Fabritius's words kept singing in my ears, and no sooner had autumn come, with the hoar-frost on the fields in the morning, than I posted myself right in his way as he came driving by. 'I say, what about those ski?' 'You'll get them all right,' he said and laughed. But I was on the spot day after day: 'I say, what about those ski?'

"At last it was winter. I can still see my sister standing in the living room with a long, long parcel which she said was for me. . . . It was the ski from Fabritius. They were red lacquered ash ski with black stripes; and with them was a long stick with a gleaming blue lacquered shaft and blue lacquered disk. I used those ski for ten years. They were the ones I had on when I made my first big jump at Huseby Hill. It was there that the big skiing match used to be held. We were not allowed to go there, we brothers; we could go to all the other hills round about, but Huseby Hill was forbidden. We could see it from Fröen, and it tempted us until we could no longer resist. At first I started

[1] Nordahl Rolfsen: *Children's Christmas Tree.*

from the middle of the hill, like most of the other boys, and everything went well. But then I noticed that one or two were going from the top. I simply had to try that. Off I set, came at furious speed to the take-off, soared through the air for a long time, and then caught my ski fast in a snowbank. At that time we did not have bound ski. My ski remained sticking up in the snowbank and I cut an arc head first through the air. I was still going at such speed that when I came down again I bored into the snow to my waist. There was dead silence on the hill. The boys thought I had broken my neck. But when they saw that there was still life in me and that I was beginning to crawl out, interminable shouts of derisive laughter resounded from top to bottom of the hill.

"Some time later I entered a skiing competition at Huseby and won a prize. I did not take it home with me, however, for I was ashamed of myself this time too. It was the first time I had ever seen Telemark men on ski, and, of course, I realized at once that I was nowhere beside them. They used no sticks and dared to take off without having a thing to rely on but the strength of their muscles and the firm, lithe carriage of their bodies. I saw that this was the only proper way. I would accept no prize until I had mastered it."

WHILE he was still an apprentice in the new way of skiing, he took part in a school match. He jumped straight and true, with narrow gauge and without a stick, but stumbled and broke both ski, while his brother, who was still following a more conservative policy, took the first prize.

Nordmarka was the boy's training field and developed the feeling for nature that was such a marked feature in Nansen at all times. He practised especially those sports which can be pursued in the open—skating and skiing, fishing and hunting; and early proficiency in swimming stood him in good stead later

when he had to swim after the drifting kayaks in the Arctic
Ocean.

In after life he always sought recreation in nature and sport
when his work had kept him shut in too long. Prolonged devotion to sports in youth built up a reserve of strength, a solid
basis for work and enjoyment. Without this store of energy he
could never have withstood the tremendous pressure of work,
the superhuman demands on mind and nerves through so many
years.

When I met him for the last time in November, 1929, he
had just returned from a hunting trip; it was imperative for him,
he said, to get out to the woods and mountains, "Otherwise it
will be a poor lookout for my health." I reminded him of the
trip he made in 1884 across the high mountain plateau from
Bergen to Oslo and back again, all alone. He made the same trip
a second time at the age of fifty-five, and descriptions of both
expeditions are to be found in his wonderful book *Sporting Days
in Wild Norway*. He replied that next year, his seventieth, he
would make the trip for the third time; and indeed, he looked
as though he might.

Of his first fishing trip in Nordmarka, Nansen says: "Great
was the rejoicing as we set off with coffee-pot and fishing-rods to
live a pioneer life in the forest. Never shall I forget the days
we spent up there. I can still see before me the wooden hut on
the shore of Lake Langli with the long sweep of talus behind it
and the great monkshoods growing round the hut. There was
freedom up there and we could be savages to our heart's content. There was no father or mother to tell us when it was
bedtime or to call us in to meals. . . . The night was light and
long, and sleep was brief. At midnight or thereabouts we would
creep into the hut and lie down for a couple of hours on the
juniper branches; and long before the peep of day, we would
be down at the pool catching trout, wading in the river, skip-
ping about on the stones. . . . While I was still in my 'teens, I
used to pass weeks at a time alone in the woods. I disliked hav-

ing any equipment on my expeditions, and managed with a crust of bread and fish which I broiled myself on the embers. I loved to live like Robinson Crusoe up there in the wilderness."

Often, however, he went with his brother and an older relative who happened to be an enthusiastic huntsman and fisherman. From the age of twelve the Nansen boys were trained in Nordmarka, from spring till fall, from fall till spring, with stiffer and stiffer tramps.

"When the oak leaf is like a mouse's ear, the trout will jump for the fly." So every Saturday from about the end of May, as soon as they had gulped down their dinner, the three young fishermen would set off on a five hour hike. They took no time for rest or food, either on the way or at the river. As soon as they reached their goal, they got out their rods and cast away as long as it was light. At the darkest part of the night they took a nap for an hour or two in a log cabin or in the shelter of a tree or rock. Then to work again at dawn, often up to the waist in the river. The next night they trudged off home, their shoes full of sand and water, and tired to death; but with a few hours' sleep they were all right again, and the mess of trout on the kitchen table was capital. Next Saturday at three o'clock they would be off again.

The hikes became still longer when the boys grew big enough to go hare hunting at Krokskogen. One time the brothers stayed up at Fylling for eleven days hunting hare. Provisions ran short, and finally they had nothing left but potato cakes. Both they and their dog had to go hungry, but when the time came to go home Fridtjof had bagged seven hares and his brother six.

Whatever sport he indulged in, it was the outdoor life that made the strongest appeal to Nansen even as a boy. He was a first class skater, but ski were and continued to be his greatest love. His tall frame was no advantage to a jumper, and the proficiency which he nevertheless did attain in jumping was acquired only at the cost of persistent effort. In skiing matches it was the long distance running which gave him his surest points.

Fridtjof Nansen's connection with the Christiania Ski Club deserves some mention here. Deriving its importance from the prestige, rather than from the number, of its names, for the membership was limited to fifty, this club, founded in 1877, revived the sport of skiing in Norway. The founders had already for some time made a practice of coming together for skiing trips in Vestre Aker, and the meeting place was often the Nansen home, Store Fröen. Fridtjof had been present from the first moment. He and his brother, both school boys, were always allowed to go along on the trips, and at the age of twenty they became members. Bright and cheerful, fearless to the point of recklessness, and the best ski runner of them all—such did Fridtjof show himself to be in this circle of sportsmen, and he was heartily welcome there.

In 1879 the club, with the support of the central association, held the first national skiing match at Huseby Hill. The Christiania Ski Club gave the impetus to the formation of the National Ski Society in 1883 which then took over the big national matches.

Although the Christiania Ski Club has since led a more private existence, its members have helped to advance the sport in many ways, especially by force of personal example. The "Old Fellows" were not satisfied with Sabbatical ease in their cabin "Volden"; they went on long skiing trips in the high mountains of Jotunheimen and Rondane. The party of "Old Fellows" who crossed Jotunheimen on ski, in 1911, had an average age of fifty-eight. And summer and fall they went far afield fishing and hunting. These men realized the ideal of sport.

It was no small matter for the young Nansen to have won friends for himself among these mature sportsmen. He was encouraged by them in a great many ways, and has frequently acknowledged his debt to the Christiania Ski Club. Among the many and staunch friends he made there, we may mention particularly Thomas Fearnley, the ship-owner, and Consul Axel Heiberg, who became his lifelong friends. When the first *Fram* expedition was in preparation, it was Fearnley, Heiberg, and Ellef Ringnes who were the sponsors of the expedition. Thomas Fearnley was one of the original members of the club and its president for forty-three years, from 1884 until his death in 1927. Nansen, who after his Greenland expedition was honorary member of the club, on several occasions took the opportunity of pointing out publicly the services of the club and of Fearnley. Nansen's speech in honor of Fearnley at the celebration of the club on its fiftieth anniversary, in 1927, will never be forgotten by any who was present. He paid homage to the club and to President Fearnley, and pointed out how the club with the president at its head had shown the youth of the country the way out to the great forests and to the great open spaces. When Nansen finally turned to Fearnley and said: "Now stand up, old man, and accept our homage!" there was a tremendous ovation.

Nansen was a member of the Christiania Ski Club for forty-nine years; its ideals and example were after his own heart, and the club recognized in its famous honorary member the best man in Norwegian sport. In his later years he was so extremely busy that he visited Volden only occasionally. But to the celebrations of the club he came if it were at all possible, and among these comrades Nansen would be the life of the party.

In February, 1902, he attended the twenty-fifth anniversary at Volden. There were thirty men in the great hall, and it was a feast of memories. At nine o'clock in the evening entered a procession of youth, a band of thirty ski runners bearing torches with greetings from the younger ski clubs. After homage and thanks had been exchanged, Nansen took the stand. When Nansen's mind was stirred on such occasions and in such surroundings, the barriers fell away; a vision of Norway, the Fatherland, spread before his eyes and he spoke in moving words. All sixty of them sang the national anthem till the rafters rang.

Then the torches were lighted, and out over the hill went the procession, man after man over the take-off in the flaring light of the torches.

Nansen frequently expressed his views on sport. At a meeting of the Pedagogical Society at Oslo in 1910, he spoke of the real purpose of skiing: "Skiing has lost a part of its value owing to the fact that the competitive spirit has been allowed to dominate. The goal of all manly exercise should be, of course, the building up and strengthening of body and soul, and it should, at the same time, lead us out into the open. But many of our sportsmen have become mere muscle machines, race horses, bending all their strength and energy towards making records and getting in a few meters ahead of their competitors."

At the Norwegian Tourist Society's convention for school children in June, 1921, reported in the 1922 Year Book, Nansen told of how in his youth he could go on skiing trips in Nordmarka and return to find his own tracks two weeks later. While outdoor sports were advancing at quite a different pace now, he said, not everything in the modern development was desirable. There was too much emphasis on sport for sport's sake, losing sight of the fact that sport is not an end in itself, but a means to an end. Its true aim is the old one of a sound mind in a sound body.

"There is also another aspect of sport that has come too much to the fore, and that is the social aspect. It seems as though sport can no longer be carried on except in large parties. There must be clubs and societies and meets with continual gatherings in club houses and cabins. But an important part of outdoor sport should be, of course, the life in the out-of-doors, the escape from the many, from the eternal hubbub, the confusing din, to the world of nature, to the great open spaces. . . . The wise men of India said that every man should spend at least one hour of every day in solitude and devote it to meditation, to finding himself. The eternal whirlpool where men incessantly rub up against each other until they become round, smooth ciphers and men about town, is not qualified to develop individuality and character. In this noisy society, the young people are more or less drawn into a feverish round of pleasure. They never have time to stand face to face with themselves, no time to harken to the inner voices. Open air life becomes merely a new form for sociability. Pleasures and diversions we must have, but it is important to choose sensibly those which give lasting happiness and recreation.

"That which should compensate us and lead us back to a more natural human existence is and remains the simple outdoor life in wood and fell, on moor and heath, in the great solitudes, where new and larger ideas flow in on us and make marks that are not soon obliterated. It is in the wildernesses, in the solitude of the forest, within sight of the wide expanses, far from the madding crowd, that character is formed. And it is men of character that our age most sorely needs.

"Those who have experienced the free and unhampered life of the wilderness, independent of everything and everybody, do not readily turn back to the crowd. . . .

"Have you not slept many a night quite as well with moss for a couch and the carpet of stars for a canopy as in the softest hotel bed? And did you not waken feeling fresher in the gentle soughing of the woods in the breeze of the dawning day than you did in the clatter from a hotel kitchen? And then there is the training in relying on one's self, without being dependent on others, in being self-sufficient and looking after one's self under all circumstances. We learn that primitive joy in the simple, natural life from which we have now got away, and not least, the joy of contentment, of having the fewest possible wants— free as a bird under heaven.

"I can remember a time when I was very young, and it seemed to me that a box of matches and a fishing rod were about all the equipment one needed to spend several weeks out in the woods and fells.

"With the years this has been added to somewhat. But one

does not need very much to be an outdoor man: some food, a crust of bread, butter, a little cheese, some flour and condensed milk, a woolen blanket or a light sleeping bag, a pair of heavy stockings or puttees, a water-proof, a cooking utensil, and if one is to be out long, a tent that one can pitch one's self. Then maps and compass, and that is about all, you see, besides the box of matches and the fishing rod with which it is always possible to catch a few fish. And what pleasure a trip with such an outfit can give one!

"Should not the ideal for the Norwegian youth of the future be the friend of nature, the sportsman, the free, independent man who knows what he wants, with hardened will and hardened body, who knows himself, his people and his country, making the greatest demands on himself and the fewest on his surroundings?"

This ideal for the youth of the future, exemplified in Nansen's own figure, was not, in 1880, typical of the sons of alma mater. Stamped by a life of sport and outdoor life from his boyhood days, Nansen stood out from the ordinary in stature, and in dress. He was exceptionally tall, six feet, straight and slender; taut, swift, and strong; agile and elastic in his movements. He usually wore sporting clothes: a tight fitting suit which set off his powerful, slim, lithe body. He never wore an overcoat. Fairhaired and fair-skinned, he was a pronouncedly Germanic type, but his face, long with large, open features, was weatherbeaten and tanned. His head was not purely dolichocephalic, a mixture rather. In later years as he grew bald and his face became thinner, his skull seemed still larger, the seat of a mighty brain. His voice was deep, resonant, and powerful. His eyes were greyish blue in color, strong, expressive, and changeful: now hard as steel, now bright and beaming, sometimes veiled and dreamy, and again mild and tender as when he was talking to children. And the intellectual equipment contained in this mould was equally great. It often happens that genius is limited to a single sphere; it is often purchased at the expense of under-development in other fields. Nansen's endowment of genius consisted in the large total of many great abilities and in the balance and harmony among them. An all round man both in mind and body, he recalls the versatile geniuses of the Renaissance with whom, indeed, he has often been compared.

Still another trait: although he, less than anyone, set out to make friends, no one who came near him could help delighting in his company.

The artist, Erik Werenskiold, his friend and neighbor, has frequently drawn and painted him, from his youth to his death bed. These pictures of Werenskiold's, so characteristic of Nansen in various moods, give us in sum the Nansen whom nobody knew better than he.

THE FIRST SIGHT OF THE ARCTIC SEA

IN 1880 Nansen matriculated from the technical high school with a high aggregate, and the next year entered the University where he took up the study of zoology. His scientific interests were very broad, and later in life he sometimes regretted that he had not made physics or mathematics his specialty, for both these subjects attracted him. When instead he chose zoology, it was largely because he hoped that his work in this field would take him out into the open. Actually it was this choice that gave him his initiation into arctic exploration through his first northern trip, which opened his eyes to the Greenland problem and led to his later investigation of the polar basin and his achievements in the field of oceanography.

Professor Robert Collett, knowing, of course, that Nansen was a clever hunter and sportsman, advised the future zoologist to accompany a sealer up to the Arctic Ocean and obtain his first experience there as a research student in descriptive natural science, making observations and notes on wind and weather, sea and ice, and animal life. Provided with all sorts of equipment and instructions for his scientific work, Nansen installed himself on board the *Viking*, a large new sealing vessel putting out from Arendal under the command of Captain Krefting. The *Viking* stood out in the sound off the Torunger islands just as the sun was rising on March 11, 1882. Nansen gazed back regretfully at the islands and capes and cliffs, golden in the rays of the sun.

This would be the first spring that he would not paddle

in and out among the islets and skerries to welcome the birds
on their flight northwards, the first spring that he would not
hear the blackcock screaming and the cuckoo calling in the
great forest.

His heart ached within him.

But now a new and even greater adventure was luring him

WAVES WASHING OVER THE DECK
Drawing by Nansen

on: the sea and, away in the far north, the world of ice. And
the sea gave him an impressive reception. Filling full her bel-
lows, she trod out a mighty fugue on the pedals of her great
organ, an overture worthy the entry of a Fridtjof Nansen into
the world of ice.

For seven days and nights of furious tempest, they ploughed
through the heaving billows of the northern sea. They rushed
madly onwards past an abandoned wreck. Gigantic waves tum-

bled like mountains over the ship. They reeled till the main-yard snapped.

Nansen, who never became a good sailor, suffered the agonies of seasickness for five days. Then it wore off, and he was able to hurry out on deck in great excitement at the first cry of: Ice ahead! Everything was blackest night. Then suddenly something large and white shot out of the darkness, intensely white against the jet black sea. More sheets followed, gliding past with the waves swishing over them. Others ran up against the vessel and were tilted endwise, thrust aside, or crushed under the strong bow. The ship careened and lurched so that one had to hold on for dear life not to be knocked head over heels. Far to the northwards Nansen became aware of a strange illumination, brightest near the horizon, mysterious and ghostly, like the light of a distant fire. It was the ice sky, the reflection from the mist over the ice fields. And the boom of the meeting between ice sheet and sea filled the air far out to sea and far in over the ice.

The elements of arctic scenery are few but impressive: the ice, the sea, the sky. Similarly with animal life, the species are few, but the individuals within the species are myriad.

This arctic scenery, with its limited but powerful range, captivated the young man's sensitive feeling for nature, particularly the play of light on air, ice, and sea. In his *Hunting and Adventure in the Arctic* he writes: "The northern sky is a radiant bath of colors, now bright with the reflection from the ice, now darker over the open water, now red with the glow of the sun, now more golden where the red blends with the light from the snow. Low purple clouds, yellow rimmed. Higher up, pale green shading into the pale blue of space. Round about, the white floes drift across the smooth, dark surface of the water. Close at hand they have shapes and colors, here greenish down through the water, there verging into blue at the edges and in the fissures; in some places ultramarine in the deep chasms that the sea has eaten out underneath the hummocks.

"They are so unreal, so delicate and pure, these colors. But in towards land is the endless expanse of drifting ice, and out towards the sea the endless dark surface of the water.

"A solitary white gull wings lightly through the great luminous space, a blue gull hovers afar off, uttering its long-drawn, melancholy, flute-like note. The big black head of a seal rises noiselessly above the glossy surface of the water, stares round-eyed at the ship, then pointing its snout skywards, sinks down again just as noiselessly.

"This is indeed the realm of infinite solitude. All the work of man vanishes like the track of a ship through the ice."

Here in the region of the drift ice, northeast of Jan Mayen Land, the seals congregate at the breeding grounds. The arctic current that goes southward along the east coast of Greenland sends an arm over to the east. This arm carries the drift ice out in a point to the northeast of Jan Mayen Land, the "Point," the sealers call it. In the ocean between Jan Mayen and Spitzbergen the warm North Atlantic Drift flows in like a whirlpool from the coast of Norway forming the Great Bight to the north of the Point. It is to the nucleus of the Point that the seals usually resort to breed. The location of both point and bay may vary considerably, however, from year to year. It is important to get there while the young have only their soft under coat, because they do not like to go in the water then and may be clubbed down by the thousands. The adults usually have to be shot. It is essential to shoot them stone dead with one shot, for if one of them goes into the sea, the others all follow. The skin with the blubber is removed; the rest is left as food for bears and birds, Greenland sharks and grampuses.

For weeks the *Viking* cruised round without finding the rookeries. They encountered storm and tempest. It was like a dance of death between ice floes and waves. Krefting was a dare-devil sailor.

But on one such day when the vessel was pitching and tossing under the combined assaults of storm and ice so that the mastheads cut long arcs, Krefting himself was frightened when he saw Nansen clambering down from the crow's nest.

On Sunday, March 26, somebody announced: "A sail to the leeward!" It was the famous *Vega,* which three years before had taken the Swedish explorer, Nordenskiöld, through the Northeast Passage. She was now engaged in sealing and a fair sight she was, as she lay there with her high, slender rigging darkly outlined against the cloudy sky where the moon was just breaking through.

Nansen stood looking at the famous ship for a long time. He tells about it in his book *Hunting and Adventure in the Arctic* (1924), though without revealing what he thought and dreamed. But seven years after this encounter Nansen stood before the Swedish Anthropological and Geographical Society in Stockholm and received from King Oscar the Vega medal. This was on the completion of his Greenland expedition.

On May 2 they sighted Spitzbergen, and by the 25th reached Iceland where they made a brief landing. Finally after five weeks they struck the rookery. And now all hands were busy day and night. The scientist was transformed into a seal hunter and soon showed himself as sure and quick a man with a rifle as any of them. Before long he was made leader and gunner on one of the largest sealing boats. The records of the catch from day to day show that Nansen's boat was one of the best and often the very best. His prowess won him the respect of the crew.

This learned youth with all his curious contraptions, glasses, and instruments, and dip-nets that hung along the side of the ship and came up filled with all sorts of filthy stuff over which he would pore all day long with the microscope, was at the same time the best seal hunter and boat leader and the boldest arctic seaman of them all.

He was popular with the crew. He used to sit in the forecastle chatting with them far into the night. This cruise of 1882 always shone with a peculiar lustre in the memories of these arctic seamen afterwards: That was the time they were on "the Nansen trip."

At the end of June they froze fast in the ice and drifted down with it towards Greenland, then southwards along the coast of Greenland until on July 17 they got free and sailed home. This long delay meant a big loss for the company, but for Nansen it was a glorious time. Now he had a chance to satisfy his appetite for polar bear hunting. In his diary, and later in the *Norwegian Sporting News* for 1883 and in his book *Hunting and Adventure in the Arctic,* he has given vivid descriptions of these bear hunts.

The man in the crow's nest would cry: "Bears to the leeward!" In the morning in his berth somebody would shout in his ear: "Better turn out. There's a bear right beside the ship."

One evening as he was sitting in the crow's nest painting the glacier coast of Greenland, the watch shouted: "Oh, look at the bear!" There it was right under the bow. Nansen slid down the rope so fast that it burned his hands, and dashed in for his gun. But the bear was gone. The captain teased him: "You're a fine fellow to have in the crow's nest, can't even see a bear when he's sitting right under the bow!" But four days later Nansen redeemed himself. It was the last bear hunt.

Three men set out after a huge bear who was hobbling off as fast as he could go. Nansen, as usual, was more lightly clad than the others, in gym shoes and a woolen sweater, without a coat. At a stretch of open water the others went round, but Nansen made a leap for it. The ledge broke, he plunged in, swam across, and threw his gun up on the ice. It slid back into the water, he dived for it, threw it farther in, and swam to a lower ledge. A quick inspection of his rifle and ammunition, and he was away. Rounding a hummock, he came upon Master Bruin, who, leaping aside, got the shot in his back, jumped into the water, and swam away, keeping far down below the surface. Nansen had to cross the open water to be ready for

him on the other side. Landing with a broad jump on one of
two small floes in the middle of the space, he tottered a moment,
regaining his balance just as the bear popped up beside the
other floe and jumped up on it, roaring. The next moment
meant life or death. But Nansen was too quick for him, the
shot burnt into his breast, and Nansen, grabbing him by the

BALANCING ON AN ICE FLOE AS THE BEAR STICKS ITS HEAD
OUT OF THE WATER
Drawing by Nansen

lugs before he had time to sink, held him up until help arrived.
   The captain ordered him back to change, for he was, of
course, wet through. But as he was nearing the *Viking* he caught
sight of two riflemen out after three bears. They wounded one
of them, and it started off. Now it was Nansen's turn. He pursued
and felled it, and started after the next one. This race was
always recounted with great gusto by the men of the *Viking*
afterwards. The heavily clad men were soon outdistanced, and

Nansen and the bear were alone. The one ran for his life, the other for his honor. Away they went over floes and lanes and open water. Where the open water was too broad to jump over, Nansen plunged in and swam across. On they raced mile after mile, but when they had done four or five miles the bear's speed began to slacken. Nansen closed in on him and felled him with two shots.

There he was with a dead bear, a rifle without ammunition, and a penknife as his only weapon. He set to work with the penknife to skin the bear, and had almost finished when Oluf came up. Together they dragged the pelt with the blubber back to the ship—a heavy burden. They were met on the way by an embassy from the captain bringing them beer and food. It tasted wonderful. That was the last hunt.

On July 26 Norway emerged from the sea. "Surely the mountains of Norway are lovelier than all others, especially when they rise up thus out of the sea!" he writes. The next day they cast anchor in the harbor of Arendal, and the *Viking's* first and Nansen's first arctic voyage was ended.

That night the men of the *Viking* painted the town of Arendal red. When Krefting and Nansen came out of the club with the chief constable, the crew were busy throwing the town constables into the sea because, unlike the police of Tönsberg and Sandefjord, these fellows had no proper sense of the privileges which should be accorded to newly landed arctic seamen. While they stood there trying to make peace, Nansen relates, one of the crew compared the speed of the constables' retreat with Nansen's race for the bear, saying that Nansen ran fast, but the constables ran faster.

Nansen, on parting, gave the crew this fair character: "What good-natured fellows our Norwegian sailor lads are at bottom, when they are the right sort! Living with them both in storm and stress and in fair weather, one learns to appreciate their warm-heartedness. A stauncher or more unselfish comrade does not exist—he will give you the very shirt off his back if you need it, and will gladly risk his life for you if you are in danger. But if they get excited and begin to run amuck, there is no knowing where they will stop; though even then their latent sense of humor is always ready to flash out like a ray of light through the storm clouds."

It was hard to part from Krefting—"he was a staunch, gallant fellow, an able and fearless Norwegian seaman and arctic voyager, a good friend." The friendship and influence of this splendid captain were perhaps not the least important benefits of the *Viking* trip.

Then, too, the Arctic Ocean itself had taken possession of his mind with all the magnetic power of its beauty and wildness, its riddles and problems. The coast of Greenland, along which they spent those twenty-four days, was to the others a death's causeway strewn with horrors from all the sealers crushed in the ice, but to Nansen it was the proscenium to the land of adventure. The peaks and glaciers which no human foot had ever trod lay glistening beyond the drift ice. "In the evening and at night, when the sun on his celestial journey touched them and set the air and clouds ablaze behind them, their wild beauty was still further enhanced."

The longing and desire to explore that mighty, unknown land behind the inhospitable barriers of arctic currents and terrifying glaciers was already strong in him on board the *Viking*. He was not granted permission to go ashore, but at least his Genius had shown him the country.

YEARS IN BERGEN. SCIENTIFIC WORK

NO SOONER had Nansen got home than he received a message from Professor Robert Collett asking him to become curator of the zoological collection in the Bergen Museum. The twenty-year-old youth had not yet produced any scientific work, but Collett had already formed a very high opinion of his character and abilities.

The head curator of the museum was the famous Dr. Daniel Cornelius Danielssen, a highly talented man of great originality and keen sensibilities. As a physician he was known all over the world for his fundamental studies on leprosy. Director of the Lungegaard hospital for lepers, he was a man of many interests. He had been a member of the Storthing, and was a leader in the cultural and community life of Bergen. He possessed an amazing power of work with an indomitable courage in the face of many sore trials and adversities, and was still young of mind in spite of his sixty-seven years. He had exactly the right sort of personality to be the chief and friend of a man of Fridtjof Nansen's temperament.

Dr. Danielssen soon realized of what stuff he was made, this tall, fair giant with the rough-hewn features and the steady eyes. The relation between them is clear from their letters. On July 16, 1893, Nansen, under way in the *Fram*, sent a greeting to Dr. Danielssen from Kjöllefjord in Northern Norway which concludes:

"Dear Danielssen,—Everything that I have to tell you I

shall save up for another time, and just thank you once again for all that you have been to me, my dear, fatherly friend. Fate has parted our ways so that we may no longer work together; but whether I am with you or far away from you, you have ever my greatest respect and my greatest admiration. You are now in the evening of life, but it is a beautiful evening, and you have a great and beautiful day's work to look back upon. I am still in the middle of my life's day, and have still much left to do. You will always stand before me as a shining example. If I grow tired and relax, your strength of will and your never flagging energies will spur me on, as they have done so many others."

The transition from a healthy, outdoor life of bear-hunting and all sorts of exciting adventures to a life of quiet confinement, chained to a microscope in a laboratory, can scarcely have been easy, but the desire to do scientific research was strong in Nansen. The idea of tracing the courses of the spheres through the oceans of space in the great eye-piece of the telescope had attracted him strongly to the study of astronomy and mathematics. Now, however, he descried in the worlds under the microscope much in little; he apprehended in the microcosm a mighty world of riddles and problems equally fascinating to investigate.

It was not, of course, the simple tasks adapted to the novice that interested him. He threw himself into the largest and most difficult problems in his field, and the results of his labors over the short period of five years, presented in long, prize-winning dissertations, are commended by specialists with emphatic recognition of his acuteness, independence, and energy. Such great hopes did scientists place in his future that they saw with regret his desertion of the laboratory for the field of polar exploration. As early as 1883, an English zoologist who had spent considerable time with him at the museum in Bergen sounded him on the subject of joining the staff of young scientists which the palaeontologist, Othniel Charles Marsh, was building up at Yale University. In 1887 David Starr Jordan, at that time presi-

dent of Indiana University, wrote to Professor Collett asking
him to recommend a young zoologist, and when Collett gave
Nansen's name with a warm endorsement, Dr. Jordan offered
the young man a position under very favorable conditions.

Such offers were tempting. At that time, and for many years
to come, it was not easy to feel sure that the path he had chosen
was the best, the one that would lead farthest towards the goal
which beckoned, distant and dim. To get out into the open,
far out, was to Nansen like finding himself again; but for the
time being he concentrated all his energies on the work at
hand. In a hitherto unpublished part of a diary, he writes about
his work in Bergen: "Shut off from all the life around me, I
lived for my studies alone. Night and day I worked at my microscope. It was like a fever. I scarcely think anyone can ever have
worked harder. I refused to think of anything else."

His father had never before had to worry lest this passion-
ate hunter, fisherman, and sportsman should not take proper
care of his health, but now he was worried. His son had to
assure him that he was an active member of two gymnastic
societies, and that he frequently dashed off to the hills, right
out into Jotunheimen, to give himself a real airing.

One Saturday evening in January 1884, when the rain was
teeming down in good Bergen style, Nansen read in his sporting
paper: "Skiing Match at Huseby Hill February 4." It gripped
him with irresistible force: "The spruce forest stood there
alluringly white under its mantle of snow; the valleys, with slopes
and ridges and fells round about, lay there smooth and white,
glistening in the sunlight, fresh and fair in the ringing frost of
winter."

He obtained leave of absence and started off on ski across
the high plateau from Voss to Oslo. There he took part in the
Huseby match, won a prize, and then went back over the fells
through Hallingskeid and Vosseskavlen to Voss with no other
companion on the trip than his dog. This was the first time that
such a journey over the mountain plateau had ever been made

on ski. He described the trip in *Aftenposten,* March 1884, and this account was incorporated in his book *Sporting Days in Wild Norway,* 1916. In the same book he tells how he repeated the trip over Hallingskeid and Vosseskavlen thirty-two years later, and it was his intention, as has already been mentioned, to make it again in 1931, his seventieth year.

The return trip, for which he chose the most difficult but the most glorious route, was the more exciting. He lost his way. After marching for eighteen hours, he dug himself into the snow, slept for five and a half hours, and then tried to find his bearings, but the moonlight was dangerous. He dug himself in again, and slept until dawn. When he reached Vossevangen at one o'clock the next morning, a stiff hike lay behind him. There had been many a thrilling moment, before sheer precipices, pulling up just at the edge of an abyss, hanging by his ski-staff to the edge of a steep snow drift with a cataract or a gorge just beneath. Endurance, preparedness, courage—all that his boyhood and youthful training in sport had built up in him was put to test and use. Without skiing and the high mountains, we should never have had a Fridtjof Nansen or a Roald Amundsen.

When Nansen was sitting quietly beside his microscope again after such trips as this, he felt refreshed and for a time had peace in his soul. His mountain exploits provided an outlet for his superfluous energy, but his greatest debt to the mountains was for their solitude, their silence, their immensity.

Back of that vision of the Norwegian fell, on which Nansen lived until the next time, lay hidden another vision—the arctic glacier country beyond the drift ice with icy pinnacles and fields of perpetual snow on which no foot had ever trod. The unknown called him.

One evening in the preceding fall, as he was listening indifferently to the news of the day being read aloud, he had suddenly wakened up. A telegram stated that Nordenskiöld had returned from an excursion on the Inland Ice of Greenland,

and that his two Lapps had been far in across the endless snow fields on excellent skiing roads. "It flashed on me like lightning: an expedition across Greenland from coast to coast on ski." The plan was ready in his mind just as it was later set forth and carried out.

The first written proposal for the Greenland expedition is in a letter dated June 17, 1884, written from Gardermoen, where Nansen was doing his military service, to Captain A. Maurier in Copenhagen.

Maurier had written to thank Nansen for an article entitled "Along the East Coast of Greenland," which Nansen had written for a geographical periodical. Maurier mentioned that Nordenskiöld had landed on the east coast of Greenland, and that a Danish expedition was in preparation.

Nansen's answer was in part as follows: "Yes, Nordenskiöld really landed on the east coast, as you say. You can imagine how excited I was to hear this. Apparently it has been a good ice year this year, although according to what the sealers say there must be excellent chances of getting very close to the shore any year, at least towards the end of the summer. Some have even told me that they have been so close in July that they could have rowed to shore without any great difficulty. I thought it an exaggeration at the time, but have since come to believe that it may well have been possible.

"Since Nordenskiöld's last expedition particularly, although it had occurred to me long before, I have been steadily ruminating a plan which I cannot but believe is possible of execution, and that is to cross Greenland on ski.

"From all that I can discover, from all the information that I have been able to procure about the interior of Greenland, from the results of Nordenskiöld's last expedition, and finally from my own—I think I may say not inconsiderable—knowledge of ski as a means of locomotion for a man with good skiing legs, I cannot get it out of my head that this might be a comparatively easy and practicable way of investigating the many interesting problems presented by the polar regions at the present time. Should such an expedition be undertaken, it could most easily be managed in connection with an expedition to the east coast, for it would certainly be best to go from east to west. On the west coast one could always count on striking a settlement, and would consequently not need to provision for more than the anticipated duration of the crossing, which I hardly think would be long, with a small, select party of expert ski runners. The provisions would have to be drawn on ski sledges."

Four and a half years elapsed before the plan could be carried out. Nansen wrote to his father, in the same year, of his longing to get out into the open, to have some adventures again. The feeling of unrest was hard to quell, but work is a good antidote, and was applied in this case with its customary success.

There were two things holding up the Greenland expedition. Nansen had a big scientific work on hand that he wanted to complete first, a work which should prove what he was capable of. Then there was his father, old and ill, whom he desired to spare all anxiety. His mother had died some years earlier, in 1877, after which the family had left Store Fröen and moved in to town to a house in Incognitogaten. In 1883 the father suffered a stroke. He died in April 1885 while his son was on the way home to see him.

From the old man's letters we can seen how he tried to keep himself posted about his son's work, and how delighted he was at his progress.

"When I get a letter from you, the tears often come to my eyes, not tears of sorrow, but of mournful joy. May God bless your work and direct it to good results."

Nansen's friend, Dr. Lorentz Grieg, who was much in his company in Bergen, contributes something to our knowledge of his character as revealed in this period of his life:

"I admired the way in which he followed and acted upon his convictions. The spirit of compromise was absolutely foreign

to him. The reason why those who were close to him were so sincerely fond of him, in spite of the fact that he made few allowances and could be extraordinarily stubborn, was that at other times one caught a glimpse of a disposition exceedingly tender and warm-hearted. When this side of his nature was uppermost, it manifested itself in peculiarly attractive and characteristic traits, that showed him to be capable of deep feeling. The child was always strong in him. I remember how in the Christmas holidays we used to sit in the living room at home with a box of cakes between us and wrangle over the contents while we listened to my sister's singing. The best and warmest side of his nature came out at such times; he was never so likable as then. He would sit hour after hour with a pensive air, comprehending and entering into the tenderest, gentlest moods. Schumann, and Schubert with his vehement passion, interested him, but our own poets and composers were his chief delight. These moments of softness and susceptibility always seemed surprising in a youth who the next moment would be as firm and hard as steel. He loved music and poetry.

"Seldom does one find at his age such a pronounced love and yearning for the good, the just, the pure; seldom such unflinching determination in following it to its uttermost consequences. To seek was for him always connected with constant unrest, yearning, and struggle; to accomplish, in spite of everything and everybody, was his highest joy in small things as well as in great."

The Rev. Vilhelm Frimann Koren Holdt, in whose home Nansen lived all the years at Bergen, writes in the Norwegian *Kirkeblad*, July 11, 1930.

"These were good and happy years we lived together, and the ties of friendship which were woven between us then grew firmer and stronger as time passed. Fridtjof was a clean and idealistic youth, and his love of work and capacity for it were a delight to witness. His ability to suffer severe privation and endure without complaining was strikingly illustrated a number of times. Consequently I had to tell him, when he was planning the Greenland expedition, that if he found any men to follow him on the trip, he need not count on making the same demands on them that he made on himself. I recall an example of how easily satisfied he was. We were trying, in 1883, to find a place on Askö [an island near Bergen] where we could live for the summer. It seemed hopeless, for we could not get more than one room. However, when Fridtjof opened a door on the other side of the entry, we saw that there was a little shed with an earthen floor. 'I can take this,' he said, 'I shall buy a hammock and sleep here.' And he did. Since he and I both had to go to town every day, and connections were poor, he bought a light boat, and on those days when we were free to come back at noon, he would take the oars and we would go home pleasantly and safely."

Holdt and Nansen were kindred spirits in many ways. Holdt was minister to the lepers—victims of that dread disease which must be treated in complete isolation. Holdt showed these sufferers the most touching care, and they loved him like a father. His Samaritan labors for the lepers and others on the darker side of life were certainly not without their influence on the young Nansen. Sympathy for suffering and unfortunate people was awakened in him here—that capacity for compassion which was later to turn Nansen himself into a Samaritan on a grand scale.

Holdt had also keen literary interests. The literature of the Golden Age in both Norway and Denmark was fully represented in his large library, especially Ibsen, Björnson, Kielland, and Jonas Lie. Holdt used to read these works aloud in the evenings, and there was no more eager and captivated listener than Nansen.

It was no mere lodging house, it was a home that Nansen found with the Holdts, a home with a rich intellectual life, and one in which love and goodness held sway; and he always looked back to it with great affection and gratitude. The Bergen years, and especially the life in this home, have had more influence on Nansen than we have hitherto known. He kept up the connection by correspondence all his life, and we have letters, right up to his last year, in which he stresses the importance of these youthful years in the Holdt home for the whole of his subsequent development.

One of the few who are still left of his contemporaries in the Bergen years is the curator of Bergen Museum, Dr. James Grieg. They were together during the last two years that Nansen was at the museum. Nansen was very busy at the time with his doctoral thesis and his preparations for the Greenland expedition. The first tests of sleeping bags and of much of the other equipment were made on Blaamannen and Storfjellet, mountains above Bergen. Grieg accompanied him on skiing trips, hunting woodcock, and fishing. It happened that there were bears at that time in the mountainous tracts near Bergen. One day Nansen got word of bears in the wild regions east of Hamlegrö and Blaakoll towards Björdalen and Bjölvefossen. They set off, and were away for a whole twenty-four hours in the most terrible weather. It made a refreshing interval in the work at the museum, and they both escaped without injury.

During these years there were several large schools of whales seen in the neighborhood of Bergen, both toothed whales like the sperm whales and dolphins, and small baleen whales like the rorquals. The latter were shot with bow and arrow in Nansen's day, but the sperm whales and dolphins had to be harpooned. Nansen, of course, was along, not only as zoologist, but also as a keen harpooner.

One year a substitute teacher of nature study was required at Amalie Hansen's School for Girls, and the young curator was persuaded to take the position. My feminine informant tells me that he was very bashful and blushed for nothing at all. The hero of the *Viking* could certainly have lain down in a cage of

polar bears with greater tranquillity of mind than he could
pass an hour at the desk before a class of girls. He usually took
the class along to the museum, where he felt more at home, and
could manage to divide the girls' attention between the dead
wonders inside the glass cases and the living wonder outside
who was telling them marvellous things about the animals.
Nevertheless he did not escape the obvious fate of having the
whole class fall in love with the substitute teacher.

In August, 1904, Nansen, cruising on the *Veslemöy*, spent
a few days in Bergen. I quote from his diary: "Bergen, strange
to be here again where I spent five and a half lonely years, years
which were perhaps among the most important in laying the
foundations of my life. The only friends to whom I was attached were far away. Here I lived my hermit's life with my
many dreams. How rich and full of promise life was then! It
seems to me almost as though the man who lived here at that
time were somebody else of a generation ago, so far away does
that whole world of ideas now lie. How changed everything is
now! I look upon everything differently, from quite another
point of view. And how the town has changed! It is certainly
beautiful. And these alleys and hills with rendezvous and late
hours and solitary lights in the windows—it is all so picturesque
and characteristic. I did not see this then, but did I see anything
at that time except my own eternal problems?"

Nevertheless he did experience something there, something
which, experienced in youth, is never forgotten: the coast and
skerries of West Norway. In a page of his diary from the
same cruise, while he is still in the east, he writes: "Why is it
that when I hear beautiful music, or dream myself off into the
realms of beauty, it is always to the rocky West coast after sun-
down? The sea shines like a mirror of copper, airy blue islands
swim far out on its burnished surface, and the sky arches over-
head, high and clear with golden rimmed sun clouds. I am
borne softly on dream waves out towards the kingdoms of ether,
and everything earthly vanishes away—away—."

Sixteen years later he saw the place again; "but my fairy land I did not find." No, it was no longer there, but it lived in his mind; Welhaven's poems and Kjerulf's melodies sung by his wife's voice could call it up, this youthful fairyland from the coast of Bergen and Florö.

IN ORDER to advance his scientific investigations further than was possible with the methods he had hitherto known, Nansen went to Italy in the spring of 1886. He first studied at Pavia under Golgi, and then went on to Naples. Most of the time, from April until June, was spent at the biological station on the bay of Naples under the direction of the founder, the brilliant and energetic Anton Dohrn of Jena.

Everybody knows now what a biological station is, but at that time nobody knew. The idea was Dohrn's, and because it was so new, it cost him a four year struggle against the greatest obstacles from both Italians and Germans, and his whole fortune was spent before he could open the world's first biological station. Up to this time sea creatures had been studied in the form of dead, distorted specimens preserved in alcohol. The life of these animals was a closed book. With the new facilities as Nansen describes them "the research student spends hours before the great reservoirs face to face with the rarest forms of sea creatures, in close companionship with the life of nature, and in this time learns more about the world of live things than by ploughing through many volumes of printed knowledge or poring over the dead treasures of museums. He learns to use his eyes and his powers of observation on living nature itself, and learns to consider life itself as the real subject of investigation."

Nansen realized the importance of such an institution for Norway, and suggested the establishment of a biological station at Bergen, but his Greenland expedition prevented further development of this idea. Later he was instrumental in establishing the biological station at Dröbak which was inaugurated in 1894.

These spring months beside the beautiful bay of Naples were a warm and fruitful season of growth in the young man's mind. The observations and the life at the biological station gave a powerful impetus to his scientific studies. The example of Dohrn's great life work, and no less that of the man himself, whose powers of will and endurance reached the ideal which Nansen was later to realize in his own life, exerted a strong influence on him. The impressions of the country, its luxuriantly beautiful scenery, its merry, carefree people, the joy in existence that flourishes in emulation of the oranges and roses on that lava soil, its art, its history—all sank like a seed in deep and receptive ground.

One of his friends at the station sketches him as he was then:

"The blonde Viking with the slim, lithe, well-trained body was an excellent dancer and the gayest of the company. Every supper was a miniature feast, a musical, carefree social hour in the highest degree refreshing. One time we were going to Sorrento and hired a carriage to drive along the famous highway. On the way, another carriage with two ladies in it came behind us. They amused themselves by overtaking us and laughing at us. Then Nansen jumped out of the carriage and ran alongside the horse for a long distance, so we caught up with the ladies amid shouts of laughter from both sides.

"At other times he was quiet and thoughtful, and would sit for hours without uttering a word. I can still see him at the foot of Vesuvius among the ruins of San Sebastian in the desolate lava fields. San Sebastian had been destroyed in 1874 by an eruption of Vesuvius; only a church remained. I can still see him sitting there on a block of lava, hour after hour without moving. He simply sat and stared into the distance. Time after time we shouted and called to him. He did not move. On the way home we two walked together arm in arm and I tried to get him to talk, but in vain. He did not utter a single word."

Nansen's first major work, *On the Anatomy and Histology of the Myzostomidæ,* eighty-six folio pages illustrated with a large number of his own drawings, had appeared in 1885.

The myzostomidæ are a group of worms which live as parasites on certain radiata and which, owing to their mode of life, undergo remarkable changes. A number of prominent investigators had worked on these creatures, and Nansen confirmed and expanded the results of his predecessors. He showed that he had mastered completely all the technical resources of his day. He made his preparations according to the newest methods, drew exceptionally well, and thoroughly understood the various arts of reproducing his drawings. He had plenty of initiative, energy, and perseverance, an unusual ability to see to the heart of a matter and to make straight for it regardless of any authority other than truth itself.

In 1886 he produced a new work, studies on *The More Minute Structure of the Central Nervous System.* He extended these investigations not only to the worms but also to the Crustaceans, mollusks, and the lower vertebrates, the lancelet and the hagfish.

This field was still very much in darkness in spite of the work of many investigators. The search for the fibers and cells of the nervous system led here into the great mystery, the hidden secret of life.

Nansen plunged into this difficult and weighty problem with all his energy, but was forced to a standstill because the methods he was using were not adequate to lead to definite conclusions. He cast about for new ways and means to expedite his research, and it was then he heard of the Italian scientist, Golgi, who had discovered new methods of exposing nerve cells and fibrillæ by applying a silver nitrate stain. Most histologists condemned the new methods with harsh criticism, but Nansen set out for Pavia to study Golgi's methods on the spot. He utilized them successfully, and carried them further than Golgi, in his study of the nervous system of the invertebrates, in which field he was a pioneer.

Nansen now succeeded in penetrating farther into the secrets of the central nervous system than any of his predecessors. His great work published in English, *The Structure and Combination of the Central Nervous System,* will, therefore, always have a place in the literature of this subject, according to the opinion of a specialist in the same field, Professor Magnus Gustav Retzius, the eminent Swedish histologist.

After this work Nansen turned to another problem which had hitherto defied the efforts of investigators: the development of the hagfish, a sort of archetype of the most primitive vertebrates. Nansen found that the hagfishes were male in their early days, and later became females. The question of the development of this remarkable animal has not yet been completely solved, but Nansen's work was an important step towards a solution.

Then finally he seized on a biological problem which had long interested him, the development of the whales. These remarkable mammals are descended from animals which formerly lived on land, and offer many problems to the student. With his usual energy, Nansen procured the necessary materials for his research by increasing the Bergen Museum's collection of embryo whales. After his return from Greenland, he resumed the study of whales together with another investigator in this field, Professor Gustav Guldberg, but the preparations for the *Fram* expedition took up so much of his time that the completion of the work had to be left to Guldberg.

The first part of the work was published in 1894: *On the Development and Structure of the Whale. Part I. By Gustav Guldberg and Fridtjof Nansen.*

The friends of biological research always hoped, says Professor Retzius, that after his exploits at the North Pole, Fridtjof Nansen would again give his undivided attention to the field of research in which he had already done such significant work and which offered opportunities, for an intellect of the caliber of his, to solve the greatest problems, to "make expeditions of exploration into the far-reaching and still only partly charted domain of biology, beyond which increasingly greater unexplored territories open before the mind."

THE GREENLAND EXPEDITION. PREPARATIONS

IN THE field which for the time being he forsook, there were others to take his place. In the field to which he turned, all his predecessors had been foiled. And beyond this new problem lay a still greater one, the exploration of the Arctic. The saga of his forerunners was a terrifying series of tragedies.

By the power of genius he solved both problems.

The years of his growth and development, his youth, the Bergen years, all seemed to be a preparation for this career. The many-sidedness of his abilities, the rare fusion in him of sport and scholarship, was the necessary qualification.

Such a combination was not usual at that time. His being a sportsman was even something of a handicap; because of it, people hardly dared to put faith in him as a scholar. Nor did he look like a scholar. He had neither spectacles nor a long beard; he usually wore a short jacket and grey sport clothes; he went on foolish unnecessary skiing trips across the high mountain plateau in winter, alone. He was fisherman, hunter, rower, swimmer, gymnast, devoted to all sorts of pursuits in which physical prowess was the main thing. That this physique should at the same time house a scholar of distinction did not seem reasonable.

In the fin de siècle period, the days of the "Christiania Bohême," a man of Nansen's type was gratuitously irritating. When the habitués of the Grand Café saw the grey-clad athletic figure dart past the window, a particularly deep draught of brandy and soda was required to drown their irritation. When the budding shoots of the intelligentsia out on Drammensveien saw the same figure, bare-headed, in a woolen jersey, shoot by on a practice run, their contempt for the crazy fellow was, according to the confession of one of them, beyond words.

The brandy-and-soda intelligentsia categorically concluded that this exasperating athletic person was but a dunce in science.

One winter evening in 1887, Nansen entered the den of his good friend Dr. Grieg, then in Oslo, and set forth his plans. He was going to Stockholm.

"What are you going to do there?"

"Look up Nordenskiöld and ask him to approve my plan. I shall take my doctor's degree in the spring, and then go to Greenland. It's going to be a tough spring, old man! But never mind!"

And then he traced out on the map the route he had chosen. It lay far to the north—"the advantage of this is to show the world that Greenland can be crossed so far north"—and started from the east coast, the uninhabited east coast, which had no communication with the world, and hence offered no possibility of retreat. This was the most original idea in the plan, the most insane thing about it in the opinion of most of his contemporaries. The advantages of his plan were obvious enough to Nansen. By going in the reverse direction, from west to east, one would come to an uninhabited coast and have to turn back again, to make the journey twice. Conditions are somewhat altered in our day, since Angmagsalik, the only Eskimo town on the east coast, now has, ordinarily, annual communication with Europe. At that time it meant staking one's life irrevocably on attaining the goal.

"It was like a revelation in those decadent days to hear of a man of action ready to lay down his life for an idea. I was awed and thrilled that evening when we parted," said Dr. Grieg.

So Nansen went to Stockholm to seek out Nordenskiöld, the great Swedish pioneer in arctic exploration. The Norwegian professors, W. C. Brögger and J. N. F. Wille, were at that time at the Stockholm Högskola.

The caretaker announced one day to Brögger that there was a Norwegian asking for him. He had not given his name, but he was tall and fair, and, he added with a smile, had no overcoat; it was probably another sailor or somebody of that sort who needed a coat.

"Then in he came himself—tall and straight, his fair hair rather untidily thrown back from his massive forehead. He put out his hand with a peculiarly winning smile and introduced himself.

" 'You are going to cross Greenland?'

" 'Well, I'm thinking of it.'

"I looked straight into his eyes. Indescribably confident himself, he inspired confidence as he stood there with a good-natured smile on his strong, rough-hewn face. Although he was exactly the same all through the interview, simple, straightforward, perhaps even a trifle blunt in his manner, he nevertheless seemed to grow in stature with every word. This plan to cross Greenland from the east coast on ski, which a moment before I had regarded as a supremely insane idea, became, in the course of that conversation, the most natural thing in the world. And all of a sudden it flashed on me with absolute conviction: he will do this thing just as surely as we are sitting here and talking about it.

"This man, whose name I had not known a couple of hours before, had in these few minutes—quite naturally and inevitably as it seemed—made me feel as though I had known him all my days; and I felt, without having to think how it had come about, that I should be proud and happy to be his friend for life."

Nordenskiöld, too, considered Nansen's plan foolhardy but not absolutely impossible of execution. Nansen's personality made a deep impression on him; he became more and more interested, and gave Nansen much valuable advice. When they met again, the foolhardy plan had been carried out and the ice of Greenland crossed for the first time.

On November 11, 1887, Nansen applied to the University Council for a grant of 5000 kroner for the expedition. His application begins thus: "It is my intention to undertake during the summer a trip across the Inland Ice of Greenland from the east to the west coast"; and it concludes by quoting Nordenskiöld's words: "The investigation of the real nature of Greenland is of such great and fundamental significance for science that it is scarcely possible at the present time to set a more important goal for a polar expedition than just the investigation of the natural conditions in the interior of that country."

The University Council warmly supported Nansen's application, but the Government said No. One of the papers wrote that there was no reason why the Norwegian people should pay so large a sum as 5000 kroner to enable a private citizen to make a pleasure trip to Greenland. Others considered it downright wicked to aid and abet suicide. Still others found amusement in the comic paper in Bergen which announced: "Exhibition! In the month of June next Fridtjof Nansen, curator of the Museum, will give an exhibition of ski-running with long distance jumping on the Inland Ice of Greenland. Good seats in the crevasses. Return tickets unnecessary."

Aside from young people and a few scientists, the consensus of opinion was that Nansen's plan was the scheme of a madman.

Expeditions from five countries, including polar experts such as Peary and Nordenskiöld, had tried to penetrate the Inland Ice from the west side, but all had been forced to turn back. On the east coast a return journey would be certain death. Besides this, a number of competent authorities, former Greenland travellers who were in a position to know conditions, believed that it was practically impossible even to land on the east coast.

A strong current flows southwards along the east coast of Greenland, bearing with it great masses of rough old arctic ice. A number of attempts to land on the southern part of the east coast, south of 66° N., had already been made in vain. Farther north it is easier to approach the shore, but it was not until 1883 that Nordenskiöld succeeded in reaching Cape Dan by steamer.

In 1777 the whole whaling fleet had been caught fast in the ice off the east coast; ship after ship was crushed down; 320 men perished, and 155 drifted south round Cape Farewell on a floe and were rescued.

In 1868 the German polar expedition under Koldewey made the same trip; one of the vessels, the *Hansa,* was crushed between the floes and sank on October 19. The crew drifted down on an ice floe and were rescued off Cape Farewell on June 13, 1869.

Nansen had drifted in this terrible current in 1882 for twenty-four days in the *Viking.* He knew it, and he was aware that it had been too much for the others; but what constituted the main achievement of both his arctic expeditions was the conquest of obstacles which had proved the defeat of other navigators.

In January 1888 the University Council received word from Copenhagen that Councillor Gamél would donate the necessary 5000 kroner. Besides this, Gamél paid the expenses of the winter in Greenland, of the return journey to Copenhagen, and of their sojourn there. After the trip was over, this circumstance was censured: Nansen should have waited until the money could be procured from some source in Norway. There was, however, no prospect of this; and moreover the expedition cost not only 5000 kroner, but over 15,000. Nansen was prepared to make up the rest from his own small fortune, but after the trip was completed, the Students' Association collected 10,000 kroner.

It was a busy spring with the preparation and equipment of the expedition. Nansen constructed all the most important things himself. He went out to the mountains near Bergen and made long trips over the high plateau to try out sledges, sleeping bags, and cooking apparatus. He lectured in Bergen about Greenland and the expedition, and on April 28 defended his doctoral thesis in Oslo.

His subject was "The Structure and Combination of the Central Nervous System." The disputation was unusually animated, lasting for three and a half hours. All his opponents complimented Nansen on his courage in attacking a difficult problem and on the energy with which he had worked out the solution, but they doubted his conclusions. The fact, however, was that his conclusions were too new and were not wholly understood. Later researches have demonstrated that Nansen was right.

In discussing Nansen's position as a scientist, the Norwegian geographer, Professor Werner Werenskiold, wrote in the Swedish magazine *Ord och Bild*, 1927: "His doctoral dissertation seemed at first to confirm the opinion of those who doubted him; we may still hear echoes from that time. A later age has, however, given him the fullest recognition also for his zoological work. He introduced the newest methods of investigation which were then unknown here (Golgi's coloring technique) and showed great skill in making his preparations and in drawing them. Not only that, but his ideas were new and original to such a degree that his honored opponents did not understand anything. Nevertheless he did receive his doctor's degree, in 1888— it was said because he had made up his mind to go and die on the Inland Ice of Greenland anyway, so it did not matter."

During all the time that he was preparing for the disputation he was also engaged in the preliminary work of the expedition, and in selecting his men.

There were not hundreds of applicants for this trip as there were later for the *Fram* expedition, but there were quite enough—forty. It was essential to be a good ski runner. Nansen selected three Norwegians and two Lapps. He believed that the Mountain Lapps, on account of their familiarity with snow and the hardships of mountain life, and on account of the sense of location with which they were credited, would be particularly useful.

The Norwegians were Otto Sverdrup, a retired ship's captain; Oluf Christian Dietrichson, first lieutenant in the Norwegian Infantry; and Kristian Kristiansen, a peasant from the north of Norway. Sverdrup, born in 1852 in Bindalen, was at the same time farmer, fisherman, hunter, and seaman. Always cool and resourceful, he was an invaluable asset to the expedition. He later became captain of the *Fram* and leader of several arctic expeditions. Dietrichson, born in 1856 near Levanger, was meteorologist, surveyor, and cartographer of the expedition. Exceptionally hardy and active, he had traversed most of the valleys of Norway and the high plateau between Skien and Tröndelag on ski, usually going alone. He is now a major-general and lives at Soon. Kristiansen, farmer and seaman, born in 1865 at Steinkjer, was a staunch and reliable man.

When the Lapps finally arrived they did not quite measure up to specifications. Nansen had stipulated that they should be picked Mountain Lapps between thirty and forty years of age and unmarried. Samuel Johannesen Balto, aged twenty-seven, was a settled River Lapp from Karasjok, big for a Lapp, strong, intelligent and persevering. Ole Nielsen Ravna was forty-five or forty-six, a nomadic Mountain Lapp, married, and had five children. Though very small, he was incredibly strong and wiry. The Lapps knew neither the aim of the journey nor how it had come about. There was no stimulus to them in the idea that they were taking part in a scientific and sporting venture. They had volunteered simply and solely to make money, but were so terrified by what they had heard on the way down about the dangers of the expedition that they would gladly have turned back home again; and Nansen would certainly have preferred to replace them had there been time. They went. Nansen encouraged them as best he could and everything worked out nicely. They had great powers of endurance, were plucky, good-natured, and amiable, and Nansen became quite fond of them.

Their sense of location, however, at least as far as Greenland was concerned, was not superior to that of the Norwegians.

On a trip of this kind where the men themselves had to be the pack-horses, it was essential that the equipment be light and at the same time substantial. Nansen's practical mechanical ability now stood him in good stead. He was able to devise things and construct them with his own two hands. He now made use of all the experiences from his outdoor life and of all the good advice and information he received from Nordenskiöld, and from the famous Danish geologist and Greenland explorer, Dr. Hinrich Johannes Rink, then Colonial Minister in Copenhagen.

Nansen designed all the most important articles himself. He built pack sledges 2.90 meters in length and half a meter in width. Earlier expeditions had used heavy, clumsy sledges with narrow runners that sank deep in loose snow. Nansen took the Norwegian ski sledge as a model. It rests on wide runners resembling ski, is light, skims nicely along the surface, and draws easily on all sorts of roads. He built it of ash and shod the runners with thin shoes of steel. The sledge weighed 11.5 kilograms and with the steel runners 13.75 kilograms. There were no nails, just lashings, giving it the elasticity necessary to stand the stress and strain. A bar of ash bent like the back of a chair was placed at the rear of the sled and proved useful for steering and shoving.

They took along ski with leather fastenings, Indian snow shoes, and Norwegian snow shoes known as *truger* (troughs). Snow shoes were better than ski on a steep ascent in soft snow. The sleeping bags were of reindeer hide and accommodated three men each. The cooking apparatus was an important accessory, the result of a great deal of experimentation.

Their clothing consisted of a light woolen undersuit, and over that an Icelandic wool sweater, knee breeches and jacket, and thick wadmal snow socks. They had ordinary sewn shoes, ski shoes with soft leather soles, and Lapp moccasins made of the skin from the head or legs of the reindeer buck. The rest of their outfit included well-shrunk woolen stockings and over them socks of goat's hair; woolen gloves and dogskin gloves; a wind-proof canvas coat with hood, a woolen cap, and a hood of wadmal; snow goggles of smoked glass, eye-protectors of wood, and red silk veils; and a tent large enough for two sleeping bags. A saucy blizzard taught them that an arctic tent should not consist of separate pieces but should be sewn together in one piece with the floor so that the tent door is the only opening.

The provisions consisted of pemmican, chocolate, liver pâté but not the Strasburg luxury, Swedish *knäkkebröd,* English biscuits made partly of meat-powder, dried strips of halibut, meat-powder chocolate, butter, Gruyère cheese and Norwegian whey-cheese, pea-soup, condensed milk, a little tea, a little coffee, still less tobacco, and no alcohol.

Besides this they had a large number of tools, scientific instruments, tarpaulins, bamboo poles, matches, candles, some medicinal and first-aid supplies, two guns, and ammunition.

There was one grave deficiency. At the last moment it was discovered that there was no fat in the pemmican. The result was that the men suffered from a desperate craving for fat. They constantly felt ravenously hungry. Otherwise the equipment was on the whole satisfactory, better in many ways than that of any previous expedition. The equipment of the Greenland expedition, with the additions suggested by their new experiences on this trip, formed the basis for the excellent equipment of the *Fram* expedition and of all later arctic ventures.

The final preparation was a short course in Eskimo language with Dr. H. J. Rink.

The last evening that Nansen was at the Rinks', Fru Rink went with him to the door: "You must go to the North Pole too some day." He answered as though it were a familiar idea long and seriously pondered: "I mean to."

ACROSS GREENLAND

O N MAY 2, 1888, Nansen set out from Oslo to travel by way of Copenhagen to Scotland where he met his companions who had sailed direct from Kristiansand. Thence they went to Iceland, and there embarked on the sealer *Jason* which was to transport the party to Greenland, on the understanding that the sealing interests should come before those of the expedition.

On June 11 they stood off Cape Dan. Nansen had intended to start from there, but the ice belt was ten geographical miles wide. Finally on July 17, about two and a half miles distant from land, they took to the boats. Nansen had seen from the crow's nest that there was open water in towards the shore; with good luck they might manage to slip in quite easily. Luck was against them, however; one of the boats was damaged and had to be drawn up on an ice floe for repairs. While this work was going on, they drifted out into the swift-flowing ice stream and were carried at terrific speed away from land and southwards. For ten days they drifted south, from 65° 30′ N. to 61° 40′ N., right down to the island of Kutdlek. On July 29 they set foot on land. Irreclaimable days had been lost.

The ride on the ice floe had had its exciting moments. The night of July 20 came near to being the expedition's last. The ice stream hurled the floe on which they were drifting out towards the breakers where sea and current meet. The border line between life and death was indicated by the white surf out in front of them. Nansen ordered the men to turn in for a nap

64

before beginning the struggle with the breakers, while Sverdrup kept watch. The floe was being violently rushed nearer and nearer the breakers, waves and chunks of ice were washing in over it, and it was gradually being broken up into smaller and smaller pieces. Things looked bad for them. Sverdrup went over to the tent, unfastened one hook, but considered, hesitated,— would not waken before it was time—closed it, wandered back again, and looked at the ice and waves. Several times he went over to the door, opened it, and closed it again. The men in the tent slept. Nansen wakened at the sound of the waves washing against the walls of the tent and seeping into it, but hearing the quiet firm tread of the sentinel outside, he went off to sleep again—iron nerves! When he wakened again, the floe had drifted shorewards away from the breakers.

This was a discouraging beginning, and the best of the summer was gone. Nordenskiöld rightly emphasizes as the strongest proof of the energy of these men the fact that they did not for a moment consider looking for the nearby Fredriksdal and waiting until the next year, but straightway rowed north towards Sermilik Fjord, about 500 kilometers distant.

The trip northwards again followed close along the shore, past the mouths of fjords and headlands. Some parts of the coast were bare; at other parts inaccessible glaciers extended right down to the sea. Glacier calves came floating down, great mountains of ice, fantastically beautiful but treacherous. It was fearfully impressive when one of them tumbled over, setting the sea in an uproar, or when a tower of ice came hurtling down several hundred tons at a time. When one calf tumbled into the seaway several others were likely to follow it, and there was a deafening roar as though the end of the world had come; and in the midst of the cataclysm two nut shells with men in them. What were they doing here in this dance of the ice maidens? The Lapps did not like it. They were not used to this sort of thing on the expanses of Finnmark.

Toiling and rowing, with never a warm meal, nothing but

cold water and dry biscuits and dried meat, they finally landed one evening on a small island; but the fjord was as smooth as a mirror, so they had to be off again, rowing as much as possible, sleeping as little as possible, eating as little as possible and as seldom as possible. Nansen declared there was food enough, however, and that helped, said Kristiansen. Another night was spent on an island so tiny that there was no room for the tent, just enough for the two sleeping bags, and rather cramped at that it seemed to the two men from the expanses of Finnmark. On they went, toiling and rowing, or hauling the boats over long stretches of ice, squeezing in between refractory floes, insinuating themselves among the insidious ice maidens who crunched oars and tholepins or the floe they stood on. Sometimes great masses of ice plunged down just where they had been two minutes before. "A miraculous occurrence," Nansen notes when this happens for the third time.

On August 10, towards evening, they drew the boats up on land for the last time at Umivik Fjord; and Nansen made coffee—the second warm meal in twelve days.

The next day Nansen and Sverdrup went to the mountains to find a route for making the ascent. The huge moving glaciers of Greenland are badly cracked at the foot, and the fissures run at right angles to the course of the glacier. It was best to reconnoitre. The others busied themselves making repairs and packing up. With snow shoes, Alpine ropes, and ice axes the two waded and climbed their way ahead for the greater part of twenty-four hours. The snow bridges over the crevasses broke now and then, but ice axe and rope saved them. Twenty kilometers from the camp at 900 meters altitude, they turned and went back by another route. By five o'clock in the morning they were down. The problem was solved. After a few more days' preparation, they set off on August 16 at dusk. The snow was not so soft at night. The sea beyond, so impassable with drift ice four weeks before, now lay open and free from ice as far as the eye could see. Landwards, the Inland Ice reared its white arch with nunataks above and moving glaciers underneath. Now and then came a heavy boom, as of great cannon, the salute from the advancing glaciers on their eternal march.

The first night they toiled ahead for about four or five kilometers. The baggage, 600 kilograms, divided among five sledges, gave them plenty of exercise in the loose snow on the steep and crevassed terrane. Heavy rains and rough weather kept them to the tent for three days. They slept as much as possible and ate as little as possible—one meal in twenty-four hours.

On August 22 at 900 meters altitude there was night frost. The sledges ran easier, but the ice was uneven, and the sledge ropes tugged and galled until it felt as though their shoulders were on fire. From now until they reached the west coast they had no other drinking water than what they melted from snow in metal flasks carried next their bodies. At from —30° to 40° centigrade these drops were bitterly earned. Washing dishes with water was out of the question. A bath would have been suicidal; from the time they left the *Jason* until they reached Godthaab they did not have a wash of any kind nor a change of clothing. The sanitary regulations of civilized man are modified at 40° below zero and rendered superfluous, for no bacteria are found at this temperature—not even so much as a cold in the head. Aside from frost bite and the discomfort caused by thirst and the craving for fat, the health of the party was excellent; none of them had a single day of illness.

"Life had also its bright moments. If we had to toil and suffer at times, these nights with northern lights and moonlight made up for a great deal. This part of the world has its beauty too. When the ever changing aurora borealis danced light and fairylike over the southern sky, perhaps in more radiant splendor here than anywhere else in the world, it was possible to forget our trials and tribulations; or when the moon came up and followed its silent course across the star-strewn heavens, played over the tops of the ice ridges and bathed the whole of this stark world of ice in its silvery rays, then peace descended all about us and life became beauty. I am sure that our nocturnal marches over the Inland Ice of Greenland made an ineradicable impression upon all of us who were on that expedition."

On August 24 the sleighing was miserable, the snow heavy as sand and loose, the ascent steep. Every stage on the way was rewarded with a cake of meat-powder chocolate to each man. They made less than ten kilometers that day.

In the evening they had oatmeal biscuits with an icing of snow on which lemon-juice, oil of lemon, and sugar was poured —"the most refreshing and satisfying dessert one can imagine," said Nansen, "very much like the Italian dish *granita.*" A strange feeling he must have had as he sat there outside the tent enjoying this dish in small mouthfuls and watching the moon play over the snow fields, while his thoughts wandered back to the last time he had eaten granita, on a warm summer night beside the bay of Naples with the moon playing over the dark waves of the Mediterranean.

The next day the climb was again stiff and the sleighing still worse. To save time they started the cooking apparatus on the sledge. When the soup was hot they stopped, put up the tent, and carried the apparatus in. Unfortunately Nansen overturned it, and the soup with all its precious ingredients, the alcohol, and the lumps of snow from the water tank spilled over the floor of the tent. They all sprang up quickly, threw out everything inedible, and lifted the corners of the tent floor so that the soup collected in the centre. They poured it back into the cooking apparatus and boiled it again. "Hardly a drop was lost," the soup tasted fine, and the denatured alcohol merely added to the savor. The next day they had drifting snow and storm. Rigged out in all their wind gear, their hoods wrapped closely around their heads like disguised monks, they pushed on upwards, with the fine snow penetrating the pores of their garments. It was a wet mess when the snow melted after they got into their sleeping bags. The next morning they were buried in the snow which had filled the tent during the night's storm.

The sledges outside and the tent had almost disappeared in snow, but the snow made it snug inside, and they had a comfortable Sunday morning with coffee and breakfast in bed. The next morning the ascent was so steep that they had to have three men to each sledge. When they started downwards after a new load, Kristiansen, who rarely opened his mouth, said: "Good God, to think that people would let themselves in for anything as bad as this!" On August 27 they halted again on account of storm. Nansen now realized that with such bad weather and bad roads they were not going to catch the last steamer from Kristians-havn, and decided to alter his course to the more southerly Godthaab. The journey would be shorter, they would have more assistance from the wind, and a good chance of catching the last ship.

The next day they lashed the sledges together into two rafts, rigged up masts, and sewed the tarpaulins together for a sail. It was a cold job working with bare hands for seven hours.

The most grievous work up on the ice was pitching the tent, for it had to be put up with bare hands. Nansen froze all his fingers twice. The second time he did not get them thawed out until he was in the sleeping bag—"almost unbearable pain," he says, and that means that it was bad indeed. Once he froze his nose and his throat, but discovered it in time. The protection of the region of the stomach was a difficult problem in a storm, but was solved by the insertion of a felt hat. The sun in this thin air is just as harmful for the face as the frost. Kristiansen's cheeks broke out with nasty blisters and sores. The Lapps suffered from snowblindness until they learned to use veils and goggles.

"It looked very strange to see these fine silk veils fluttering in the blue air. It instinctively brought up recollections of promenades in spring, of glittering carrriages and elegant ladies with sparkling eyes; while here we saw instead six men, anything but elegant, drawing equipages which suffered just as little from that weakness, and behind the veils, only six grimy, weather-beaten faces."

On August 29, Nansen, Sverdrup, and Dietrichson put on their Indian snowshoes. At first they fell headlong repeatedly, but they soon learned to manage them, and found that they held them up better than the Norwegian snowshoes or "troughs," and gave surer footing. Kristiansen could not get the knack of using them, and stuck to the Norwegian troughs. The Lapps refused to use snowshoes of any sort and almost wore themselves out until on August 30 they put on their ski. From September 2 on, after the worst of the climbing was over, all the men used ski.

On August 31 the last nunatak disappeared below the horizon behind them, and until they saw land again on September 21 there was nothing to be seen week after week but the interminable flat desert of snow. One day passed like another with oppressive monotony and steady toil. From that day on, the surface of the snow was as smooth as a mirror, unbroken except by the tracks of the ski. The going was heavy; the average day's march was between ten and twenty kilometers. Had they reached the top of the Inland Ice in the middle of summer, they would have had a smooth and solid crust to travel on; but now they had loose, new-fallen snow, fine and dry as dust and packed together into drifts as heavy as sand or clay. The colder it got the worse it was. And now in September it became very cold, −40° C. inside the tent, −45° outside, the lowest temperature which has been recorded on our globe at this time of the year. Even in the sleeping bags it was so cold that in the morning their heads were covered with rime and ice. Beard and hair gradually froze fast to their clothes so that it was sometimes hard to get their mouths open to speak. In the thin dry air the midday sun, even at this time, could become so hot that the snow became sloppy and wet their feet. Their shoes, heavy outer stockings, and socks were often frozen together in a solid mass. The change in temperature between day and night was sometimes more than twenty degrees. The same phenomenon occurs

in the Sahara where it is suffocatingly hot in the sun, but cold
enough at night to freeze water.

On these evenings on the Inland Ice, at an altitude like that
of Gallhöipiggen, Dietrichson was not to be envied. With a
hardihood and determination which Nansen himself had to
admire, he carried out his meteorological observations with bare
hands until his fingers were horribly frostbitten.

Violent physical exertion in such cold is very exhausting
and disagreeable, and when storm was added to a temperature
of —40° C., even these hardened men felt the strain. One time
they had such weather for four days, but kept to the tent for
only one of them. The snow buried the tent so that they were
snug and warm and they cheered themselves up with a cup of
coffee and a smoke. During this time their craving for fat became particularly strong, and one day Sverdrup asked if it would
do to drink the grease they had for their shoes—old boiled lin-
seed oil. Nansen discovered that chewing a splinter of wood
relieved thirst: it kept the mouth moist. He and Sverdrup almost ate up the Norwegian snowshoes which were made of
bird-cherry. This kind of wood was good, and the bark especially was excellent.

On September 14 they began gradually to descend towards
the coast. The highest point reached was 2716 meters. Every day
they watched eagerly for land. Ravna's face got sourer and
sourer. One evening in the tent he said: "I old Mountain Lapp,
I silly old fool. I think we don't never come to the west coast."
To this Nansen answered: "Yes, that's true, Ravna, you silly old
fool." Then Ravna burst out laughing: "Yes, that's true, Ravna
silly old fool." He was apparently comforted by being answered
in this way.

The next day the temperature was —18° centigrade, which
seemed fine and mild to them.

The seventeenth was one of their big days: it was on that
day exactly two months before that they had left the *Jason*.
Butter was dealt out as a special treat. A snow bird came twitter-

ing round them, lighted in the snow, and followed them a while on their journey. "Anyone who believes in good angels would certainly regard as such these two snow birds, the one which bade us farewell on the east coast and the one which bade us welcome here; their cheery twittering was a blessing: it put life in all of us and with renewed strength we pushed confidently ahead."

A favorable wind blew up, they set sail and went off at terrific speed mile after mile across the snow. The sledges were lashed together in twos with a steering rod projecting out in the center between them. Here one of the men stood on ski and steered, the other two either sat behind or were towed along behind on their ski. Well on in the afternoon they saw land and kept on sailing, faster and faster, right down on to the crevassed terrane, where they almost sailed their last. Nansen suddenly perceived a dark shadow in front and managed to luff just at the edge of a chasm some hundred meters in depth. In the uncertain light of the moon they did not venture to sail farther but pitched camp. Nansen's fingers were frozen through and he put in a bad night with them before he could get to sleep. When they stuck their heads out of the tent in the morning, they saw the whole country south of Godthaab Fjord lying spread out before them. "Do you remember when as a child you beheld for the first time the high plateau with glistening glaciers and drifts of snow lying before you? Do you remember how it attracted you, all this unknown world? If you do, you will understand how we felt at the sight of this country. We were like children; something came up in our throats as our eyes followed along the valley, vainly searching for a glimpse of the sea. It was a beautiful country, wild and grand, just like the west coast of Norway."

That day, and for several days following, they had a hard time of it. The crevasses of the border region were ready to swallow them up. Once or twice the heavy sledges almost keeled over, and several times the men themselves hung suspended in mid-air over an abyss and had occasion to make use of their gymnastic arts with bars and ropes. There was constant need here for the "snap up" and the "pull up," for strength and agility and speed, for an eye in every finger and for steady nerves. The aforementioned Genius had her hands full these days, but she had a great deal of amusement too; it was a regular "devil's ball room" she turned them loose in.

One day they found water up in the clefts of the ice, and Nansen's pen waxes lyrical over the joys of repletion.

On September 24 they finally came down from the ice and set foot on bare ground. "Words are powerless to describe what it meant to us just to feel earth and stones beneath our feet, or the sense of wellbeing that surged through us when we felt the heather spring beneath our steps and smelt the delightful fragrance of grass and moss."

That night the tent was pitched on bare earth for the first time. What a delight to stretch out on the soft heather! A fire of heather outside the door cast Rembrandtesque shadows into the tent where the men sat and contentedly ate their fill. It was a beautiful mild evening, and Nansen lay on his back on the heather dreaming while Sverdrup smoked a pipe of moss. Sverdrup declared it was the finest evening he had ever spent in his life.

To reach Godthaab by land was impossible. The next day they carried the baggage down through Austmanna Valley to Ameralik Fjord. While the other four continued at this work, Sverdrup and Nansen contrived a boat from the tent floor on a frame of willow branches. The oars were made by stretching canvas across forked willow branches for blades and attaching them to bamboo shafts. The thwarts of bamboo were, Nansen says, "the scantiest seats it has ever been my ill luck to sit upon, and I devoutly hope never again to have to go through a similar penance." It was no very elegant craft, but they rowed away in it and six days later, October 3, were in Godthaab where a salute was thundered forth as soon as it was known who they were.

It was a grand pull—one day they sat for twenty hours on the uncomfortable thwarts until their backs could stand no more. The weather was good with glorious sunny evenings and northern lights. There was no lack of food. They shot big blue gulls and ate them lock, stock, and barrel—heads, feet, everything. For dessert they had black crowberries which they put away standing, sitting, lying down; finally they did not even bother to use their hands but gobbled them off with their lips until they fell asleep. "If it be true that gluttony is one of the more grievous sins, then we two who ate crowberries that day in Ameralik Fjord will surely suffer a terrible punishment." The vitamin investigators of our day will have the indulgence ready.

But the last ship had sailed two months before they arrived at Godthaab, and the nearest vessel lay 700 kilometers away and was leaving in a few days. Two speedy kayak men were dispatched and reached the ship with letters from Nansen to Gamél and from Sverdrup to his old father.

The four men who had been left behind at the fjord were brought to Godthaab on October 12, and the expedition was at an end.

"We had toiled hard and undeniably endured much to attain the goal, and how did we feel about it now? Did we feel like joyous victors? No, the goal that we had so long looked forward to had nothing of the unexpected." The joy lay in the exploit itself. It was experienced at moments on the way to the goal, in the struggle for the goal. When the goal was attained, the chief joy consisted in eating one's fill, stretching one's self out on a real bed, and immersing one's head in a wash basin full of water. When one beacon was reached, he instantly put hand to brow, striving to catch sight of the next, the new goal, the one he had in mind when he answered Fru Rink: "I mean to."

The spirit of youth—
Like a fierce hawk in the blue,

It must hunt, it must pursue,
Ever seeking beacons new.

Nansen and his comrades, then, were forced to pass the winter in Godthaab where the Danish families showed them the greatest hospitality.

Nansen spent most of his time in studying the Eskimos. His method of studying them was characteristic: he lived the life of an Eskimo himself. He dwelt in their huts for weeks, worked with them, accompanied them on their long journeys, learned to paddle a kayak and to use their tools and weapons, ate their food, learned their habits and customs, and became so proficient in their difficult language that he and they understood each other very well. He liked them and they him.

They were impressed by his becoming such an able, full-blooded Eskimo. As a matter of fact it did not go against the grain: all he had to do was give free rein to his real nature. The original savage, the primitive, the call of the wild within himself, developed by his outdoor life to a fully recognized need and craving, made the transition to the Eskimo quite easy. "I am coming more and more to realize that it would not be at all impossible for a European to become an Eskimo if he had time enough."

In the book *Eskimo Life,* written con amore, he pictures understandingly and sympathetically the life of these children of nature.

"The Eskimo constitutes the extreme outpost towards the eternal silence of the world of ice. He took possession of the tracts disdained by all other peoples. By constant struggle and slow development he has learned what none has learned better."

Nansen is filled with admiration for this people which has overcome such untoward natural conditions. Primitive peoples can take care of themselves as long as they are left alone, as long as they are spared the so-called blessings of civilization. They are better and happier without them. It is not before they come in contact with civilized races that they degenerate both physically and morally.

In Nansen's opinion this is also true of the Eskimos. They are naturally endowed with a high moral sense. He does not agree with the missionary, Hans Egede, who calls the Eskimos "demented, phlegmatic people living without knowledge of any sort of religion, in animal stupidity, without order or discipline." "How base we really are," writes Nansen, "and what a perfect right these savages would have to look down on us with scorn if they knew that we use the most vulgar language of abuse against each other in the public press, such expressions as fool and blockhead, liar, traitor, perjurer, filthy rag, scandal sheet, boor, while they themselves have never a term of abuse on their lips. Their language, indeed, entirely lacks this class of words so richly developed in ours."

According to his opinion, expressed at the conclusion of the book, the whole stock in trade should be packed up and shipped, together with the tradesmen themselves, back to Denmark. This is what will happen some day in any case; but by that time there will probably be no Eskimos left to inhabit this land. "In the long winter nights the dead will play their shining game over the eternal silence of their land of snow." According to the belief of the Eskimos the northern lights are the sports of the dead.

On April 15, 1889, the ship *Hvidbjörnen* arrived and with it the time of departure. "It was not without regret that some of us left this place and these people among whom we had been so happy." One of Nansen's Greenland friends said to him: "Now you are going back to the great world from which you came to us; you will meet many people there and find much that is different. You will soon forget us, but we shall never forget you." Those who have known Nansen know that he never did forget them. Every Christmas he sent gifts and greetings to the Eskimo who had taught him to paddle a kayak.

They reached Copenhagen on May 21. A year ago a candidate for suicide upon whom Norway would not risk 5000 kroner, he was now a world famous man.

After a week of festivities in Copenhagen, he came home to a welcome such as no Norwegian had ever before experienced. On May 30, in perfect weather, the *Melchior* glided in under the castle of Akershus which thundered out a welcome. The harbor swarmed with steamers, torpedo boats, and white sailboats by the hundreds. Akershus and all the bridges were jammed with people. Even Ravna was not unmoved. "Isn't it a wonderful sight with all the people?" asked Dietrichson. "Yes, wonderful, very wonderful, if only they had been reindeer!" answered Ravna.

Up at the window of the Larsen sisters' hotel where he was to stay, stood Martha Larsen, once housekeeper at Store Fröen. She waved and beckoned and her tears fell fast. Martha, good motherly Martha, had bound up his bleeding face after his first encounter with the ice, and had helped him in many a tight corner. Now he came storming up the stairs and threw his arms around her. It was as though in her he embraced father and mother and the home at Store Fröen—yes, and old Mother Norway herself.

* * *

Of Nansen as leader of the Greenland expedition and of the relations among the participants, Major-General Dietrichson writes as follows in a letter which is quoted here with his permission:

"Nansen's plans and preparations for the Greenland expedition were so thoroughly considered that he was prepared and equipped to meet every obstacle which could possibly be thought of as likely to meet the expedition." He describes Nansen: "Tall, slim, and powerful, he was well fitted to stand the physical strain. In disposition he was calm and self-controlled. Clear-headed as he was, it was easy for him to make a quick and at the same time well considered decision. Hardy and fearless, he possessed a dauntless energy, an exceptional strength of will, and admirable powers of work and endurance.

"A matter of no small importance in bringing to a successful conclusion an expedition of this kind, where it is necessary for a number of participants to live uninterruptedly for a considerable time in such close proximity, is the preservation of friendly relations among them. This rests largely with the leader of the expedition. With his frank, simple, amiable disposition, and his gay humor, it came quite natural to Nansen to be companionable with the various members without losing any of his authority as leader. He placed himself on equal footing with his comrades, shared every trial and tribulation with them, and often took the heaviest end of the work himself; he never spared himself. This contributed to a remarkable harmony among the members of the party who all regarded Nansen, not only with esteem, respect, and admiration as the distinguished chief in whom we all had unlimited confidence, but also with genuine friendliness. Nansen thoroughly reciprocated this feeling and gave frequent proofs of it as the years passed by, right up to shortly before his death."

RESULTS OF THE GREENLAND EXPEDITION

FOR THE public at large, the sporting element in the Greenland expedition was of paramount importance. The daring and ingenious plan, the superb preparation, the skilful execution, the dangerous situations, the brilliant victory gave an epic quality to the whole enterprise.

But this epic was at the same time a chapter in the saga of scientific research. The investigation of a region which is in the same condition now as were Norway and Sweden, and indeed the whole of northern Europe and North America, in the great ice age, was, of course, intrinsically of great significance.

Until a few years before Nansen's expedition, little more was known about Greenland than our forefathers knew 900 years ago. For reasons not yet clear to us, there have been two great ice ages with a longer and milder period intervening. In Europe about five million square kilometers were under the ice sheet. The glacier, which was constantly advancing, carried with it rock and gravel from the mountains. The surface of Norway was striated to an average depth of 25 meters. Quantities of Norwegian rock were borne southwards to Jutland and northwestern Germany, while Sweden supplied the Danish islands and Germany. The "Swedish Stone" at Leipzig where Gustaf Adolf fell is literally a block of Swedish granite borne thither by the glacier.

As it melted the glacier frequently deposited great boulders on mountain peaks and ridges, balancing them so delicately and

79

nicely that they tremble at a touch. They are called rocking stones, and there is a farm in Maridalen near Oslo called the Rocking Stone after one of them. In the mountain landscape north of Egersund there are many of these curiously poised boulders on ridges and peaks. By striation and transportation the glacial ages remodelled the country, moulded fjords and valleys, and helped to chisel out the beautiful features of Norway. And these same glacial periods stored up deposits of sediment in great plains at the bottom of the sea which have since emerged and become dry land.

The human race persisted through the ice ages. It was a critical period for the development of life in a large part of the world. Many animal and plant species became extinct. Gigantic animals equipped with terrible weapons and means of defence, beside which the tigers of our day seem like mere harmless kittens, the mammoths, the woolly rhinoceros, the aurochs, the Irish elk, colossal reptiles and lizards were unable to hold their own. A relic like the musk ox survives with the ice age of which it has remained in possession in Greenland.

As far as the scientific results of Nansen's Greenland expedition are concerned, it must be remembered that the one great aim of the expedition was to succeed in crossing the country from coast to coast. Expeditions from five countries had been forced to turn back without having solved the riddle of the interior of Greenland.

It would never have occurred to the Greenlanders themselves to explore the Inland Ice. Why should they do so? There were neither seals nor whales to be found there, merely a desert of ice without a trace of life, a kingdom of death where the souls of the dead and evil spirits and, of course, the ghosts of the old Norsemen had their abode. For this reason it was not easy, either, to get the Eskimos to venture in on to the ice.

There was a tradition of an ice free interior, and the great polar explorer Nordenskiöld seriously believed it to be more than a myth. It was his opinion that the possibility of an ice free interior might have a sound scientific basis.

Nansen discovered that the ice forms an unbroken covering from coast to coast, with no oases or open stretches. Nor are there any projecting peaks: these nunataks, as they are called, are found only in the coastal region. The interior of the snow fields on Nansen's route presented a level surface rising very gradually towards the highest ridge of the glacier, which runs north and south approximately along the central line of the country. Later expeditions going straight across the country at various latitudes confirm this description of the glacier's form. The highest point touched on Nansen's route was 2716 meters. The surface of the Inland Ice, then, does not reproduce the relief of the substratum. The thickness of the glacier varies considerably; over the deepest valleys it must be at least 2000 meters thick.[1]

The ice divide does not necessarily lie where the watershed would be if the land were free of ice. The plastic mass of ice will be highest where the resistance to the outward advancement is greatest, and that will usually be in the middle of the ice mantle.

How was the Inland Ice formed? As the temperature fell, the amount of melting did not correspond to the snowfall. The wind swept the snow down from the mountains and gradually filled the valleys until finally even the highest peaks disappeared. The glacier continued to grow until the loss from the calving of the advancing arms and melting brought equilibrium with the snowfall. This thick, viscous mass glides from the interior out towards the coasts at a slow rate of speed in the interior, but increasing towards the margin where some advancing glaciers have a speed of over thirty meters in twenty-four hours.

Besides these observations of the extent, form, and movement of the glacier, of the nature of the ice and snow, Nansen's party made such meteorological observations as were possible without interfering with the headway of the expedition.

This was left mainly in Dietrichson's charge, and regarding

---

[1] The Wegener expedition recorded 2700 m. by echo sounding.

the work and the way in which he carried it out, Nansen writes: "The self-sacrifice and zeal with which he performed this task was beyond praise. What it means to produce a work such as he produced under such conditions can only be fully appreciated by someone who has tried to make his observations and keep his meteorological diary with the thermometer at —30° C. or below. It requires more than ordinary energy and determination to do this when one is dead tired or when destruction is threatening all around, and to write when one's fingers are so swollen and devastated by frost that one can scarcely hold a pencil."

His series of observations of temperature, the first that was ever made in a desert of snow and ice at a high altitude, is of great interest. The radiation in this thin dry air in the interior of the Inland Ice was found to be unexpectedly great. From September 11 to 15 the temperature fell at night to —45° C. (at an altitude of 2600-2300 meters above sea level), but rose in the daytime to —20° C. Such extreme variation of temperature is known only in the Sahara and similar desert stretches where radiation is great on account of the dry air.

Professor Mohn calculated that the tempature on the Inland Ice of Greenland sinks in the coldest months to —65° or —70° C. The Wegener expedition which wintered on the Inland Ice recorded —65°. This means that Greenland has the second pole of cold of the globe at the same distance from the pole as the one formerly known in Siberia. The climatic conditions on the Inland Ice of Greenland are a highly important factor in determining the weather in large parts of the northern hemisphere.

Another discovery made on this expedition was that the surface of the interior of Greenland is covered not with ice but with deep snow. The snow never melts there.

Not the least important results of Nansen's expedition were the establishment of the superiority of the ski runner and the demonstration of the equipment and technique which has been the model for all subsequent expeditions in the arctic regions.

BETWEEN THE BATTLES

ABOUT two months after his arrival home Nansen became engaged.

On the night of August 12, according to Nordahl Rolfsen, a shower of sand and small stones rained on the window panes of the house in Eilert Sundtsgate where Fridtjof Nansen's half sister Ida lived. Her husband, Axel Huitfeldt, who had been Fridtjof's instructor in the use of gun and fishing-rod in Nordmarka, sprang out of bed and opened the window. "What do you want?" he cried furiously out into the night.

"I want to come in," answered a tall, grey-clad figure. From the window fell epithets of abuse such as used to be exchanged in Nordmarka. But the grey-clad figure continued with his, "I want to come in."

And at three o'clock at night Fridtjof stood in the middle of the floor in his sister's room, his long legs astride and his hands in the pockets of his trousers, and looked fiercely at her. She sat up in bed:

"But Fridtjof, what is the matter?"

"I am engaged!"

"To whom?"

"To Eva of course!"

He then announced that he was hungry, and his brother-in-law had to go to the pantry for cold roast beef and down cellar for champagne. The nocturnal feast was spread on his sister's bed, and with it a new chapter in Fridtjof's saga was begun.

Eva Sars was the daughter of the clergyman of Florö and Manger, later the famous professor of zoology, Michael Sars. Her mother was a sister of the poet Welhaven. Her brothers were the historian, Professor Ernst Sars, and the zoologist, Professor Ossian Sars; her sister, Fru Mally Lammers, the singer. This highly talented and energetic family has a great name in the intellectual life of Norway, both in science and in art.

Eva herself was, in the opinion of a Swedish critic who is an authority on the history of song, the greatest romance singer that Norway had ever produced. She had a voice of marvellous warmth and was capable of complete abandonment to the mood of a song. She interpreted with a thorough musicianship the gayest and liveliest songs as well as the fanciful, the tragic, and the sublime. "It is by reason of the wealth of her voice in inner variations which are not the result of technique or training," writes the Swedish critic, "that Fru Nansen is so distinguished as a romance singer." She appeared with great success in Stockholm and also in London while Nansen was minister to England.

Fridtjof Nansen and Eva Sars were married in 1889. It is said that when he proposed, he added: "But I must take a trip to the North Pole."

The day after the wedding they set off on his lecture tour to Gothenburg, Hamburg, Vlessinger, London, Newcastle, Paris, and later Stockholm, where he was awarded the Vega medal, a great and rare distinction. In the autumn of 1890 they took a similar trip to Copenhagen, Berlin, Dresden, Munich, and Hamburg. Nansen described his Greenland trip and his plans for the new expedition. He was greeted everywhere with full houses and stirring ovations. If one follows his itinerary in contemporary newspapers, one is struck by the powerful impression of Nansen's personality which stamps all accounts. The words of Baron Ferdinand von Richthofen, one of the most eminent geographers in Europe, bear witness to the impression he created in scientific circles:

FRIDTJOF AND EVA NANSEN

THE NANSENS IN THEIR FIRST HOME, GODTHAAB

"The peculiar magic of Nansen's personality, which never fails to affect those who stand face to face with him, was strongly felt during the delivery of this lecture. He took us all captive by the strength of his immovable will. We saw in him a strong man marching towards a clearly realized goal, and clinging with tenacious energy to a well weighed and carefully projected plan. In him were found, in happy combination, unusual enterprise and scientific sense—qualities so often found divorced. Especially in our age of sport, it may almost be said to be the rule that the most daring feats of strength, such as the conquest of our high mountains, are carried out solely for their own sake and merely to satisfy the lust for adventure. All the more worthy of recognition is it, then, when the greatest physical difficulties are overcome in the service of a higher goal. He has shown both perception and understanding of the problems connected with arctic research."

When he came home from his lecture tour, the last volume of his great work *Across Greenland on Ski,* 700 large octavo pages, was published. This work and the one following, *Eskimo Life,* took up most of the first half of the interval "between the battles." Besides this, he accepted the position of curator of the zoological collection at Oslo University, and began the enormous task of preparation for the expedition to the North Pole.

He also built himself a house. He refused to live in the city, even on Drammensveien where they tried living in apartments for a time, and bought a lot at Svartebukta behind a point near Lysaker, where as a boy he had lain in wait for wild ducks. Here he was out in the midst of wild natural scenery and yet not far from the city. While he was building, they lived in a shack at Lysaker station where the painter Otto Sinding later established his house and studio. The shack had never been lived in, and now in winter it was certainly cold enough. "That winter," says Fru Nansen, "cured me of the habit of feeling cold!" The water pitcher was like a polar calotte every morning.

In this wretched abode Nansen sat and wrote his book about Greenland. In the intervals he ran down to Svartebukta to watch the building. It was Fru Nansen's cousin, the architect Hjalmar Welhaven, who built the house, a characteristically Norwegian home in all its appointments.

Björnson was present at the house warming. Rising up from the seat of honor, he lifted his champagne glass and christened the new home *Godthaab*.

In the leisure moments of these strenuous years, Nansen loved to gather his friends about him here—never-to-be-forgotten occasions for those who were privileged to be present. The painters Erik Werenskiold, Eilif Peterssen, Skredsvig, Munthe, Sinding—these were men of humor and wit and intellect! Nansen, and Fru Eva too, had tried their hand at painting. Old Schiertz in Bergen, with whom Nansen drew and painted, was seriously convinced that Nansen should become an artist.

At these gatherings Nansen, who was a master of the art of verbal narration, used to tell stories. The following description of a New Year's Eve excursion on Norefjell with Fru Nansen, who was fond of skiing and accompanied her husband on some rather stiff hikes, was given by Nansen at lunch the day after the launching of the *Fram*.

"It was New Year's Eve, in 1890. Eva and I had gone up to Kröderen for a breath of fresh air, and we made up our minds to climb Norefjell—to the top of course. We stayed the night at Olberg, and were rather lazy in the morning, so that it was well on in the forenoon before we got away from the farmhouse. We did not hurry at all at first and the day slipped by. It is quite a long climb even in summer when the days are longer, but in winter you have to look sharp if you want to get to the top while it is still light. Then, too, we had taken a route which may perhaps have been the most direct, but was certainly not the quickest. The snow was very deep and we had no guide. Such a peak is always tough climbing, especially in winter.

Finally it became so steep that we had to take off our ski and carry them; but we simply had to go on. You can't turn back half way be it never so slippery and icy. The last stretch almost beat us. I had to go ahead and cut our way step by step with my ski staff. It reminded me of what the little girl wrote in her school essay: 'For every step we went forward, we went back two. At last we reached the top.'

"Well, we too reached the top. But by that time it was dark, and we had been at it steadily from ten until five with nothing to eat. We had plenty of food, however,—a mixture of whey-cheese and pemmican—and we set to munching it up there in the midst of the snow in the murky darkness."

"You may thank heaven we don't treat you to that today," interpolated Fru Nansen.

"Yes, Eva, you make wry faces over it," growled her husband, "but it is really just a matter of getting used to it.

"Well, there we sat, we two alone on the top of Norefjell, some 5,000 feet above sea level. The snow stung our cheeks, the darkness grew denser and denser. Far away in the west there lingered a faint, faint afterglow from the last day of the year. It was time for us to be moving.

"The only thing for us to do now was to head more or less in the direction of Eggedal. From Högevarde, the top of Norefjell, down into the valley is about ten kilometers, which would not have been anything to speak of in daylight. But now it was not so easy to find our way in the darkness up in the midst of the wild mountains. We had to take a chance on it, and off we started in the pitch blackness, I ahead and Eva following. We went like the wind over rocks and hills, and it was no joke to keep our balance, I can tell you. When you've been out in the dark for a while, a sort of faint illumination seems to rise from the snow; you can hardly call it a light, but it is a sort of glimmer at any rate. Heaven knows how we managed to get along sometimes, but manage we did. All of a sudden I had to stop short and shout to Eva. It was too steep for ski, and there was nothing for it but to sit down and slide. It's not very good for your trousers, but it's safer in the dark.

"The snow blew about our ears till they tingled, for it was freezing like anything, and on we went.

"Suddenly, as we were going at full speed, my hat blew off—a little grey hat of the sort I usually wear. So I had to put on the brakes and get on to my legs again. Far up I caught a glimpse of something black upon the snow. I scrambled up, grabbed for it, and dashed my fingers against a stone. The hat must be still farther away. Yes, there it was. Again I clutched at a stone. The place simply swarmed with hats, hat after hat, as far as I could see. But when I went to put them on my head they all turned to stone. Stones for bread may be bad enough, but stones for hats are not a whit better.

"There was nothing for it but to go ahead hatless.

"Eva sat just where she was. 'Eva!' I shouted, 'Eva!' The answer came from far below. The distance seemed endless, especially with this mode of travelling. Now and then, of course, we were able to use our ski. But the snow was deep, and when that is so you can clear incredible distances. We no longer had any idea of direction; we knew only that we must go down. At last we came to a dead fix. Eva had to sit and wait again while I groped for a way out. I moved step by step in the inky darkness and was away for a long time. Suddenly the thought struck me: suppose she were to fall asleep. Such things have been known to happen—and she must be dead tired. 'Eva, Eva!' I shouted. To my intense relief she answered this time too, but from far, far above. If she had fallen asleep, I don't know how I could ever have found her again. As it was, I groped my way up to her bringing with me the good news that I had found a watercourse. I won't say that a watercourse is the best possible skiing hill, especially in pitchy darkness, when your stomach is empty and your conscience ill at ease. For this was really a reckless piece of work. But somehow or other we did continue to make our way down the watercourse.

"Now we were among the birch trees, and finally we struck upon a road.

"Far down we came to a hut. I thought it looked cosy enough, but Eva said it was dirty and horrid. And now she was quite lively; she wanted to push on. Just like a woman.

"Finally we reached the parish clerk's house in Eggedal. It was very late in the evening, so we had to wake the people up. The parish clerk was quite frightened when he heard we had come from the top of Norefjell.

"This time Eva was not so fastidious about her night's lodgings. She had no sooner sat down in a chair than she fell asleep; but, of course, it was twelve at night and she had been at it for fourteen hours.

" 'He's quite worn out, the little lad you've got with you,' said the parish clerk, for Eva was wearing a grey skiing costume with a short skirt, trousers, and a Lapp deerskin coat.

" That's my wife,' I answered. And then how they laughed!

" 'Oh Lord, oh Lord, you don't mean to say so! Think of dragging your wife along with you over the top of Norefjell on New Year's Eve!'

"But now came supper, and as soon as Eva smelled that it was not whey-cheese and pemmican, she wakened up.

"We rested up there at the parish clerk's for three days. So that was our trip to Norefjell on New Year's Eve. I thought it great fun, but I don't know what Eva would say. . . .

"A few days later the little lad and I drove down through Numedal to Kongsberg in twenty-three below zero, and the lad almost froze to death on my hands.

"But you have to go through a little hardship now and then in order to enjoy life properly after it. If you don't know what cold is, neither do you know what it is to be warm."

THE LURE OF THE POLE

THE NORSE vikings were the first arctic voyagers. Long before other seafaring peoples had ventured out of sight of the coast, our forefathers put right out to sea. In their square-rigged viking boats they fared across the ocean, northwards and westwards, to Nova Zembla, and Spitzbergen, to Baffin Bay, Newfoundland, and North America, half a millennium before other peoples found their way to the same regions of the ocean. They discovered and settled the Faroes, Iceland, and Greenland.

It was these daring navigators who for hundreds of years bound together the ring of islands and lands around the Norwegian Sea into *Noregsveldet* or the Norwegian Realm. In open, thin-walled ships and without compass, they ventured forth and discovered—or failed to discover and perished.

What were the motives that drove them forth? The same that have always animated voyagers—lust for adventure, desire for freedom, economic reasons; but also sheer curiosity and thirst for knowledge. We learn that Ohthere of Hologaland, who was at the court of King Alfred in England, sailed north of Norway right up to the White Sea, because, as he himself says, "he wished to find out how far the land extended due north, and whether any man dwelt north of the waste tract."

But the sea-bound ring of the Norwegian Realm broke. The viking ships rotted on the beach. Other races, the Dutch and the English, became the masters of the Norwegian Sea.

The discoveries and experiences of the Norsemen were largely forgotten, and fantastic notions about the northern oceans replaced them. Thus from the fifteenth century on there prevailed a belief in an open Polar Sea and, together with that, a belief in an ice-free Northeast and Northwest Passage to the treasures of China and India. Gradually, as the ice blocked the hoped-for passage towards the northwest and northeast, routes farther north were followed, finally pointing towards the Pole itself. It was a via dolorosa. And yet such a way may lead to victory, as England's history shows. In 1540 England had only four vessels of more than 120 tons burden. Then awoke the idea that it might be possible to find a short route to China north of Norway and Russia. A London company sent out three ships in 1553; two of them wintered off the Kola Peninsula. Russian fishermen coming aboard the next spring found only dead men. All had perished from scurvy. These two ships were sent home with new crews. One of them went down off the coast of Norway with all hands; the other disappeared, but the third vessel, which had got separated from the others in a storm, came through. It was commanded by one of those men who never give in, who keep their eyes open, and take immediate advantage of every chance.

He heard of the White Sea and the old trade between the Norwegians and the Russians, and went thither against the advice of many wise people. This journey became the great turning point in the development of English commerce and shipping. A new market for English goods was opened; the mercantile marine developed rapidly and helped England to become a world power. Thus an Utopian dream became the star to which England's Genius hitched her chariot; the white ice portal opened a great new era for England.

To find a short cut for England's trade with the productive countries of Asia was also a motive for polar exploration in the first period after the sixteenth century. No available trade route was discovered, but substantial results were obtained in the course of the search: the Newfoundland fisheries; the fur trade of the Hudson Bay region, the greatest in the world; and a rich whaling ground in the Greenland Sea. Coasts and sounds and islands that no one had known of before were also discovered. During the Thirty Years' War Baffin discovered the land and bay which bear his name, and reached Smith Sound, the entrance to the channel dividing the north coast of Greenland from Grinnell Land and Grant Land. Hudson gave his name to Hudson Bay where his treacherous crew put him with his son and a few faithful sailors adrift in a boat and let them perish.

In the Northeast Passage we have the Dutchman, Barents, whose name remains in Barents Sea. He was forced to winter, the first wintering in the history of polar exploration. For ten months he lay fast off Nova Zembla and experienced all the hardships of the arctic night. The next spring, shortly after the break-up, he died on an ice floe, lying with his map before him, giving good advice to his surviving companions. The Dane, Bering, in the service of Peter the Great, made two big expeditions along the coast of Asia and out through the strait which bears his name. He sailed out into the Pacific Ocean, was shipwrecked on a little island, and died after great sufferings.

After Barents', Hudson's and Baffin's time there was no longer any interest in polar expeditions in the service of commerce. A long pause of about two hundred years intervened. In the next period, the nineteenth century, the goal of polar expeditions was scientific knowledge and sporting adventure: to reach the Pole itself, to plant one's country's flag on the very axis of the earth.

We have Parry's famous attempt in 1827 with boats drawn on sledges to 81° 45', a record which stood for a long time. He was stopped by the south-flowing current. On Nares' expedition 1875-76, Markham reached 83° 20'. On Greely's expedition 1881-84, Lockwood reached 83° 24', the highest degree of latitude attained before Nansen. These two started from Smith

Sound. In the ocean between Greenland and Spitzbergen, where Hudson in 1607 reached 73°, the German Koldewey 1869-70 reached 77° before the south-flowing current stopped him. There is an easier route along Spitzbergen where the warm current off the west coast goes northwards. It was here that Parry made his attempt in 1827. Farther east it is less favorable again. Here the Austro-Hungarian expedition under Weyprecht and Payer 1872-74 made a dash on sledges to 82° 05'. This expedition discovered Franz Josef Land.[1] The Dane, Hovgaard, tried in 1883 to reach the North Pole from Cape Chelyuskin. He was caught fast in the ice in the Kara Sea, lay there over the winter, and turned back home the next year.

Not very many attempts have been made through Bering Strait and northwards. The first is Cook's in 1776, and the other before Nansen is the *Jeannette* expedition in 1879-81, led by the American De Long. The *Jeannette* froze fast in the ice in Bering Strait and drifted for twenty-two months in a north-westerly direction. The pumps were kept going night and day for seventeen months. Finally the vessel was completely crushed and sank June 12, 1881, north of the New Siberian Islands at 77° 15'. A remnant of the crew came to land near the Lena River. De Long and twelve men struggled across the tundra until hunger and cold killed them.

From the saga of the Northwest Passage we have the ill-fated Franklin expedition of 1845. Not one of the 135 came back. An Eskimo woman saw perhaps the last of them alive. He was sitting on an ice hummock with his head bowed down in his hands. She spoke to him, he raised his head and looked at her, then toppled over dead. For from twenty to thirty years England continued to send expeditions out to rescue or find traces of the Franklin men. Gradually they found them, the graves, the crosses, the bodies. The crew had left the ships and pressed southwards in scattered bands through many degrees

[1] According to more recent investigations this group of islands was discovered by Norwegian fishermen from Hammerfest in the middle of the seventeenth century.—J. S.

of latitude until the last, the strongest of them, fell down in front of the sledges and remained lying face downward on the ice. They died while they walked, said the Eskimos.

Another sad Arctic saga is that of the Kane expedition 1853-55. He wintered in Kane Basin in Smith Sound north of Greenland. It is the old story of the effects of the cold, darkness, hunger, and scurvy. At last they had not a pound of fresh meat and scarcely a barrel of potatoes left. There were none free from scurvy except two, and as the leader looked round at the pale faces and fearful looks of his men, he felt that they were fighting the battle of life with the odds against them, and that an arctic day aged a man more rapidly and severely than a year elsewhere. With the cold and the night came sickness, freezing, tetanus, scurvy, death, and burial—the "funeral service," with a little snow strewn upon the coffin.

All too often before Nansen's time the Arctic sagas of heroic men had ended with "a little snow strewn upon the coffin." But one expedition before Nansen's stands out by itself, a brilliant success, and that is the Swedish *Vega* expedition of 1878-79, led by the great polar explorer, Nordenskiöld. He laid his plans on a correct basis. He waited until the end of the summer when the great volume of water from the Siberian rivers had swept the ice away from the coasts. On July 20, 1879, Nordenskiöld sailed through Bering Strait, and with that the Northeast Passage had been successfully navigated.

That most ill-fated of all polar expeditions, De Long's *Jeannette* expedition, was the one which had the greatest importance for future polar exploration. The important "result" of this expedition was that a pair of oilskin breeches and some other articles from the *Jeannette* were found on the southwest coast of Greenland in 1884, three years after the *Jeannette* sank off the New Siberian Islands.

The noted meteorologist, Professor Henrik Mohn, wrote an article about this in the Norwegian daily *Morgenbladet* in November 1884. He conjectured that the things from the

Jeannette must have drifted on an ice-floe right across the Polar Sea, down along the east coast of Greenland, and followed the current round Cape Farewell up to Julianehaab.

Nansen had early realized, in reading the history of arctic exploration, that to wrest their secrets from the inner unknown regions of ice would be difficult along those routes and with those means which had hitherto been tried.

But where lay the way?

Then he "chanced" to read Mohn's article. It suddenly occurred to him that here was the route: with the current right across the Polar Sea—the same way as the oilskin breeches.

We are reminded of that autumn evening in Bergen the year before when he also "chanced" to hear a telegram read about Nordenskiöld's venture on the Inland Ice of Greenland. "It flashed on me like lighting, the plan was ready."

It was only in that one brain, however, that this lightning flashed. The Greenland idea—across the Inland Ice on ski from the east coast—was simply suicidal in the eyes of the Norwegian people. During the four and a half years that the idea had to wait, no one thought it worth his while to forestall him. This idea which came as it were drifting on a floe across the Pole had no other bidders in all the nine years it lay on the stocks in Nansen's mind. The greatest aggregation of polar experience in the world—the Royal Geographical Society of England—did not believe that the oilskin breeches in Julianehaab heralded a new era in polar exploration, in spite of the fact that they appreciated the conqueror of the Greenland ice according to his merits, and had the greatest respect and admiration for Nansen personally.

It was only when the facts came in contact with Fridtjof Nansen's brain that they struck fire, burst into ideas and plans which grew into the two greatest original achievements in polar exploration.

In February 1890 Nansen set forth his plan before the Norwegian Geographical Society at Oslo. He began with a brief

résumé of the history of polar exploration, and then said: "If
we pay attention to the actual forces of nature as they exist
here, and try to work with them and not against them, we shall
find the safest and easiest way of reaching the Pole. It is useless
to work, as previous expeditions have done, against the current;
we must see if there is not a current we can work with. Substantial evidence points towards the existence of such a current."

This evidence he set forth. Besides the articles from the
Jeannette expedition, there were other things which must have
travelled by the same route. A "throwing stick" such as the
Eskimos use in hurling their arrows at birds, but quite unlike
those used in Greenland, was found by an Eskimo and brought
to Dr. Rink. It proved to be the kind used by the Alaskan
Eskimos in the region of Bering Strait. Further, all the driftwood which is found along the east coast of Greenland, and
which is such an essential to the Eskimos there, was found to
be of Siberian origin; and finally the sediment which Nansen
had collected on the drift ice east of Greenland proved upon
investigation of its content and of the remains of living organisms
in it to have originated in Siberian rivers. Nansen concludes,
too, from the fact that Payer, who made his dash for the Pole
north of Spitzbergen, encountered Siberian driftwood floating
southwards from the Arctic, that the current must flow north
of Spitzbergen and therefore across the Polar Sea.

"By means of this same drift-ice and by the same route, it
must be possible to transport an expedition," concluded Nansen.

The ship that was to travel this route would have to be
small in order to be manœuvered easily among the ice floes,
strong enough to resist the screwing of the ice, and at the same
time large enough to carry supplies of coal and provisions for
twelve men for five years. With this vessel he proposed to sail
past the Siberian islands and force his way northward as far
as possible; then moor there between suitable floes and drift
across the Pole in two or three years.

Whether they drifted across the exact point of the North

Pole or a short distance from it mattered little. "We are not setting out to seek the exact mathematical point which forms the northern extremity of the earth's axis, for to reach that point is intrinsically of small moment. Our object is to investigate the great unknown region that surrounds the Pole, and these investigations will be equally important from a scientific point of view whether the expedition passes over the exact polar point or at some distance from it." Nansen emphasized in conclusion the importance of polar exploration for science and for geography, for the study of the earth's magnetism and the electricity of the atmosphere, the northern lights, the solar spectrum, morning twilight, the physical geography of the ocean, meteorology, botany and zoology, paleontology and geology.

The Norwegians, he pointed out, had already made various contributions to the exploration of the arctic regions. Our bold men of Tromsö and Hammerfest in particular had much to their credit. But up to that time no Norwegian had been able to seek the Pole on board a Norwegian ship. He hoped that "it might be Norwegians who should show the way here! That it might be the Norwegian flag which should be the first to fly over the Pole!"

Nansen set forth his plans and reasons again in 1892 both at home and abroad, and as was to be expected, he says, they met with the greatest opposition especially outside of Norway. In 1892 he lectured before the Geographical Society in London, where almost all England's famous authorities on Polar exploration were present. The renowned arctic explorer, Admiral Sir Leopold M'Clintock, opened the discussion by saying: "I think I may say this is the most adventurous program ever brought under the notice of the Royal Geographical Society." Although he admitted the correctness of Nansen's theories, still he doubted that the plan could be realized, and he had no faith in the possibility of constructing a ship which could resist the pressure of the ice. Most of the other authorities thought like Sir Leopold that there was no probability of ever seeing the *Fram* again.

Absent experts sent letters of similar purport to the meeting.

On the other hand, however, Nansen received the support of so eminent an authority as the German scientist, Professor Supan, editor of *Petermann's Mitteilungen,* of the Scotch naturalist, John Murray, and of the president of the Royal Geographical Society himself, Sir Clements Markham, who was not present at the meeting where Nansen spoke, but who later expressed his faith in a successful outcome. And finally let us quote Captain Wharton's words at the meeting: "People sometimes ask: what is the use of arctic exploration? Amongst other things I think it may be said that its use is to foster enterprise and bring gallant men to the front. To-night we have an excellent example of that in Dr. Nansen. I can only say to him: God speed!"

It was late in the evening when Nansen got a chance to make a brief reply to all the many doubts and objections and warnings. His conviction of the rightness of his plan was as firm as ever. Admiral Sir George Nares had remarked that an arctic expedition should always have a safe line of retreat. To this Nansen answered: "I am of the opposite opinion. In my Greenland expedition I proved that it is possible to achieve a goal without a line of retreat, for there we burned our ships and succeeded in crossing Greenland in spite of this. I hope for success this time too, when we destroy our bridges behind us."

It was this same dauntless spirit that gave a ship the name *Fram*—Forward.

To the chorus of objections may be added an article in the American *Forum* for August 1891 by General Adolphus Washington Greely, leader of the ill-fated expedition of 1881-84.

In the same number of the *Forum* appeared an article by Nansen himself, "A New Route to the North Pole." "Many people think," he writes, "that the North Pole can be reached through the air by a balloon or by balloon-ships, and that it will be so reached one day. I do not deny the possibility of this; on the contrary I regard it as very probable. But the only way at present would be to entrust one's self wholly to the wind, and this is no certain way as long as we have no knowledge of the wind-currents of these regions. . . . To go in a submarine boat under the ice would be rather risky as long as submarine navigation is as little developed as it is at present. But is there no other way to reach the North Pole?" After a careful development of his theories of the current and a detailed formulation of his plans, he concludes: "It will be no holiday trip, this drift through regions where the days last six months, and the nights are no shorter; but it is not to seek pleasure that we go out. People perhaps still exist who believe that it is of no importance to explore the unknown polar regions. This, of course, shows ignorance. It is hardly necessary to mention here of what scientific importance it is that these regions should be thoroughly explored. The test of the human race is a continual struggle from darkness toward light. It is therefore to no purpose to discuss the use of knowledge; man wants to know, and when he ceases to do so, he is no longer man."

Immediately following Nansen's article is Greely's critical and rather caustic comment on it. He remarks that Dr. Nansen "has had no arctic service; his crossing of Greenland, however difficult, is no more polar work than the scaling of Mount St. Elias. It is doubtful if any hydrographer would treat seriously his theory of polar currents, or if any arctic traveller would indorse the whole scheme. There are perhaps a dozen men whose arctic service has been such that the positive support of this plan by even a respectable minority would entitle it to consideration and confidence. These men are: Admiral M'Clintock, Richards, Collinson, and Nares, and Captain Markham of the Royal Navy, Sir Allen Young and Leigh-Smith of England, Koldewey of Germany, Payer of Austria, Nordenskiöld of Sweden, and Melville in our own country. I have no hesitation in asserting that no two of these believe in the possibility of Nansen's first proposition—to build a vessel capable of living

or navigating in a heavy arctic pack, into which it is proposed
to put his ship. The second proposition is even more hazardous,
involving as it does a drift of more than 2000 miles in a straight
line through an unknown region, during which the party in its
voyage (lasting two or more years, we are told) would take
only boats along, encamp on an iceberg, and live there while
floating across." General Greely then proceeds to prove the
falsity of all Nansen's assumptions and concludes by remarking
that "arctic exploration is sufficiently credited with rashness and
danger in its legitimate and sanctioned methods, without bearing the burden of Dr. Nansen's illogical scheme of self-
destruction."

NANSEN MAKES READY

AND WHAT had the people here in Norway to say to this polar expedition? There was on the whole great excitement over the scheme among the public at large, an excitement which concealed considerable anxiety.

If the generality of people did not know the history of all the polar explorers by heart, still they knew more than enough of the tragic tales of the Pole, of the many who had wooed the princess on the glass mountain and had had to pay with sadly nipped ears and noses, and sometimes with their lives. That it was Nansen's Genius herself who was sitting up there, and that she had given her chosen prince a hint of the right route and the right method, the average man in the street could hardly have been expected to surmise.

But there were many who were enthusiastic about the plan and did not doubt that Nansen was the man to carry it out. The Government and the Storthing responded without question this time to his application for support and granted what he asked: first 200,000 kroner and later 80,000 kroner. King Oscar gave 20,000 kroner and most of the rest was made up by private subscribers, some wealthy and some people of small means. The total expense of the expedition up to the time of its departure was 444,339.36 kroner.

The most important item of the equipment was the vessel which was to navigate this difficult route. The well-known shipbuilder, the creator of the modern pilot boat and life boat,

Colin Archer, undertook the difficult task. This was the first ship in the world to be built with the express purpose of being able to resist any amount of ice pressure. It was to be of such a shape that when the ice screwed in on it, the vessel would slip out of its grip and be hoisted up free of the pack. Greely, Nares, and others pointed out that this idea was not a new one, and there they were right; but, says Nansen, "what might be said to be new is perhaps the fact that we not only knew the ship should have such a shape, but that we gave her that shape, and with it the necessary strength to resist the pressure of the ice, and that this and this alone was the dominant idea which guided her construction."

Never before was such care taken in the designing and building of a polar ship. The sad experiences of previous expeditions presented problems, and Nansen, with his ability as designer solved them and gave directions, while Colin Archer thoroughly understood how to carry out his part of the work at the draughting board and on the stocks. It was an instance of the splendid cooperation of two men equally competent for the difficult task.

The ship was 402 register tons. She had very sloping sides and was short and broad—something like a pilot boat. The hull was pointed fore and aft and both ends were made especially strong. Both rudder and propeller were protected and could be hoisted up each through its own well. The stem consisting of three oak beams was 1.25 meters thick. On the outside of the bow was an iron sheathing and outside of this again were transverse bars of iron running some distance backwards on either side as in sealers. The frame timbers of seasoned oak, 28 centimeters thick, were built in two tiers. The frames were 56 centimeters wide and close together, the interstices being filled with a mixture of pitch and sawdust from the keel to a little distance above the water-line. The outside planking consisted of three layers, two of oak and an outer ice-skin of greenheart. The inner lining of the frames was of pitch pine planks in three layers. The total thickness of the sides of the ship was 70-80 centimeters. In order to make her still stronger, the inside was shored with heavy beams, stanchions, knees, and braces. The hold was divided into three compartments by water-tight bulkheads. The principal dimensions were: Length from stem to stern, 39 meters; length of keel, 31 meters; breadth, 11 meters; depth, 5.25 meters; displacement, 800 tons; weight of hull, 420 tons. She was rigged as a three-master and the crow's nest was 32 meters above the water. She was driven both by sail and steam.

The living room, a saloon abaft, was surrounded by four single and three four-berth cabins. Everything was done to protect these quarters from cold and dampness; the sides of the ship were lined with tarred felt, cork padding, thick felt, linoleum, and finally panelling. The ceiling of the saloon and cabins was similarly constructed and was 40 centimeters thick. The floor was of cork, wood, and linoleum. In front of the saloon was the cook's galley and beyond that, on the half deck, were the chart house and work room. Electric light was furnished by a dynamo which could be driven by the engine or by a "horse mill," but was usually driven by a windmill.

The ship carried eight boats and warm, substantial tents to be used if the men lost the ship and had to resort to ice floes and boats. Kayaks were later taken on board for the same purpose.

The ship was launched on October 26, 1892, from Colin Archer's yard at Rekevik near Larvik.

The thermometer had shown ten degrees below zero in the night;[1] snow had fallen, and a thin white veil lay over hill and valley. Gradually the mist dispersed, and the morning sun shone out with the strange, subdued splendor peculiar to clear winter days.

Nansen was at Larvik station to meet the guests. In the

[1] From the account of Professor G. Retzius in the Swedish *Aftonbladet*.

harbor lay a whaler with a crow's nest at the masthead; it carried the guests to Rekevik. There stood a great hull with its stern towards the sea—a tall and broad ship, the lower part black, the upper white. Three flagstaffs rose from the deck of the vessel, two with flags, the one in the middle without. It was reserved for the pennant bearing the ship's as yet unknown name which was to be hoisted during the christening.

Thousands of spectators had gathered at the yard, thousands had clambered up on the cliff. But around the great vessel stood groups of sturdy figures in working clothes, with grizzled hair and furrowed features, carefully examining her lines and build. They were whalers who had gone year after year to the Polar Sea and braved its dangers. There were also many workmen among them, ship's carpenters who had had a hand in building the ship and who now stood proudly looking at their work. And there was the master builder himself, the dignified man with the serious, noble features and the long white beard—Colin Archer.

Then Nansen followed by his wife mounted a platform which had been erected beside the stem of the vessel. Fru Nansen stepped forward, with a sharp blow broke a bottle of champagne against the stem, and said in a loud, clear voice: "I name you *Fram*." At the same moment the flag, with the name in white letters on a red ground, was hoisted on the empty flagstaff. The last ropes and cables were loosed, and the great, heavy ship glided slowly at first, then faster and faster, stern foremost, down the steeply inclined slipway into the water.

Just as the whole bulk of the ship took the water and the stern righted itself, a huge wave swept shorewards deluging the cliff and the spectators who had rushed down to the edge of the sea. Like wet flies they crawled up over the slippery rocks.

On the platform by his wife's side stood Fridtjof Nansen, tall and straight, looking down. All eyes were fixed on them. But in Nansen's bright, calm, frank, steady glance there was not the slightest trace of anxiety, doubt, or fear. He had that faith in his cause and that strength of will which can move mountains.

*   *   *

Many there were who were eager to go along—hundreds of Norwegians and 150 from other countries. Of course the members of the expedition must be Norwegians, and of course Otto Sverdrup must be the *Fram's* commander. The other members were: Sigurd Scott-Hansen, first lieutenant in the navy, who took charge of the meteorological, astronomical, and magnetic observations; Henrik Blessing, ship's doctor and botanist; Theodore Claudius Jacobsen, mate; Anton Amundsen, chief engineer; Adolf Juell, steward and cook; Lars Pettersen, second engineer; Hjalmar Johansen, lieutenant in the Reserve, stoker and meteorological assistant; Peder Henriksen, arctic skipper; Bernhard Nordahl, gunner in the navy, electrician, stoker, and meteorological assistant; Ivar Mogstad, man-of-all-work; and Bernt Bentsen, mate of several arctic voyages and the thirteenth man on the *Fram*. Bentsen came on board at Tromsö to speak to Nansen at 8:30, and at 10 o'clock the *Fram* set sail. He was really to go only as far as Yugor Strait, but as a matter of fact went the whole voyage. His ability as a seaman, his cheerful disposition, and faculty for making witty observations made him a decided acquisition. Eight of the thirteen were married.

The rest of the equipment was as carefully chosen as the ship and the crew. Special attention was paid to the food supply. Professor Torup, a specialist in the physiology of nutrition, was indefatigable in giving assistance and advice. The fat famine which occurred on the Greenland trip was not allowed to repeat itself and the well-known bogey of polar expeditions, scurvy, never set foot on board the *Fram*. Professor Torup also attended to the medicinal preparations, and Professor Schiötz to the physics equipment; Professor Otto Petterson of Stockholm and Mr. Thornöe of Oslo superintended the hydrographic department, Dr. Neumayer of Hamburg the magnetic, and Professor Geelmuyden the astronomical. Professor Mohn, who had taken such an interest in the *Fram* expedition from the start, saw to the meteorological instruments and gave valuable assistance in many other ways. Mr. C. J. A. Dick, a tireless friend of the expedition, attended to the photographic equipment.

The distinguished Siberian traveller, Baron Eduard von Toll, of St. Petersburg, arranged for the purchase of fifty-nine sledge-dogs. The same man established on his own initiative three supply depots on the New Siberian Islands in case the *Fram* should meet with disaster and the expedition be obliged to return home that way. Nicolai Kelch of Irkutsk offered to bear the expense both of the purchase of the dogs and of the establishment of the depots.

Never before had a polar expedition set out with such carefully considered equipment. Every eventuality that could be imagined was provided for, every detail was given thorough consideration. All the material and all the work were first class.

Nansen was once asked after the expedition whether anything had happened for which he had not provided. "No," he said, "I had provided for at least five times as many contingencies as arose. Before I left, I used to lie awake at nights and imagine everything that could possibly happen. Then I would light the candle and note it down. This must have happened fairly often, for Eva once said to me: 'Aren't you ever going to get any sleep, man?' But to foresee all possibilities is precisely the secret of being a leader; nothing must come as a surprise."

THE DEPARTURE OF THE *FRAM*

ON MIDSUMMER Day, 1893, the *Fram* lay ready to sail. The year of ceaseless toil was over, but the hardest part was still to come—the parting from his wife and little daughter.

Nansen writes: "A dull, gloomy day and with it came the inevitable leavetaking. The door closed behind me. For the last time I left my home and went alone down the garden to the beach, where the *Fram's* little petroleum launch pitilessly awaited me. Behind me lay all I held dear in life. And what before me? How many years would pass ere I should see it all again? What would I not have given at that moment to be able to turn back, but up at the window little Liv was sitting clapping her hands. Happy child, little do you know what life is—how strangely mingled and how full of change. Like an arrow the little boat sped on. . . ."

The *Fram* had waited long past the time set for sailing, but there was his boat at last. Now it came alongside. He quickly stepped on board, and without greeting anyone, went up on to the bridge and gave the signal to start. Those who saw his face did not soon forget it—calm, hard as stone, grey. Ponderously the *Fram* swung her bow towards the fjord. From the bridge Nansen gazed in towards Svartebukta to his home, Godthaab. Beside the bench under the fir tree he caught sight of a light-clad feminine figure. "It was the darkest hour of the whole journey."

The next day the *Fram* glided into the harbor at Rekevik

where her cradle had stood. There Archer came on board, took the wheel, and steered his child a little distance on her way before disembarking with Nansen's brothers. A salute from the *Fram's* guns thundered forth in honor of Colin Archer— "a worthier inauguration they could not well have had."

They sailed on in good weather, calm and bright, as far as Lindesnes. There the ocean gave him a mighty welcome as it had done on the *Viking* trip in 1882. The *Fram* was built for ice and pressure, but in a swelling sea she rolled like a log. Casks and timbers on the deck were washed from rail to rail. "Seasick I stood on the deck occupying myself alternately in making libations to the gods of the sea and trembling for the safety of the boats and the men, who were trying to snug down what they could on the foredeck. Often I saw only a whirl of sea, floating planks, arms, legs, and empty barrels. Now a green sea weltered in and knocked a man's legs from under him so that he fell and the foaming torrent washed over him. Now I saw the men leaping over hurtling spars and barrels so as not to get their feet crushed between them. There was not a dry stitch on their bodies. Juell, who was lying asleep in the "Grand Hotel," as we called one of the long-boats, awoke to hear the sea roaring under him like a cataract. I met him at the cabin door as he came running down. It was no longer safe there, he thought; best to save one's clothes—he had a bundle under his arm. Then he set off forward to secure his sea-chest, which was swimming round in the salt sea on the foredeck. He tugged and hauled it aft while one heavy sea after another swept over him. Once the *Fram* buried her bows and shipped a sea over the forecastle. One fellow was left sprawling on the anchor davits over the frothing water. It was poor Juell again. We were hard put to it to secure our goods and chattels. We had to throw all our good paraffin casks overboard, and one prime timber balk after another went the same way, while I stood and watched them sadly as they floated off. The rest of the deck cargo was shifted aft on to the half deck. I am afraid the stock of the expedition stood rather low at this moment."

But the storm subsided, and from the next day until they reached Bergen the weather was fine. The whole voyage along the glorious coast of Norway was a sheer pleasure trip and for Nansen in particular a welcome relief.

At Bergen "the sun was holding high festival in the sky. The Bergen hills, Ulrikken, Flöien, and Lövstakken sparkled and glittered and greeted me as of old. A marvellous place it is, that old Hanseatic town!"

Nansen lectured in Bergen, and the town festivities kept up well on into the small hours of the morning. The next day the *Fram* had her deck filled to capacity with Bergen friends who were eager to accompany them a little distance.

They sailed past Mangerland, where a lonely pastor, one of Norway's greatest naturalists, made his great discoveries—Nansen's father-in-law, Michael Sars, later professor of zoology at Oslo University. It was here too that Nansen himself took his first steps along the path of zoological research.

Next came the Florö coast with the large rocky islands of Kinn and Batalden and other fairy lands bathed in the fiery glow of evening over sea and sky. "Tired as I was, I could not seek my berth. I must drink in all this loveliness in deep refreshing draughts." And as they sailed on, this enchanting coast presented its changing panorama in sunny days and, farther north, in nights still more beautiful than any day.

"A glorious land! I wonder if another fairway like this is to be found the whole world over. Those never-to-be-forgotten mornings when nature wakens to life, the silvery mist wreathing the mountains which lift their tops above it like islands rising from the sea! Then the brilliant day gleaming on the dazzling white snow peaks! And the evenings with the sunsets and the pale moon! Mountains and islands lay hushed and dreamy like a youthful longing. Here and there we passed friendly little havens with houses round about smiling among the green trees.

Ah! how they waken the longing to return to life and warmth, these snug homes in the lee of the skerries. You may shrug your shoulders as much as you like at the beauties of nature, but it is a fine thing for a people to have a fair land, be it never so poor. Never did this seem clearer to me than now when I was leaving it."

All along the fairway they met people who greeted them, from sloops and row-boats, fishermen and peasants, women and children. Steamers crowded with people came out from all the towns to hail them and wave good-bye and bid them God-speed on their journey with music and song and cannon salutes.

Far up north in Helgeland an old woman stood out on a bare crag waving and waving. She must have come from some place in behind the mountain. "I wonder if it can really be us she is waving to?" said Nansen to the pilot. "You may be sure it is," was the answer. "But how can she know who we are?" "Oh! they know all about the *Fram* up here, in every cabin, and they will be on the lookout for you when you come back, I can tell you."

That evening Nansen sat looking at the land and thinking: Here the Norwegian people toil their lonely lives long in the struggle with the rocks, in the struggle with the sea; and it is these people who are sending us out into the great hazardous unknown, the very folk who stand there in their fishing boats and gaze wonderingly after the *Fram*. What do they really think of the expedition, of its value? "Perhaps there dawns before their minds a momentary vision of a new and inconceivable world, with aspirations after a something of which they know naught. . . .

"And here on board are men who are leaving wife and children behind them. How sad has been the separation! What longing and privation await them in the coming years!

"It is not for profit that they do it, nor yet for fame. There may be little enough of either. It is the same thirst for achievement, the same craving to go beyond the limits of the known, which inspired our people in Saga times, that is stirring in them still today. In spite of all our toil for subsistence, in spite of all our parish politics, utilitarianism is perhaps not so dominant among us after all."

On July 19, they reached Vardö where there was a sumptuous banquet, music, speeches, and rivers of champagne. The next day the bottom of the *Fram* was scraped, while all the men performed their last civilized rites of purification before entering on a life of savagery: at the bath-house of Vardö the Finn girls lashed them with birch twigs till the last vestiges of the morning after headache were gone.

Early the next morning, July 21, while the town and the harbor still slept, the *Fram* stood out from Vardö.

This last impression of Norway was just the right one for them to carry away with them—such beneficent peace and calm, and none of the turmoil of people with their cheers and salutes. Just then the sun broke through the mist and smiled over the shore—rugged, bare, and weather-worn, but still lovely—dotted here and there with tiny houses and boats, and all Norway behind it.

The land faded slowly on the horizon. "I wonder what will happen to her and to us before we again see Norway rise up over the sea."

For four days they steamed ahead through fog, dense, bleak arctic fog. Then the weather became clear, extremely mild and calm, and the sun shone over the smooth, gentle swell. "It was a delight to relax and yield one's self to the peacefulness of the sea."

After another day of fog, they encountered ice. They had not expected it so soon and the prospect was discouraging. When the fog lifted, however, it proved to be just an ice belt. The *Fram* had had her first trial in the ice and had come through with flying colors. She twisted and turned among the floes "like a ball on a platter." At Khabarova on Yugor Strait the Russian, Trontheim, met them with the dogs which had been ordered,

and wild creatures they were. Nansen and the Russian took some
of them out for a trial run with sledges on the bare ground. It
was a mad ride and fine sport, but they came within a hair's
breadth of landing in the river. The dogs were tied up on the
fore deck where they furnished more musical entertainment
than was desired.

The country here about Yugor Strait is an undulating plain
covered with a brownish-grey carpet of moss and grass, strewn
with flowers of rare beauty. During the long, cold Siberian winter the snow lies deep over the tundra; but no sooner does the
sun get the better of it than hosts of tiny northern flowers burst
forth, saxifrages and poppies, forget-me-nots, cloudberry blossoms, and cottongrass, and small forests of blue-bells ring softly
in the wind on their delicate stalks.

Over these mighty tundra-plains of Asia, stretching infinitely onward from one sky-line to the other, the nomad wan-
ders with his reindeer herds, a glorious, free life! When he
wills, he pitches his tent and has his reindeer around him, and
when he wills he goes on his way. "I almost envied him."

They became rather well acquainted with the nomads of
the tundra, the Samoyedes, who, during the days the *Fram* lay
there, were doing honor to their St. Elias in the wildest of orgies.
Their blessing in the form of lice seemed long afterwards on
the *Fram* to have been endowed with immortality.

The departure from Khabarova, August 3, meant also
the parting from Nansen's secretary, O. Christoffersen. He left
bearing the last post home, and with his going the last link was
broken.

With the petroleum launch going ahead to take soundings,
they entered the dreaded Kara Sea. The launch, which was
always causing excitement, created the first sensation. Some oil
caught fire and in a moment the stern was a sea of flame. Both
Nansen and the boat were almost burned up. The Kara Sea
brought them both storm and current, ice and dead water. Dead
water is no pleasant phenomenon to have to deal with; it is

shallow pools of fresh water lying on top of the salt water, and if a vessel runs into it, it drags along with her and can hardly be got rid of.

Occasionally they anchored and the expedition went ashore for a lively hunt for deer, bears, and birds. Dr. Blessing collected plants, and Nansen made geological studies of the traces of the glacial age and stratifications, coast lines, and the changes in level which the whole north coast of Siberia together with Scandinavia has undergone since the great ice age. Geographical discoveries were made and islands were named after the members and patrons of the expedition, besides King Oscar Peninsula and Eivind Astrup Mountain.

On September 9 and 10 they rounded Cape Chelyuskin, the most northerly point of the Old World. When the northern extremity was passed on the morning of the 19th, the flags were hoisted and a salute thundered out. "We had escaped the danger of a winter's imprisonment on this coast, and we saw the way clear to our goal—the drift-ice to the north of the New Siberian Islands."

All hands were turned out, and punch, fruit, and cigars were served in the saloon to the accompaniment of music on the organ. "Something special in the way of a toast was expected on such an occasion," says Nansen. He lifted his glass and said: "Skoal, my lads, and congratulations on passing Chelyuskin!"

And the *Fram* scudded ahead with sail and steam, breaking all her previous speed records as though she understood what it meant.

For the first time since Vardö they sighted mountains as high as 500 meters.

A new chapter now opened in the hunting annals of the *Fram:* walrus hunting. Early one morning Henriksen, an expert in arctic hunting, announced that there were walruses on a floe just beside them. Nansen, Henriksen, and Juell set off. "Soon we were so near that we had to row carefully. . . . Body to body they lay close-packed on a small floe—enormous masses

of flesh. 'Good gracious, what a lot of meat!' exclaimed Juell,
who was cook." Henriksen got ready with his harpoon, Nansen
stood behind with the gun, and Juell manœuvred the boat.
Off flew the harpoon, but struck too high and glanced off their
backs. Now there was some excitement. "Ten or twelve huge
ugly heads glared at us all at once, these mountains of flesh

ATTACKED BY A HOODED SEAL
Drawing by Nansen

twisted themselves round with incredible celerity and came wad-
dling with lifted heads and hollow bellowings towards the edge
of the floe where we lay. It was undeniably an imposing sight.
I laid my gun to my shoulder and fired at one of the biggest
heads. There was a thud, and the animal staggered, but fell
head foremost into the water. Now a ball into another head;
this one dropped too, but managed to fling itself into the water.
And now the whole herd dashed in so that the spray flew round
about us. It had all happened in a few seconds. But they soon
came up again, all around the boat, the one head bigger and
uglier than the other, their young close beside them. They

stood up in the water, bellowed and roared till the air trembled, plunged towards us, now on their sides, then upright again, and new bellowings filled the air. They rolled over and disappeared with a splash, then bobbed up again. The water foamed and boiled for yards around—the ice-world that had been so still before seemed in a moment to have been transformed into a raging bedlam. Every moment we expected to have a walrus tusk or two thrust through the boat, or to find ourselves heaved up and capsized. Something of this kind was the very least that could happen after such a terrible commotion. But the uproar continued, and nothing came of it. I again picked out my victims. They went on bellowing and grunting like the others. Another bullet, and one of them tumbled over and floated on the water; now a bullet to the second one, and it did the same. Henriksen was now ready with the harpoons, and secured them both. One more was shot but sank."

In the afternoon they shot two more. This hunting was not only a change in the monotonous voyage; it procured the expedition a welcome supply of fresh meat, which is of great importance on a polar trip. The preservation of the meat offered no difficulties in the cold, bacteria-free air: it kept fresh for any length of time.

On Tuesday, September 19, Nansen wrote in his diary: "This is the most beautiful sail I have ever had. Northwards, steadily northwards, with a good wind, as fast as sail and steam can take us, and open sea mile after mile, watch after watch, with the sea becoming clearer of ice all the time! How long will this last? As I pace up and down the deck, my eye is constantly drawn towards the north. I gaze and gaze into the future. But there is always the same dark sky ahead, which means open sea. My plan is standing the test. Luck seems now to be on our side."

On September 20 they came to the edge of the ice at 77° 44'. On the 22nd they made fast to an ice block, and the *Fram* yielded herself up to the embrace of the ice. The frost came, and the ice closed in more and more solid around them. The *Fram* was transformed from a vessel into snug quarters in the drifting ice.

At 77° 43′ north and 134° east the polar drifting had begun.

DRIFTING OVER THE POLAR SEA

IN THE preface to his great work *Fram over Polhavet* (*Farthest North*), Nansen says: "This book has taken on too personal a coloring to be a travel narrative in the ordinary sense." But he hopes that the story will emerge from the personal elements. As a matter of fact it is precisely this personal coloring which gives the book much of its peculiar value. Now that his life is ended, his own countrymen and his admirers all over the world feel the need of viewing his career connectedly, of seeing his achievements as the manifestations of an extraordinarily rich and strong personality.

During the sail from Vardö until they moored in the ice at 77° 44′, there was not time for more than a running account in the diary of their experiences from day to day.

Only a single entry tells of the dream rider saddling his horse. One night after twenty-four hours of strenuous hunting for bears and fleeing reindeer, finished off with a row against the current—"the worst row I ever had in my life—" and more coffee and cold tea than he was used to, Nansen was unable to sleep. "And now memory's airy visions steal softly over my soul. Gleam after gleam breaks through the mist. I see before me sunlit landscapes—smiling fields and meadows, green, leafy trees and woods, and blue mountain ridges. The singing of the steam in the boiler-pipe turns to bell-ringing—church bells—ringing in Sabbath peace over Vestre Aker on this beautiful summer morning. I am walking with father along the avenue of small birch-trees that mother planted, up towards the church, which lies on the height before us, pointing up into the blue sky and sending its call far over the countryside. From up there you can see a long way. Nesodden looks quite close in the clear air, especially on an autumn morning. And we give a quiet Sunday greeting to the people that drive past us, all going our way. What a look of Sunday happiness dwells on their faces!

"I did not think it all so delightful then, and would much rather have run off to the woods with my bow and arrow after squirrels—but now—how fair, how wonderfully beautiful that sunlit picture seems to me! The feeling of peace and happiness that even then no doubt made its impression, though only a passing one, comes back now with redoubled strength, and all nature seems one mighty, thrilling song of praise! Is it because of the contrast with this poor, barren, sunless land of mists, without a tree, without a bush—nothing but stones and clay? No peace in it either—nothing but an endless struggle to get north, always north, without a moment's delay. Oh, how good it would be to have plenty of time!

"One lives on memories. When I dream now, it is never of the Polar Sea, always of home; sometimes of childhood, sometimes of her who is behind it all giving the dreams a deeper meaning. No, sleep, sleep, you need it! And closing my eyes I banish thought and try to cradle myself in sleep. But through the shutters gleam a rocky cape and a bridge with a light boat and a flat shore and fir trees; and among the fir trees she stands in a light-colored dress, her big straw hat shading her from the sun. With her hands clasped behind her back she is looking out across the tranquil blue sea and smiling sadly. Then she turns and goes up towards the house. A big, black dog lifts his head, looks up at her with his faithful eyes, and follows. She lays her hand playfully on his head, then bends down to talk to him. Now someone comes down carrying a happy baby and she reaches out for the child and lifts it high. The baby crows with delight and waves its arms. This is life, the very kernel of life, the home and family."

Through three long years there was ample time to dream and yearn.

THEY now prepared for the long winter night. They got ready to meet the depredations of cold and drift ice and other natural forces to which, it had been prophesied, they would succumb.

The engine was taken apart, greased, cleansed, and put away, and the rudder was hauled up. The hold was converted into workshops: a carpenter shop, smithy, machine shop, and tinsmith's shop. Shoemaking and sailmaking were carried on in the saloon.

Everything from the most delicate instruments down to wooden shoes, axe-handles, ski, sledges, and kayaks, was made on board the *Fram*. Uniform employment was given every man. Idleness is not a good thing in the arctic winter. It is the devil's handmaiden and the scurvy's best ally.

A "horse-mill" brought along to drive the dynamo, or rather to give the men exercise, was never used: there was always plenty of other physical work. The dynamo was driven by wind or motor.

To these tasks was added, "most important of all," the taking of scientific observations, which occupied a good many hours. The meteorological observations were taken every four hours night and day, at night by the men on watch.

Every second day they took the astronomical observation by which their position was ascertained. This was certainly the work which was followed with most interest by all. Among the other scientific pursuits may be mentioned the determining of the temperature and salt content of the water, the investigation of currents, ice, and samples of the bottom. The sounding of the surprisingly great depths was a laborious task. Furthermore, they observed the northern lights and estimated the amount of electricity in the air.

The only one who had little to do in his own field was Dr. Blessing. When it proved impossible to obtain patients, he turned in despair to doctoring the dogs. His scientific work consisted in weighing every man once a month, counting the blood corpuscles, estimating the amount of haemoglobin and pigment, and studying the effect of arctic life, and especially the dark winter, on the blood and health in general. Thanks to the excellent food, the steady occupation enlivened by two hours' training on ski when possible, and the good quarters on the *Fram,* they all enjoyed splendid health throughout. There was an occasional toothache, Nansen had a little touch of lumbago, and Sverdrup suffered an attack of intestinal catarrh one time after he had lain in wait for bears too long on the ice. These were the main entries in the doctor's case-book.

Everything was done that could be done to keep the men in good trim and in good humor.

To this end the *Fram's* large and varied collection of books contributed. Violins, gramophone, accordion, and organ enlivened many an evening and "song resounded at the viking board." Nor were the playing cards allowed to get musty.

There was still another factor which Nansen stresses: the quarters were arranged so that there was one saloon for all, and during mealtimes and leisure hours they were together, but, if they got tired of each other's company, there was plenty of room to spread themselves outside of the *Fram.*

One day passed very much like another. At eight o'clock all hands turned out and breakfasted on hard bread, butter, various cheeses, corned beef or mutton, ham or Chicago tinned tongue or bacon, caviare, anchovy roe, oatmeal biscuts or ship's biscuits, and orange marmalade or jelly. For beverages coffee alternated with tea and chocolate. After breakfast every man went to his work. At one o'clock all assembled for dinner which generally consisted of three courses. With the meat course they always had potatoes and either green vegetables or macaroni. Tall stories were served with the dinner. Bentsen in particular had an inexhaustible fund. He served new ones every day and never ran out. Nor was Sverdrup far behind when it came to spinning a yarn. They had beer as long as it lasted; otherwise spirits were not forthcoming except on the most momentous occasions when a little drop might be brought from the doctor's medicine chest.

Except on festive occasions smoking was not allowed in the saloon or cabins. Ordinarily they had a smoke in the cook's galley, and then after a brief nap, worked until 6 o'clock. Supper at 6 was about the same as breakfast. Then after a smoke in the galley, they transformed the saloon into a silent reading room. The library of books and pictures was, says Nansen, a real boon and did a great deal towards making the *Fram* the fertile oasis that it was in the midst of the vast desert of ice. After 8 o'clock cards and other games were played. Those who were musically inclined entertained on the various instruments. At midnight they turned in. Each man kept watch one hour. The nastiest job for the man on watch was going out on the ice to take the meteorological observations. Besides this he had to keep an eye on the dogs, listen for bears, and write up his diary. On the whole the time passed pleasantly: "The regular habits which were forced on us were certainly beneficial."

On December 18, 1893, Nansen was reading about Kane's expedition. Kane complains of the enervating and aging effect of the arctic night. After having experienced this night for three months, Nansen says that he has not noticed any such effect. "I do not remember ever having been in better health physically or mentally than just now. I should be inclined rather to recommend these regions as an excellent sanitarium for cases of nervousness and general breakdown. I mean this in all seriousness. . . . The whole secret lies in arranging things sensibly, and especially in being careful about the food."

In the Kara Sea the *Fram* had brilliantly stood the test in the loose drift ice.

On October 9 while they were sitting chatting after dinner, a deafening noise began, and the whole ship trembled. This was the first ice-pressure. All the men rushed out on deck. The *Fram* behaved beautifully. The ice pressed hard, but it was forced under, and the ship was lifted up as much as two feet. "On the 11th it began to creak and moan along the sides of the ship, softly at first, then gradually growing louder through every key, now wailing with a high plaintive sound, now growling and snarling. Then it would crack, and the ship would give a sudden lurch ahead. The noise increased steadily until it was like a full organ. The ship shivered and shook, rose by fits and starts, or was gently hoisted up. It was a pleasant comfortable feeling to sit inside and listen to all this uproar and know the strength of the ship. Many a one would have been crushed long ago. But outside the ice was ground against our ship's sides, the piles of broken-up floe were forced under her heavy, invulnerable hull, and we lay as if in a bed. Soon the noise began to die down; the ship sank into her old position again, and all was silent as before."

The men no longer bothered to go up on account of the pressure. They felt that after all nothing but the ice was going to be hurt by it.

The ice slackens twice and packs twice in twenty-four hours in connection with the tidal waves, especially at springtide and new moon. In the interval between new and full moon there is little or no pressure. The tidal pressure was more noticeable in the *Fram's* first autumn and the third year when she was in the neighborhood of the open sea. In the interior of the arctic basin the pressure occurs more irregularly and is caused by the wind driving the ice. If heavy masses of drifting ice encounter resistance in other masses of ice drifting in the opposite direction, owing to a change in the direction of the wind in some more or less distant quarter, tremendous packing may result.

"Such an ice conflict is undeniably a stupendous spectacle. One feels one's self to be in the presence of titanic forces, and it is easy to understand how timid souls may be over-awed and feel as if nothing could stand before it. For when the packing begins in earnest it seems as though there could be no spot on the earth's surface left unshaken. First you hear a sound like the thundering rumbling of an earthquake far away on the great waste; then you hear it in several places, always coming nearer and nearer. The silent ice world re-echoes with thunders; nature's giants are awakening to the battle. The ice cracks on every side of you, and begins to pile itself up; and all of a sudden you too find yourself in the midst of the struggle. There are howlings and thunderings round you; you feel the ice trembling, and hear it rumbling under your feet; there is no peace anywhere. In the semi-darkness you can see it piling and tossing itself up into high ridges nearer and nearer you—floes 10, 12, 15 feet thick, broken, and flung on the top of each other as if they were featherweights. They are quite near you now, and you jump away to save your life. But the ice splits in front of you, a black gulf opens, and water streams up. You turn in another direction, but there through the dark you can just see a new ridge of moving ice-blocks coming towards you. You try another direction, but there it is the same. All round there is thundering and roaring, as of some enormous waterfall, with explosions like cannon salvoes. Still nearer you it comes. The floe you are standing on gets smaller and smaller; water pours over it; there can be no escape except by scrambling over the rolling ice-blocks to get to the other side of the pack. But now the disturbance begins to calm down. The noise passes on, and is lost by degrees in the distance."

Walks over such an exciting terrane would certainly be a rigorous regimen for the nervous and debilitated patients for whom Nansen recommends these regions!

It was the winter pressures that the earlier arctic explorers thought no ship could withstand whatever it might be made of. The *Fram* had more experience of these than any other ship had had without losing a sliver. She could not be crushed, but there was another danger—that of being buried under a pressure-ridge. On January 3 and 4, 1895, a pressure-ridge of extraordinary height and bulk bore down on the *Fram*. The floe under the *Fram* was nine meters thick, but it gave way before the enormous weight of the ridge. The possibility of having to leave the *Fram* had been foreseen and provided for. Boats and tents, sledges, dogs and ski, provisions, clothes, sleeping-bags, and tools were moved to safe places on the ice. All hands slept with their clothes on that night. On January 4 the ridge came in on the port side and buried part of the ship to a depth of two meters over the gunwale. Twelve of the men were standing out on the ice looking on. But the thirteenth, Sverdrup, where was he? Nansen dashed on board and found Sverdrup in the steam bath. "Are you crazy? Don't you know the ship is going to be crushed into splinters? The others are out on the ice; we are just waiting for you." "Oh!" answered the imperturbable captain, "I thought it might be a long time before I got a bath again, so I had better make a thorough job of it now."

This was the most villainous form of attack the ice could have hit upon, says Nansen. The floe which was being shoved by the pressure across the ice towards the *Fram* was three meters thick and caught the *Fram* amidships. Any other ship would have been crushed. The *Fram* took the blow according to program, converted her ram into a jack-screw, wrenched herself loose, and raised herself up. Her powerful sides crushed the floe and broke it into blocks and chunks of ice which gave the crew plenty of exercise with picks and shovels for several weeks.

This was the final death grip of the ice. The men of the *Fram* got no further practice in turning out, but they learned to respect the fearful might of the ridge. It also increased their respect for their beloved *Fram*—for the triumphant idea which her form represented. To be on the safe side, however, they allowed the equipment which had been carried out, to remain on the ice.

The polar bear was another exciting element in the life on

board the *Fram*. This widely roving sealer is found everywhere in the drift ice regions about the Pole and far in on the polar ice cap itself. For Nansen the polar bear was an old acquaintance from the famous bear hunts of the *Viking* expedition, and many bears fell before his sure aim on the *Fram* expedition too. He

THE BEAR HAD CAUGHT SIGHT OF US
Drawing by Nansen

really displays his talent for narration when he describes adventures with bears.

Bears on the fasting cure were strongly attracted by everything that was edible or odoriferous on board the *Fram*, from the dogs and the men to the frying pan in the cook's galley. When Juell would set a frying pan with fat and onions on the deck, a bear's sensitive nose could get a whiff of it a good many miles off on the ice. The bear is so near-sighted that if he wishes to satisfy his curiosity by a sight of the object he must come very close.

One day when Scott-Hansen, Blessing, and Johansen were out putting up an observation tent near the *Fram,* a bear came along.

"Hush! Keep quiet, so we don't frighten him," said Hansen. They crouched down and watched him. "I think I had better try to slip on board and announce him," said Blessing. "Yes, do," said Hansen. And Blessing tiptoed carefully away so as not to frighten the bear. By this time Bruin had seen as well as scented them, and came jogging along, following his nose, towards them. Hansen now began to get over his fear of startling him. The bear caught sight of Blessing slinking off to the ship and made straight for him. Blessing also was now much less concerned about the bear's nerves. He stopped, uncertain what to do; but a moment's reflection brought him to the conclusion that it was pleasanter to be three than one just then, and he went back to the others faster than he had left them. The bear followed at a good rate. Hansen did not like the look of things, and thought the time had come to try a dodge he had seen recommended in a book. He raised himself to his full height, flung his arms about, and yelled with all the power of his lungs, ably assisted by the others. But the bear came on quite undisturbed. The situation was becoming critical. Each snatched up his weapon—Hansen an ice-staff, Johansen an axe, and Blessing nothing. They screamed with all their might, " Bear! bear!" and set off for the ship as hard as they could go. But the bear held on his steady course to the tent, and not until he had examined everything there, did he set out with enormous strides after the fugitives. Nansen was now running towards him. "When he saw me he stopped in astonishment as much as to say: 'I wonder what sort of little creature you are?' I got well within range, and he stood quietly, staring stubbornly at me. Finally he turned his head a little to one side, and I sent the bullet through his neck. Without moving a limb he crumpled up." It was a lean he-bear. A bullet through the cervical vertebrae or through the brain is the only thing which will kill a polar bear instantly.

Even with a bullet through the heart, he may run for many yards and cause trouble.

After that day the men never went out on the ice unarmed, and they were still more careful after Peder was bitten in the hip by a bear in 1895.

One night a bear stole on board twice, and each time took a dog with him. One of these dogs was vicious and had a special spite against Johansen. If he sat up in the crow's-nest and whistled in the winter darkness, Svarten would howl with rage far out on the ice. When they found his remains, Nansen asked: "Are you happy now that your enemy is done for?" "No, I am sorry." "Why?" "Because we did not make it up before he died."

It was this same dog-killer that wanted a rump steak from Peder when he came out with a lantern to see what was causing the row at the side of the ship. It was a bear with a dog in his grip. When the bear made for him, Peder gave him a whack on the head with the lantern. The bear sat down and stared at him, and Peder made use of the pause to run and cry the alarm. Everyone who could get his hands on a gun rushed out. There was need for haste; a bear lay gnawing at a live dog. "Shoot! Shoot! Mine won't go off!" screamed Peder. His gun was full of frozen vaseline. Nansen's gun was plugged with tow which he could not get out. The mate's gun was also plugged. Mogstad was waving an empty rifle in the air and shouting to some one to shoot the bear. Scott-Hansen, the fifth man, was lying on his stomach in the passageway groping for ammunition through a chink in the door; the door would not open because of a dog kennel behind it. At last Johansen appeared and sent a ball straight down into the bear's pelt. That did some good. The dog was released, but it took five bullets to kill the bear. They often teased Peder afterwards about having screamed so horribly when the bear bit him. "H'm!" said he, "I wonder if there aren't others who would have yelled just as loud. I measured the steps of the fellows who were so 'fraid of frightening the bear, the other day, and there was seven yards to a step."

The dogs, as they increased in number, made plenty of work as well as fun. There was a great commotion in the camp when they were let loose to tumble in riotous delight in the snow. They often went along on hikes across the ice. Very quick to give warning of bears, they were nevertheless very cautious about making any closer acquaintance with them. They had to be watched carefully, as their play was likely to turn into a serious fight. If two were fighting, the others always threw themselves on the weaker combatant and would bite him to death if no higher powers intervened with firm hand.

To break these wild creatures in for sledge dogs was exciting sport. Nansen tells of his first attempt. The dogs took charge of everything—direction, steering, speed. Off they went over hill and down dale, then back to the ship, around it, over all the dust-heaps and boxes they could find with Nansen dangling after, now on his hinder-end, now on his stomach, now on his back. It was a regular circus, and yet Nansen was egotistical enough to be glad that no one was on deck to enjoy it.

In the monotony of their life every occasion for festivity was a welcome change. All birthdays were celebrated with fine food, music at dinner, and speeches. On the *Fram's* birthday, October 26, there was a big and well-earned party for her. After the celebration Nansen sat alone, and his thoughts went back over the year that had passed "since we stood up there on the platform, and she dashed the champagne against the bow, saying: I name you *Fram!* and the strong, heavy hull began to glide. I held her hand tight; the tears came into our eyes and a lump into our throats, and we could not get a word out. . . . Never shall I forget the moment we stood there together, looking out over the scene. And to think of all that has happened these last four months! Separated by sea and land and ice, and the coming years lying between us too. . . . How long is it to last? It is hard for me to believe that I shall not see home again soon. . . ."

The same day the sun took its departure for that year, and

the long arctic night began. Every degree of latitude that was passed was celebrated, as were Christmas and New Year's and the day in February when the sun reappeared after the long night, and Norway's Constitution Day, the Seventeenth of May. Christmas Eve, especially the first one, was something quite apart. It was a happy, pleasant evening. The chef surpassed himself, and there were boxes of Christmas gifts, Christmas papers, and music.

And candles, candles everywhere! It was not, as in the Christmas hymn, mothers' hands that lit the candles for the boys on board the *Fram,* but it was mothers' sons who lit them. A slightly forced cheerfulness was necessary to conceal the thoughts that went out to those at home. In thousands of homes that Christmas the people were in a state of suspense that was not free from unrest and anxiety. Those thirteen on the *Fram* must have wished they could tell their families that they were sitting safe and sound on board the impregnable fortress of the *Fram.*

Then came the New Year, Janus-headed, bringing a day of reckoning—first and foremost the *Fram's* reckoning. How far north and how far west? And how far still to go? The first New Year they were about 80° north latitude and longitude. There was still far to go in both directions.

In February there was a joyous celebration, the sun festival, when the sun reappeared bringing new life and hope and a yearning that stretched the wings of the soul.

In May came Constitution Day which during these years drew its glory rather from a great hope than from memories. The arms that bore the flag in those days were filled with spirit and determination. The men of the *Fram,* too, had their grand flag procession on the Seventeenth of May. Nansen went first bearing a Norwegian flag. Then came Captain Sverdrup with the *Fram's* pennant three meters long. Next came the band on a sledge—Hjalmar Johansen with the accordion—and then the others with various timely banners and symbols. Peder carried a long harpoon, and the cook had a saucepan on his back. Blessing, the unemployed doctor, carried at the top of a very long pole a banner demanding a normal working-day. It consisted of a woollen jersey, with the letters 'N.A.' (*Normal arbeidsdag*) embroidered on the breast.

Behind him came the meteorologists and then the dogs, Suggen with a bow of ribbon around his neck, and all the other four-legged members. They, too, sensed the idea of the procession, for they walked with becoming gravity.

From the highest ice hummock a speech was made in honor of the *Fram* who had so successfully carried them past 81° north latitude. Then they returned to the *Fram,* where Nansen made a speech from the bridge in honor of the day while the twelve stood on the ice with banners displayed. This was followed by thrice three cheers and a thundering salute of six shots. At this the dogs, frightened out of their wits, ran away and hid themselves for several hours.

There was powder in the air in those years—even mobilisation in 1895. The following dream which Nansen relates from December 28, 1893, is indicative of the apprehension that was lying concealed in the subconscious mind of many Norwegians during those years. "An unpleasant dream. The Swedes made a sudden night attack on Bergen. The whole bay was filled with mud scows, crammed full of soldiers. I thought I was travelling in a train across the German Quay with an officer. We had a cannon in the carriage and shot at the mud scows with shrapnel. I ducked well down in the carriage after the shot, expecting a salvo from the Swedes. But they were hushed and still in the moonlight. We went on in the train, and I was uneasy and quarrelled with the officers because they had not fallen upon the Swedes, while they were landing, with the miserable troops which we had. Later would be useless.

"Later in the dream I was living out in the country, and a Swedish officer came and informed me that they were now marching all together on Christiania. An uncomfortable dream which, it is to be hoped, does not portend anything."

When Nansen came back in 1896, his first question was: "How is my wife?" and then next: "What is the state of affairs in Norwegian politics?"

The arctic night, the dreaded arctic night of all the arctic sagas, filled and possessed Nansen's soul.

"There is nothing more wonderfully beautiful than the arctic night. It is dreamland painted in all the most delicate tints of the imagination. No forms—it is all faint, dreamy color music, a far-away, long-drawn-out melody on muted strings. But is not all life's beauty high, and delicate, and pure like this night? Give it brighter colors, and it is no longer so beautiful. The sky is like an enormous cupola, blue at the zenith, shading down into green, and then into lilac and violet at the edges. Up in the blue of the cupola shine the stars, speaking peace, as they always do, those unchanging friends. Presently the aurora borealis shakes over the vault of heaven its veil of glittering silver—changing now to yellow, now to green, now to red. It spreads, it contracts again, in restless change; next it breaks into waving, many-folded bands of shining silver, over which shoot billows of glittering rays, and then the glory vanishes. Presently it shimmers in tongues of flame over the very zenith, and then again it shoots a bright ray right up from the horizon, until the whole melts away in the moonlight, and it is as though one heard the sigh of a departing spirit. Here and there are left a few waving streamers of light, vague as a foreboding—they are the dust from the aurora's glittering cloak. But now it is growing again; new lightnings shoot up, and the endless game begins afresh. And all the time this utter stillness, impressive as the symphony of infinitude. I have never been able to grasp the fact that this earth will some day be spent and desolate and empty. To what end, in that case, all this beauty, with not a creature to rejoice in it? Now I begin to divine it. This is the coming earth—here are beauty and death. But to what purpose? Ah, what is the purpose of all these spheres? Read the answer, if you can, in the starry blue firmament. . . ."

During the three arctic winters many auroras captured and filled his imagination. These visions acted on his mind as music acts, as though space were an organ and the greatest Bach of all the spheres were playing God's richest and most beautiful symphony.

Among the arctic nights which he describes there is one which has taken form in a picture of rare plastic beauty: "O Arctic Night, thou art like a woman, a marvellously lovely woman. Thine are the noble, pure outlines of antique beauty, with its marble coldness. On thy high, smooth brow, clear with the clearness of ether, is no trace of compassion for the little sufferings of despised humanity; on thy pale, beautiful cheek no blush of feeling. Among thy raven locks, waving out into space, the hoar-frost has sprinkled its glittering crystals. The proud lines of thy throat, thy shoulders' curves are so noble, but, oh! so unbendingly cold; thy bosom's white chastity is feelingless as the snowy ice. Chaste, beautiful, and proud, thou floatest through ether over the frozen sea, thy glittering garment, woven of aurora beams, covering the vault of heaven. But sometimes I divine a twitch of pain on thy lips, and endless sadness dreams in thy dark eye. Hast thou too known life, the warm love of the south? Or is it my own longing that is reflected? Yes, I am tired of thy cold beauty; I long for the warmth and richness of life."

It was on the first Christmas Day, in 1893, that he began to feel tired of the Arctic Queen's cold beauty. The thermometer registered —38° C.

He longs, "but there are worse things than longing! All that is in one of beauty and goodness grows in its shelter."

Well on in the spring the diary still admits that it is a carefree life. "There is nothing to weigh heavily on one—no letters, no papers, nothing disturbing. This is life in a cloister, far from the world, the sort of thing I used to dream of when I was younger, a place where one can devote one's self to one's studies in peace. I am happy here."

But longings and memories alone are not enough to occupy so active a nature as Nansen's for long. His rich and comprehensive mind was filled with great forests of dreams and longings where he could wander and dream and yearn and romance, finding there the rest of complete relaxation after trying periods of work and excitement. His rest was oftenest like the eagle's: rest upon outspread wings. Severe intellectual labor, like that of the five years in Bergen, was interrupted by brief and strenuous mountain trips. Even the expedition on the ice of Greenland was a recess for his brain.

In reality, of course, this sort of change of activity provides only a degree of relaxation, although a giant strength at its midday height may feel such change as rest.

The interval between the Greenland expedition and the *Fram* expedition had been a period of strain of another kind. It was a period of enormous literary productivity. *Paa ski over Grönland* and *Eskimoliv* were written. Nansen made lecture tours at home and abroad, saw to the building of his own home, and, most important of all, carried out the work of preparation for the *Fram* expedition—an endless task. The thousands of things connected with the preparations had all to go through his brain first.

After four years of unremitting toil he stood on board the *Fram* and was able at last to get his breath. The voyage along the coast of Norway was a rest. The *Fram's* meeting with the drift-ice in the Kara Sea was a strain as was also her first encounter with the packing of the ice, underlined in red in the diary. On the other hand, the first arctic night, the first arctic summer, polar bears and northern lights were all relaxation— "a carefree life."

Sometimes during that first year the wheel of Time went round very slowly. Its relation to the position of the plumb line grew steadily closer, and if the current stood still, Time stopped his wheel.

When the wheel began its second year, the gentle progress of Time became more perceptible.

Another reason for this lagging of time, too, was the fact that one of the assumptions on which Nansen's plan was based proved to be mistaken. He had counted on a shallow Arctic Ocean where great volumes of water from Siberia would make themselves felt as a definite current. Now, however, it was discovered that the *Fram's* line would not reach to the bottom, and they were obliged to piece it out with lines of steel wire from the *Fram's* rigging. The Arctic Ocean proved to be from three to four thousand meters in depth. The water from Siberia would not be able to make itself felt very strongly as a current in this. The wind played a more important rôle than had been supposed. The map of the *Fram's* drifting shows an exasperatingly irregular course with many halts and backsets.

In the spring of 1894, Nansen wrote in his diary: "When I make the calculation, it is really, to be perfectly honest, pretty discouraging." He calculated that the *Fram* would require seven or eight years for her drift with the prospect of not getting as near the Pole as they had hoped. Even if there were no scientific importance in the *Fram's* actually rubbing her side against the earth's axis, there was nevertheless a decided stimulus for them in the wish to reach the Pole itself, that coveted goal of so many attempts, and for the public at large still the most sensational goal for the trip.

This "carefree life," this passive existence on this desperately slow, tortuous drift, this test of patience was a harder strain than the most extreme exertion in a more active existence could have been.

"This carefree life, this passive existence oppresses and crushes one. No struggle, no possibility of struggle! All is so still and dead and shrunken, stark under the mantle of ice. Ah! the very soul freezes. What would I not give for a single day of struggle—for even a moment of danger!

"Still I must wait and watch the drift; but should it take a wrong direction, then I will break all the bridges behind me, and stake everything on a northward march over the ice. Then the day of action will be at hand. I know nothing better to do. It will be a hazardous journey—a matter of life or death. But have I any other choice? It is unworthy of a man to set himself a task, and then give in when the brunt of the battle is upon him. There is but one way, and that is forward. . . ."

"What joy is there in strength when there is no use for it? What is a call? Does it consist in the powers one was given at birth? Then woe to him who was born with strength to do more than merely let himself drift with the current."

"I often think of Shakespeare's Viola, who sat like Patience on a monument. Are we not like this marble Patience as we sit here on the ice letting the years roll by and biding our time? I should like to design such a monument. It would be a lonely man in shaggy wolfskin clothing, all covered with hoar-frost, sitting on a mound of ice gazing out into the darkness across these boundless, ponderous ice-fields, awaiting the return of daylight and spring."

Early in the spring of 1894, Nansen began to think of making a dash northwards with one companion, using dogs, sledges and ski—a dare-all plan with no possibility of retreat to the *Fram*. The homeward route would have to be across Franz Josef Land, Spitzbergen, or Greenland.

He threshed out the plan thoroughly in his own mind first, and not until late in the autumn did he speak of it to Sverdrup. Sverdrup agreed that the trip should be made.

It was this idle and lifeless period which led to the concentration of Nansen's mind on this new idea, a new exploit. The "idle" period which preceded the birth of the idea was in reality an adventual period, a time of rigorous self-examination. Through the long, thoughtful hours his mind vacillated between doubt and belief.

On March 26, 1894, the day after Easter, he wrote in a diary which has not been published: "But have there not been sacrifices enough? Must one sacrifice everything because one feels the powers of will within one's self? Ah, we are but tools in the hands of greater powers: ours is not the choice!"

"Alas, even if our faith were no larger than a grain of mustard seed, we would go through life like children, following the star which beckoned us over hill and dale with the trusting eye of the child. Follow the call, let life flow free, the storm will banish all your doubt. Let it bear or break. Faith can move mountains, and I have faith. I shall succeed."

April 8. He reads Eva's letters and dreams himself home to her and to the fjord, lying breathless in the lovely tints of evening. He sees the sail-boat beside the island.

"Sometimes I am seized with despondency, but you believe in me. You know that I am the chosen of Fate, and that one glorious day I shall come back victorious. . . ."

CASTING UP ACCOUNTS WITH HIMSELF

THE *FRAM* lay in her bed of ice and drifted along with it. Except for the line, "Lina," and Scott-Hansen's observations, one might have thought that the ship was not moving at all but lying fast at anchor. She lay the whole time with her prow facing south and drifted backwards as though unwillingly towards the unknown. How safe and broad and irritatingly calm she was—just like her captain whose firm, steel-blue eyes expressed inexhaustible patience.

But the chief himself—in the midst of all this calm he was filled with unrest. It smouldered, blazed up, and died down again in his large, changeful gaze. With all his will power, he was as nothing against the course and speed of the current. The enforced inactivity of such a drift towards the Pole was consuming him. The ideas and powers which could find no outlet were used to turn the wheels of the mill; they whirled round and round within him, a maelstrom, a backwater, a destructive and disintegrating life of reflection.

It was not that he was without work. On the contrary: "An incessant, restless hurrying from one task to another! Everything must be done and nothing must be neglected from day to day, from week to week. The working days are long and seldom end until past midnight. But through it all there is a feeling of futility and emptiness to which one must pay no attention. Ah, but sometimes one cannot help one's self. The hands sink involuntarily and wearily, oh, so wearily."

In the midst of the perpetual summer light he longs for the arctic night, "for the eternal wonderland of the stars, with the spritelike northern lights and the moon sailing through the deep, blue silence—it is like a dream, like a vision into the misty land of dreams." This ungracious light which extinguishes stars and northern lights, darkness and dreams and mystery, this ungracious light which lies as an emptiness over the deathlike ice fields, cuts pitilessly into the soul, into its most hidden recesses. It lays bare one's self and one's life until one feels that the whole of one's existence is merely a petty spasm, a twitching back and forth, and one's ship has no right to be called *Fram*—Forward.

It was on July 11, 1894, that he made these reflections, and they do not represent a casual, isolated attack of melancholy. They are the after-gleanings of a reckoning with himself to which he had devoted a whole day earlier in the summer, in June 1894.

These pages of his diary have no direct bearing on the epic of the *Fram* expedition, and therefore he did not include them in the *Fram* book.

But for us, now that the great drama of life entitled Fridtjof Nansen is ended, every glimpse into his rich and highly emotional inner life is of great interest. We understand him better; we perceive the truth of what his co-workers and friends said of him in their in memoriam addresses before the Scientific Association in Oslo, that he was no Aladdin. Although few have enjoyed so many victories and triumphs, few have been so richly showered with the proudest garlands the world has to offer, no Genius tossed the plums into his lap. He had to go out after them himself, often through tangles of briers, including those that were in his own mind.

I quote from his diary for June 19, 1894:

"Always the same restless yearning—impossible to settle down to anything. A few days ago I turned enthusiastically to photography, then tired of it, and now I have begun to paint again. But no sooner do I take up my painting than I drop that too. Alas, this flightiness and fumbling from one thing to another! It is the bane of my life and will never allow it to amount to anything. The old doubt as to the real business of my life has come back again, that same quest for a single great idea on which to center my life, to which I could devote the power of my intellect, my latent energy; for that the power is there I know, or at least I am conceited enough to feel that it is. Exalted ideas of my own intellectual worth have certainly never been lacking to me. But my powers have not yet found a goal that has occupied them wholly and strained them to the uttermost. My whole life has been patchwork, and it may well continue to be until the day of my death. I have lain here on the sofa this afternoon in a state of intellectual torpor, turning over the leaves of the *Skillingsmagasin* and reading the biographies of our great men. I have a bitter feeling that they all have had a unified task upon which to concentrate and that is the reason why they have made something whole of their lives. My life has been broken up and wasted.

"When I read of a great mathematician and the great problems of mathematics, I feel a barb pierce me within. It is as though there were an uncultivated power in my soul that I have betrayed. Mathematics was my first love. I have wholly and completely forsaken it. And yet perhaps that was the course which nature had determined for me and which fate has allowed me to miss. Mathematics and astronomy with their infinite paths have still a strange attraction which I can never withstand when it grips me. There are problems to be solved there that are worth a lifetime, while the one which I began and likewise forsook— was it big enough to occupy a lifetime? At other times it is geology and speculations as to the earth's past which lure me. I pursue these studies with feverish zeal; with might and main I strive to discover new and epoch-making theories about known phenomena. I believe they must come when I know everything. But I read and read, and they do not come. How could they come to such a dilettante? I tire of the subject and let it lie again for months. Alas, I am not the great research genius I once believed! I lack the divine spark. I must hunt for subjects.

"The subject no longer dominates me, although perhaps it may have done so at one time. Now no subject satisfies me. All are too small—just as when I was a boy it was not enough for me to be first in my class. I want to go deeper, to get behind it all, to the heart of things; and there is no road leading thither. I suffer in vain. Those things which should occupy my time here do not appeal to me. I take the necessary observations, but not with pleasure—rather with effort. I have to force myself to take them because I consider that they should be taken and that the opportunity which may perhaps not come again for a long time should be made use of. In other words, it is my duty, but it is petty and uninteresting, the sort of thing that I have always looked upon as drudgery. Only occasionally does the work succeed in gripping me, as for instance when I thought I was on the track of the Gulf Stream. Then I worked feverishly, almost begrudging myself sleep. Intellectually I was as I prefer to feel myself—absorbed in a single subject. Then I discovered it. It was an undeniable fact, and the charm was gone. To elaborate the minor details of the thing no longer interested me, but I did it from a sense of duty. In the meantime I promptly threw myself into the study of oceanography, believing that here there might lie great problems awaiting solution, but I found none, and my interest died down as it had before. Now life moves along at a snail's pace filled with the trifling, sporadic observations that go with such a trip. Then perhaps I am suddenly halted, enraptured by a beautiful view, a glorious poem in colors of ice and sky, with all the bold contrasts of this arctic scenery. My craving for beauty awakens and desires to create. I grapple with it, but as usual the theme is too great for me. I see something beautiful that I should like to bring out perhaps, but the power is lacking. I realize too soon that I am not going to succeed, throw the brush down in exasperation, and leave the sketch lying unfinished as usual. Indeed, when have I ever finished a drawing in my life? I always mean to come back to it later when I am more in the mood for it; then I shall correct all those defects which can easily be corrected—but never are. What good would it do? It would only be a caricature of what I want anyway.

"But what a deal of harm this stupid artistic urge has done me! Supposing I had given in to it, what would it have led to? I should certainly not have been content with little; to produce a few 'pretty pictures' would have been nothing. No, it would have had to be something big. It must at least have been something original if there were to be any point in it at all—heigh ho! But I really reach the climax when I begin to think of myself as an author, and want to write an epoch-making philosophical work on the origin of the human intellect and the awakening of life. I an author! I who have no more talent for authorship than the paper I am writing on, and no more original ideas than that bottle of photographic developing fluid which stands before me! Nay, not so many as that has, for it can at least develop something even if the picture is taken by someone else. But what can my thoughts produce? Oh, just what has been thought and said hundreds of times before. Soon I throw myself again into some scientific pursuit or other. God knows what stands next in line. Strangely enough my own field is the one which seems to attract me least now, and yet at one time it absorbed me completely. For five years I lived and breathed for nothing else. My boldest thoughts were content to solve the riddles within that field; but of course I attacked the most gigantic problems. Nothing less would do me. I could not reconcile myself to the idea of being an ordinary ant-like slave. I looked with compassion on those wretched but very useful ants who drudge away tirelessly day after day, year after year, lugging their tiny fir-needles. Sometimes they drop one to take up another, slightly better needle; but that is all. In the course of years, however, these plodders build up a magnificent ant hill. To be engaged in being 'useful' drew my soul's contempt. I must build my own structure. Instead of the thrall that I was probably created to be, I would be the giant who stormed the heavens and filled his life with a work which, when night came, could make me feel that the earth, nay rather the whole universe, had been led into new paths. Pasteur. Only then could I be content to close my eyes and enter into eternity. That alone seemed a game worthy of my intellectual power. What purpose was served by being useful? I was too sceptical as to whether evolution actually led to anything for that. It seemed to lead rather away from than towards happiness, and happiness is the only useful end. It offered no goal for the future; its goal is but a chimera. Nature is an eternal circle.

"It was vanity, I suppose. Ah, yes, I have been vain. Like all young people, I too longed to arouse the admiration of my fellowmen. But there also I was not to be satisfied with little. It must be on a large scale. To be worth an effort it must be the admiration of all mankind.— But it could not have been desire for admiration alone. Now that I have had a little taste of it, so that I can judge of what value it would actually have for me, I am no longer ambitious of admiration. It seems to me to be more embarrassing than delightful. But for all that, I still have the same longing towards the great unknown. The yearning must, then, have a deeper root in my soul; it may perhaps be a natural impulse which craves satisfaction. But stop! If you knew that the world would perish in a few years and that hence all posthumous fame would be extinguished, would you still feel the same longing? Hardly so strongly. So it is vanity then after all. Your name must not die with you.

"Ah, puny soul of man, how willing you are to deceive yourself, how prone to embellish your motives! Or was it perhaps because there would no longer be any world to follow you into the new paths into which you would lead it? Or would you perhaps find enjoyment at last in your problems now become authentically useless for the first time? Let us, in any case, cling to that belief. Why should one have a giant's longings and be created an ordinary soldier ant? Nature often has strangely whimsical fancies. I, a pigmy, would set the world moving in new courses! I remember conjuring up before myself the greatest pontiffs of natural science and asking myself if I should be content to reach their level. But none of them found favor in my eyes, not even Darwin. A Newton was scarcely big enough for me, and yet I could not manage even to steer my own course. Why did I forsake zoology just when I believed that I had really begun it in earnest? It was not I who forsook it. Rather it was fate that by prodding a little at my life with chance outer circumstances suddenly changed its whole course. That expedition to Greenland, of course, I thought was just a little recreation trip, because my brain was overtaxed. Nor was the plan new to me; but it was a long recreation, and now I am sitting here more than six years later and still have not turned back, but have jogged further along the new desert road. This is certainly the worst break in my life yet, and I may always have to suffer for it. This break will make it practically impossible for me to find a work to which I can devote myself wholly. It has split my life up into two or more parts which will not hang together; one part makes another seem like lost time which might be put to better use in making a harmonious whole.

"I seem to have been waiting all my life for the great idea for which my life was to be a struggle, the idea which was to strike down upon me like a flash of lightning. I have had a premonition of it now and then, but the great flash has never come. There have been small sparks from an artificially charged Leyden jar. I always consoled myself with the idea that I was young and the future would bring it if I threw myself fearlessly into the problems that came my way. But now I have begun to doubt. I can scarcely be called very young any longer. The time when the flashes of lightning come, if they strike at all, is in the spring and summer; but these seasons are passing, and the future will hardly bring any. Ah, it were better to be a useful ant without any flashes than a flickering northern light which spends its whole life in a search for its own equilibrium and fades away before finding it—just a wild, idle, aimless dance across the star-strewn vault of heaven! It might, perhaps, if it had pulled itself together, have become a star of lesser rank. Just a little change would perhaps have brought about the necessary concentration. Just a word, perhaps, and my life would have developed harmoniously like a quiet stream. I should probably have sat there henceforward as a respectable zoologist. I should really have found my equilibrium once and for all. Naturally I should have attacked the problem which I considered the greatest—to trace the origin of thought, to examine thoroughly the inner structure and ramifications of the nervous system. I believed that I was on the point of making new discoveries, and visions were opening up before me which seemed to lead on to something further. Who knows? Perhaps they would have done so. I still have deep within me the same visions of that which I once thought I was about to discover and which I cannot forget. It needs only that an anatomist like Retzius or a zoologist like Roghankaster tells me that it is a pity I left zoology or the microscope to make me feel the whole weight of my guilt in forsaking them. Now I am getting farther and farther away from them. There is something which is called the sin against nature. Have I committed that sin? No,—no, I merely followed my nature too much. I am guilty rather of the sin against the Holy Ghost for which there is no forgiveness.

"But would I have been happier if the break had not come? How can I tell?

"Ah, yes. I know that there would just as surely have been something unsatisfied within me still. There would have been the feeling that I could have found something in other fields, something more splendid, and this feeling would have rankled deep within me although it might never perhaps have come to the surface. I was not quite happy when I was following that path. Shut off from all the life around me, I lived for my studies alone; day and night I worked at the microscope. It was like a fever; I cannot imagine that any man has ever worked harder. I refused to think of anything else, and yet this same corroding doubt broke through then too: why should one throw away one's youth, one's whole life indeed, for anything so sterile as science which led only to insurmountable barriers? A little nearer or a little farther did not seem to make much difference, since the final goal of the road lay in the unattainable, the infinite. And when these doubts came I felt the whole bitterness of life and a burning thirst to be assuaged in the realm of beauty, a thirst for an all obliterating love. No, that life would not have brought me more happiness, or rather more harmony; for happiness—*that* I possess greater and more complete than anything I could have imagined; it awaits me at home.

"This, then, is the outcome of a life in the cradle of which such great dreams were dreamt. It is not ended yet, of course, but I see only too well that it can never be different. Suppose I should win fame, or suppose I reach the North Pole or even the South Pole, what good will it do? My life will be just as far from being welded together into a whole as ever. I see now all too clearly the justice of my father's constant warning against dissipating one's energies too much and becoming a polyhistor, and his constant admonition to limit one's self to one main study. He may perhaps have noticed that there were many small scattered talents in the boy and have been fearful for them. Myself I did not suspect the danger, nor did there seem to be any. When I took up something in earnest, I certainly concentrated on it sufficiently—so much, indeed, that I did not even give myself time to learn the fundamentals of zoology. Too late I realize the seriousness of that warning, sitting here now as one who has never learned anything thoroughly, one to whom equilibrium is denied forever. I wonder whether it would be worse to lose one's shadow than one's equilibrium. If only I could come down to earth and be satisfied with a little, then, no doubt, something might still be attained; but that is the one thing I do not feel that I can do. Only in one single thing am I

not a dilettante, but fortunately that thing is the kernel of life.
In my love for my home, I am whole, or rather in my love for
her who is my home, my all. Would it not be enough to live for
that love alone? But that which has become life itself can no
longer be the goal of life. We must proceed together towards
something else. Tear it out and life goes with it, but if I have
it, then life too must be lived fully and richly."

July 30, 1894. "Yes, science is a good friend. I try to forget
myself in it. Sometimes I succeed for a while, but it is cold,
and I long unspeakably for warmth.

"Woe to him who has seen life for a moment. . . . But what
are the privations and sufferings of an individual beside the
great whole!"

October 26, 1894. "So I was, I suppose, a child who saw
adventure in the unknown; I had dreamed so long that I believed it existed. And I found it, I found the great adventure
of the ice, deep and pure as infinity, the silent, starry arctic
night, the depths of Nature herself, the fullness of the mystery
of life, the eternal round of the universe and its eternal death.

"Death's festival without pain and without privation, itself
eternal! In this silent, starry arctic night around me I stand
in all my naked simplicity face to face with nature. I sit down
devoutly at the feet of eternity and listen, and I know God, the
all-commanding, the center of the universe."

November 14, 1894. "Ah, sometimes I have such a desire to
be able to translate this scenery into music. What grand and
simple harmonies it would make. Only music could express the
essence of its being.

". . . I seem as if I were gliding over these plains into infinite space. Is it not an image of the world to come? Eternity
and peace are here. . . .

"What are all our research and our understanding in the
midst of this infinity?"

November 18, 1894. "One day our knowledge, our science,

all our *Treiben und Leben* seem but a pitiful Philistinism, not worth a pipe of tobacco.

"The next day I throw myself heart and soul into this very research, consumed with a burning thirst to absorb everything into myself, to spy out fresh paths. I am torn with dissatisfaction at my inability to solve all the problems that should be solved on this expedition. I burn with longing to make new discoveries for mankind, for a single great problem to which I can devote all my strength."

"As if dissatisfaction, longing, suffering were not the conditions of life! Without privation there would be no struggle, without struggle no life—that is certain enough.

"But now the struggle is to begin, the great day of action is here. Direct struggle, struggle from brimming goblets with victory beckoning beyond!"

Now it is over, the reckoning and the round of melancholy thoughts in the depths of the ego. "The last step over the bridge of resolution has now been taken." The trip north, so long considered, has now been decided upon, the plan is laid, the companion chosen.

"Confounded affectation, all this *Weltschmerz!* You are happy and nothing else, my boy!" says the diary next day.

He turns out on deck, the dogs jump and dance around him, his brave and merry friends who are to storm with him the North Pole itself.

ON SKI TOWARDS THE POLE

DURING the whole summer of 1894 Nansen considered all the possibilities and impossibilities relative to his plan for a dash by two men on ski, with sledges and dogs, to investigate regions nearer the Pole.

Late in the fall he laid the plan before Sverdrup, and on November 19 he asked Hjalmar Johansen to accompany him. Sverdrup could not be thought of, as he was indispensable on board as the commander of the *Fram* and as Nansen's successor. Every one of the twelve envied but did not begrudge Johansen his job. A finer man for such a trip would have been hard to find: Norway's most famous athlete and gymnast, he was an excellent ski-runner, with great powers of endurance, brave and cheerful.

The next day Nansen addressed the whole crew. He gave a review of the purpose of the expedition, setting forth what had already been accomplished and probably would be accomplished. He pointed out the desirability of expanding the sphere of investigation by a dash northwards. All thought this a good idea.

It was a daring and difficult journey, and its success would depend largely on having the best possible equipment. They were busy the whole winter making preparations for the trip. The *Fram* became a lively workshop where several of the crew together with Nansen prepared ski, sledges, sleeping-bags, kayaks, tents, shoes and clothing, dog harness, cooking utensils, instruments, provisions and packing materials.

Nansen's experiences from the Greenland trip and from his life among the Eskimos were now useful. He constructed the first kayak himself, making it light and strong. Fully equipped each kayak weighed 18 kilograms. They were somewhat shorter and broader than Eskimo kayaks, as the main consideration was not speed but rigidity and carrying power. They had to be short, too, in order not to bunt into the ice hummocks on the sledge journey. Otherwise they were made in Eskimo fashion: there was a hull with a ring in the deck to which the coat of reindeer skin could be made water-tight so that the waves could wash over both man and boat without either getting into the boat or wetting the man through. When the kayaks were lashed together they were capable of carrying, besides the baggage, a couple of sledges and some dogs. Kayak and sledge proved an excellent amphibian in these regions.

The matter of clothing presented a difficult problem. Fur clothes were to be desired on account of the cold, but were impossible to travel in. Woolen clothes were best. They took sleeping-bags of reindeer skin. For foot gear they had Lapp moccasins, made from the skin of the hind legs of the reindeer buck, also the Lapp boots called "komager," sedge grass (Carex æsicaria), socks, snow-socks and leggings of wadmel. From this it will be seen how they profited from the experiences of the Greenland trip.

Careful experiments were made with every single article. Nansen and Johansen moved out on the ice and lived in a tent alone, prepared their own food, and tested everything carefully. By February 25 all was ready. It was a busy time: night after night Nansen did not turn in until the small hours of the morning. Everything on the *Fram* had to be left in order for the future drift. Excerpts from the journal and observations had to be copied out and taken along, and letters home had to be written by the two arctic travellers and by those who stayed in the *Fram*. There were a thousand things to be done.

On February 25 the two men set out with six sledges ac-

companied by a troop of their companions. They were forced
to turn back, however: one sledge broke, and there were too
many sledges. The sledges were made stronger, but they had
to turn back still another time. The number of sledges was
reduced to three with nine dogs to each, and the baggage was
reduced to 660 kilograms.

Finally on March 14 they departed for the third and last
time.

The march of Nansen and Johansen towards the North
Pole and their wintering on Franz Josef Land is the dazzling
climax of all the arctic sagas, an unprecedented tale, not of luck
and chance, but of ingenious preparation and unexampled execution. It is a thrilling saga of achievement, of men who do
things—a magnificent display of mental and physical strength
and prowess.

The ice which they encountered was, even for arctic ice,
extraordinarily difficult. The pressure-ridges were often eight
or nine meters high, and where it was not possible to go around
them, they caused endless toil and loss of time.

Although the expedition started three weeks later than
had been intended, the cold was very intense. Their clothes
froze so stiff that they rubbed deep sores in the wrists of the
wearer and had to be thawed out and dried on the body in the
sleeping-bag. The foot gear had to be taken particular care of—
the moccasins turned inside out, the sedge grass pulled out to
prevent it from clinging together and dried on the chest or
thighs. While the Primus lamp hummed away and heated food
and water for them, the melting process went on in the sleeping-
bag to the accompaniment of a lively chattering of teeth. The
nights were often so cold that the mercury froze, and one morning Nansen woke with his fingers frozen white. Frequently they
were so tired at the end of a heavy day's march that they could
hardly keep awake until they had eaten. Sometimes they fell
asleep with a bite of food on the way to their mouths.

Instead of becoming better, the ice grew worse and worse.

Nansen usually went ahead to find a way around the highest ridges. Then the dogs had to be helped to draw the sledges, and often had to be lifted over the ridges. There were long stretches of rough rubble ice and between the hummocks snow and water through which they had to plunge.

The travellers were sorry afterwards to think how hard they were obliged to be on the worn-out dogs, but they had to press on; the strength had to be taken out of both dogs and men. One day one of the dogs was so ill that it was let loose. Later on in the day it was discovered that the dog had not left the camping ground in the morning. Although every hour was precious, Nansen went back and got the dog.

On April 7 Nansen realized that there was no more time to devote to this impossible work. He went alone on ski some distance farther north, but from the highest hummocks he could see nothing but rubble ice like frozen surf as far as the horizon.

"They recognized the limits of the humanly possible," said Björnson.

The next day, April 8, with the thermometer at —36° C., they celebrated this nothernmost camping-ground with a banquet at 86° 14' N.,—320 kilometers farther north than any human foot had hitherto trod. They decorated the spot with two flags.

The homeward journey was headed in the direction of Franz Josef Land. It was 670 kilometers distant as the crow flies, a long first lap on the way home, and it became still longer in the game that the current and lanes of ice played with them.

Farther south the ice grew better. April passed quickly. In May the ice became worse again; the spring made cracks and lanes in it and the surface was a soft slush into which sledges, dogs, and men sank deep. The provisions were dwindling and rations were decreased. There was not a sign of life, bear, seal, or bird. Finally in June a bearded seal popped up in a water lane. It was shot and hauled up and the fortunate hunters danced round the fat carcass like happy children. Here was food for a whole month. They ate until the oil dripped from them, and fried blood pancakes in blubber until the tent caught fire and almost burned up. When another seal appeared they celebrated the event with a banquet—a piece of chocolate with blubber!

On June 30 Nansen made the discovery that they had not advanced a jot the whole of that month. They were faced with the prospect of wintering under a less snug roof than the *Fram's* and almost without provisions.

On July 6 three welcome bears presented themselves and the food question was again solved.

The temperature became milder. To Nansen, sitting patching his breeches at —28° centigrade, it seemed quite mild. They were used to —40° and when it rose to 18 degrees below zero, Nansen perspired so much in his sleeping-bag that he could hardly get to sleep. On July 24 the diary says: "At last the great marvel has come to pass after we had almost ceased to believe in it—land, land!" In the clear air it seemed very near, a day's march at most. As a matter of fact it took them thirteen arduous days to reach it.

They toiled on through the rain. For three days Nansen lay helpless with lumbago. Every step was a torture. At nights the sleeping-bag was soaked, their legs were wet, their feet like lumps of ice, and they had not a dry stitch to change into. Johansen was obliged to take off Nansen's boots and socks for him. "I have some idea now what it would be like if one of us became seriously ill. I very much fear our fate would then be sealed." The ice was a heap of blocks. There was not a flat place large enough for a tent and there were many lanes. When they finally reached land they were so exhausted that they had to rest for several days.

One of these thirteen days came near to being Johansen's last. One foggy day just as they had come to a lane which they had to cross Nansen heard a shout behind him: "Get the gun!" "I turned round and saw an enormous bear throwing itself on Johansen, who was on his back. I tried to seize my gun, which was in its case on the foredeck, but at the same moment the kayak slipped into the water. I began to pull the kayak on to the high edge of the ice again as quickly as I could, but with its cargo it was a heavy lift. I was on my knees pulling and tugging to get my gun and had no time to look round and see what was going on behind me. Just then I heard Johansen say quietly, 'You must look sharp if you want to be in time!' Look sharp? I should think so! At last I got hold of the butt end, dragged the gun out, turned round in a sitting posture, and cocked the shot barrel. The bear was standing not two yards off, ready to make an end of my dog, Kaifas. There was not time to lose in cocking the other barrel, so I gave it a charge of small shot behind the ear, and it fell down dead between us."

The bear had slunk up behind them in the fog so quietly that even the dogs had not noticed anything, had thrown itself on Johansen and given him a cuff on the ear that knocked him over on his back. Johansen tried to defend himself as best he could with his hands, seized the animal by the throat and did not let go his hold. It was just when the bear opened his jaws to bite Johansen in the head that Nansen heard the memorable words, "Look sharp!" Bruin had been very much engrossed all this time with the busy figure over beside the kayak and was speculating as to what it was so busy about, but then he caught sight of the dogs and turned to them. He gave Suggen a cuff which made him howl and caught Kaifas with a slap on the nose. Meanwhile Johansen had wriggled speedily away and got his gun just as Nansen's shot rang out. The only harm done was that the bear cut through five months' grime on Johansen's cheek so that he had a white stripe on it for a while. It has since been calculated that only the strength of a bear could have cut so deep.

There was open water alongside the land they had reached. Kayak and sledge now changed rôles. They lashed the kayaks together and placed the sledges, which they did not dare to part with, across the kayaks. Kaifas and Suggen were still with

them. Time after time they had to come up on the ice again
and tug and haul. Finally they reached open water. Kaifas and
Suggen could no longer be of use to their friends. "Poor Suggen,
he was so touchingly good, and Kaifas—how proudly and
splendidly he had kept up to the end! Faithful and enduring,
they had toiled for us the whole journey through. . . . Destroy
them in the same way as the others we could not; we sacrificed
a cartridge on each of them. Johansen shot my dog behind a
hummock, and I shot his. It was a hard task."

On August 15 the travellers set foot on bare land for the
first time in two years. They enjoyed to the full the delights
of life on land, jumped about like children among the stones,
plucked moss and saxifrage and poppies, and hoisted the Norwegian flag. With sea-weed and seals and sea birds and the blue
sea beyond it was a paradise on earth for these ice-weary men.

The occasion was celebrated by a banquet of pemmican
and the last of the potatoes specially saved for it. For dessert
they had a new hope of reaching home in the fall.

After a day's rowing, they encountered ice again, then
after a long time more open water. A whole day and night of
sailing and then—blocked! They were obliged to winter.

The food supply was low again, but one morning a bear
announced himself at the door of the tent and at once the
barrel of Nansen's gun popped out and bade him welcome.

Towards the end of August they reached the west coast of
Franz Josef Land and selected a spot there for their winter
quarters, never suspecting that just a month's journey southwards lay Mr. Jackson's expedition.

The first and most important thing to do was to secure
a supply of food and fuel. Bears and walruses in plenty had to
lay down their lives. The clothes of the hunters became quite
saturated and stiff with blood and oil. Huge mounds of meat
and blubber were stored up and covered over with canvas and
hides. Bears and foxes tried to steal from the mounds, the bears
usually having to pay with their lives. The foxes were the worst,

for they carried off all sorts of things for which they could have no possible use—thermometers, steel wire, harpoons, and lines, indeed they even dragged off the sail.

The hardest task was building the winter hut. The walls were made of stone and moss, the roof of walrus hides with a log of driftwood for a ridge-pole. For tools they used the shoulder-blade of a walrus tied to a ski staff, the tusks of the walrus made excellent mattocks. Their furniture was severely functionalistic, simple and serviceable: two benches of stone covered with bearskin as an under layer for a sleeping-bag made of woolen blankets. The stones made rather stiff springs; the sleepers got sores on their hips from the hard couch, but slept well in spite of everything. Over the hearth they made a smoke-hood of bear hide up to the roof where they erected a chimney of ice and snow. It gave a good draught, and a bit of fur served as a damper.

The entrance to the hut was on very much the same principle as the entrance to an Eskimo hut, a sort of burrow through the earth roofed over with blocks of ice and with two doors of skin. The hut was ten feet long and exactly six feet wide, so that when Nansen stretched out his arms he touched both walls. It was almost high enough for Nansen to stand upright.

On September 25 they moved from their temporary cave into their winter residence. It was heated and lighted by train-oil lamps for which Blessing's gauze bandages provided excellent wicks; though they did not give much warmth, yet the temperature would rise as high as the freezing point in the middle of the room and that seemed comfortable enough.

When the frost-covered walls shone in the lamplight with thousands of crystals and beautiful frost-flowers, the explorers could dream that they dwelt in marble halls. When the outside temperature rose, however, or when they cooked on the hearth, the marble splendor ran down in rivulets into their sleeping-bags.

They had two meals a day—boiled bear's meat and soup

in the morning and bear steak in the evening. They consumed
enormous quantities of this food—19 bears were eaten—and
never tired of it. Now and then they ate a little blubber with
it, or dipped the meat in oil, or fished out pieces of burnt blubber from the train-oil lamps. These bits were called cakes, and
were thought "uncommonly nice." They used to imagine how
delicious the "cakes" would have been with just a little sugar
on top.

They still had some of the provisions that had been brought
from the *Fram,* but these were put away in a depot to be used
on the homeward journey in the spring.

On October 15 the sun went into hiding and the bears
disappeared. The last one was up on the roof rummaging in
their store-house on November 8. Then these two Norwegian
bears also began hibernating in earnest. There was nothing to do
but eat and sleep. They would sleep as many as 20 hours out of
the 24. For exercise they went out for a walk when the weather
permitted. It was usually blowing so hard under the cliff that
their walks were short. Then, too, their clothes were not such
that they could defy a high wind at —40° centigrade, and their
wind gear was in tatters. Nansen had hoped to get some of the
account of their journey written, but his brain was sluggish and
the surroundings were not stimulating. The diary for the nine
months that they spent in the hut is very meagre. There were
weeks with nothing but the most necessary meteorological observations. I have had all the diaries from the hut to look over,
but they are so sooty and black and greasy almost all over the
pages that it is often necessary to use a magnifying glass to de-
cipher what is written on them.

From the diary for December 1: "Wonderfully beautiful
weather for the last few days; one can never weary of walking up
and down outside, while the moon transforms the whole of this
ice-world into a fairyland. The hut is still in shadow under the
mountain which hangs above it, dark and lowering; but the
moonlight floats over ice and fjord, and is cast back glittering

from every snowy ridge and hill. A weird beauty, without feeling, as though of a dead planet, built of shining white marble. Just so must the mountains stand there, frozen and ice cold; just so must the lakes lie congealed beneath their snowy covering. Now as ever the moon sails silently and slowly on her endless course through the lifeless space. And everything so still, so awfully still, with the silence that shall one day reign when the earth again becomes desolate and empty, when the fox will no more haunt these moraines, when the bear will no longer wander about on the ice out there, when even the wind will not rage—infinite silence! In the flaming aurora borealis the spirit of space hovers over the frozen waters. The soul bows down before the majesty of night and death."

Tuesday, December 24. At 2 p.m. −24° C., cumulus, 2, wind 0.7 m. "And this is Christmas Eve—cold and windy out-of-doors, and cold and draughty in-doors. How desolate it is! Never before have we had such a Christmas Eve.

"At home the bells are now ringing Christmas in. I can hear their sound as it wings through the air from the church tower. How beautiful it is!

"Now the candles are being lighted on the Christmas trees, the children are let in and dance round in joyous delight. I must have a Chrismas party for children when I get home. This is the time of rejoicing, and there is feasting in every cottage at home.

"And we, too, are keeping the festival in our poor way. Johansen has turned his shirt and put the outside shirt next him; I have done the same, and then I have changed my drawers, and put on the others that I had wrung out in warm water. And I have washed myself, too, in a quarter of a cup of warm water, with the discarded drawers as sponge and towel. Now I feel quite another being; my clothes do not stick to my body as much as they did. Then for supper we had fish pudding, made of powdered fish and maize meal, with train-oil instead of butter, and for dessert we had bread fried in train-oil. To-morrow morning we are going to have chocolate and bread." Christmas Eve and New Year's Eve were the only times they permitted themselves to take anything from the provisions for the trip.

December 31. "They are ringing out the old year now at home. Our church bell is the icy wind howling over glacier and ice fields, howling fiercely as it whirls the drifting snow on high in cloud after cloud, and sweeps it down upon us."

New Year's Day came in with the thermometer at —41.5° centigrade. The moon was shining clear and the glacier rang the old year out and the new year in with a mighty boom like a cannon salvo. A new year has come, the year of joy and home-coming!"

On January 8, Liv was three years old. "But next birthday I shall be with you, I hope. What good friends we shall be! You shall ride a cockhorse, and I will tell you stories from the North about bears, foxes, walruses, and all the strange animals up there in the ice."

It was a curious existence to lie like this in a hut underground all winter with nothing to do. How they longed for a book! They knew the navigation tables and almanac by heart, but still it was a comfort to see the printed page. It gave them the feeling that there was, after all, a little bit of the civilized man left in them. All that they had to talk about had long since been thoroughly threshed out; but they used to sit in their sleeping-bags and picture to each other by the hour how they would go into a great, bright shop where the walls were hung with clean, soft woolen clothes from which they could pick out everything they wanted. And they dreamed of Turkish baths and soap and what a high value they would set on the good things of life such as food, drink, clothes, shoes, house, home, good neighbors, and all the rest of it.

They dreamed of being able to throw off all the greasy rags they were wearing which were glued to their bodies all over. "Our legs suffered most; for there our trousers stuck fast to our knees, so that when we moved they abraded and tore the skin inside our thighs till it was all raw and bleeding. I had the greatest difficulty in keeping these sores from becoming altogether too ingrained with fat and dirt, and had to be perpetually washing them with moss, and a little water which I warmed in a cup over the lamp. I never understood before what a magnificent invention soap really is. . . . Water had no effect upon all this grease; it was better to scour one's self with moss and sand." The best cleansing material was bear's blood and moss. Their faces, hair, and beards were so black that their teeth and the whites of their eyes shone with an uncanny whiteness—the only white in the faces of these wild men from the stone age.

Nevertheless time passed endurably in this monotonous, lethargic semi-trance. Awake and half-awake, they dozed and dreamed and looked forward to the future with the ability of strong, primitive natures to adapt themselves to circumstances and thus overcome them.

In spite of the monotonous meals, the oppressive darkness, the eternal cold, and the scant exercise, their health was excellent and their spirits good throughout.

Thoughts about their own future led them to wonder how far the *Fram* had drifted. Nansen calculated that the *Fram* would reach home in August or September and by that time he thought that they themselves would also be out. Their fancy played about a sloop from Tromsö all winter long.

THE RETURN

TOWARDS spring they began to prepare for the further journey. They needed new clothes. From the woolen blankets of the old sleeping-bags they made trousers and jackets. They got thread by unravelling canvas, and made a light, warm sleeping-bag of bearskin, but they no longer had any tent; the foxes had seen to that. Most of the provisions from the *Fram* were mouldy and spoiled, but the bears continued to come as to order—the first one came right into the house. Hunting gave them exercise and excitement, and as usual Nansen's descriptions make every encounter with a bear a thrilling and entertaining tale of adventure.

Nansen now wrote a report of their journey, put it in a metal cylinder, and hung it from the roof-tree of the hut. In 1902 the Arctic explorer, Evelyn Briggs Baldwin, found Nansen's winter camp and took the cylinder with him. In 1930 he sent it as a gift to the Norwegian Department of Foreign Affairs.

On May 19, 1896, Nansen and Johansen said farewell to their winter lair and began, with kayaks and sledges but without dogs, the most hazardous journey that has ever been made.

One day when a storm was suddenly approaching, forcing them to seek land, Nansen went on ahead to find a camping-ground. The ice was nasty, with many cracks concealed by snow. Nansen fell into one of these, and owing to his ski, which were firmly fastened on, he could not get out of the slush and rubble, while the sledge harness prevented him from turning. With his left elbow on the edge of the ice and his ski-staff dug into the ice on the opposite side of the crack, he held himself up and waited for Johansen who was busy hauling down the sail on the double kayak and had not noticed Nansen's mishap. The edge of the ice began to give; the water crept up to his waist; he shouted and shouted, but no answer came. He sank deeper, the water was up to his chest, and he would soon have been submerged if Johansen had not come just then and pulled him out.

One day in June after a long sail in the kayak, they moored at the edge of the ice and went off to stretch their legs a bit. While they were standing on an ice-hummock looking around, Johansen shouted: "I say! the kayaks are adrift!" "We ran down as hard as we could," writes Nansen. "They were already a little way out, and were drifting quickly off. 'Here, take my watch!' I said to Johansen, giving it to him; and as quickly as possible I threw off some clothing, so as to be able to swim more easily. I did not dare to take everything off, as I might so easily get cramp. I sprang into the water, but the wind was off the ice, and the light kayaks, with their high riggings, gave it a good hold. They were already well out, and were drifting rapidly. The water was icy cold; it was hard work swimming with clothes on; and the kayaks drifted farther and farther, often quicker than I could swim. It seemed more than doubtful whether I could manage it. But all our hope was drifting there; all we possessed was on board—we had not even a knife with us; and whether I got cramp and sank here, or turned back without the kayaks, it would come to pretty much the same thing; so I exerted myself to the utmost. When I got tired I turned over, and swam on my back, and then I could see Johansen walking restlessly up and down on the ice. Poor chap! He could not stand still, and thought it dreadful not to be able to do anything. He had not much hope that I could do it, but it would not improve matters in the least if he threw himself into the water too. He said afterwards that these were the worst moments he had ever lived through. But when I turned over again and saw that I was nearer the kayaks, my courage rose, and I redoubled my exertions. I felt, however, that my limbs were gradually stiffening and losing all feeling, and I knew that in a short time I should not be able to move them. But there was not far to go now; if I could only hold out a little longer we should be saved—and I went on. The strokes became more and more feeble, but the distance became shorter and shorter, and I began to think I should reach the kayaks. At last I was able to stretch out my hand to the ski which lay across the sterns. I grasped it, pulled myself in to the edge of the kayak and felt that we were saved. I tried to pull myself up, but the whole of my body was so stiff with cold that this was a sheer impossibility. For a moment I thought that, after all, it was too late; I was to get so far, but not to be able to get in. After a little, however, I managed to swing one leg up on to the edge of the sledge which lay on the deck, and in this way managed to tumble up. There I sat, but so stiff with cold that I had difficulty in paddling. . . . I shivered, my teeth chattered, and I was numb almost all over; but I could still use the paddle. . . . Two auks were lying close to the bow, and the thought of having auk for supper was too tempting; we were in want of food now. I got hold of my gun and shot them with one discharge. Johansen said afterwards that he started at the report, thinking some accident had happened, and could not understand what I was about out there, but when he saw me paddle and pick up two birds he thought I had gone out of my mind.

"I could barely manage to crawl up on the ice, and while I shook and trembled all over Johansen had to pull off the wet things I had on, put on the few dry ones I still had in reserve, and spread the sleeping-bag out upon the ice. I packed myself well into it, and he covered me with the sail and everything he could find to keep out the cold air. There I lay shivering for a long time, but gradually the warmth began to return to my body. . . . While Johansen put up the tent and prepared the supper, consisting of the two auks, I fell into a gentle sleep. He let me sleep quietly, and when I awoke supper had been ready for some time, and stood simmering over the fire. Auk and hot soup soon effaced the last traces of my cold swim."

Hjalmar Johansen says Nansen looked ghastly when he got back—his face pale, his long hair and beard wet, his lips covered with foam. He had difficulty in speaking, could hardly stand, and trembled incessantly with cold.

Once more, too, Nansen's Genius played with his life. The fairway teemed with innumerable walruses, in the water and up on the floes. They had young and were not hospitable. Food being scarce, the explorers shot two of the young ones, but the mothers taking their dead young under their fore-flippers plunged into the water with them and disappeared. The next time the mother had to be killed too. "It was a touching sight to see her crouch over her dead young one before she was shot, and even in death she lay holding it with one fore-flipper."

They had to manœuver carefully past the walrus herds and it was essential to keep in close to the margin of the ice. Walruses were swarming in every direction. Suddenly one beast shot up beside Nansen, threw itself on to his kayak, and tried to upset him, aiming a blow at the kayak with its tusks. Nansen struck it a blow on the head with the oar. It took hold of the kayak once more, tilted it up, then let go and raised itself upright. As Nansen seized his gun, it suddenly turned round and disappeared. At the same moment the kayak filled with water from the big rent made in it by the tusks of the walrus. Fortunately they were close to the margin of the ice and got it hauled up; but everything in the kayak was soaked through. They wrung out the sleeping-bag and spent "a capital night in it."

The next day they patched the kayak and rejoiced that the gash was not in Nansen's leg as well.

This was the last time that Nansen's Genius played with his life on this expedition.

It was June 17, the birthday of the great Norwegian poet Wergeland. Nansen was out for a walk, listening to the noise of thousands of birds, when suddenly he thought he heard something resembling the barking of a dog. Dogs? Here? It could not be possible! And then he heard it again, clearly and unmistakably—dogs!

He called to Johansen. Johansen started up. Dogs? Impossible! He thought Nansen had lost his mind and was having hallucinations. But Nansen strode off as fast as his long legs would carry him. He found tracks, many tracks—dogs' tracks. Suddenly he thought he heard a voice, a human voice. He ran up on a hummock and hallooed with all the strength of his lungs.

In that one human voice which he had heard in the midst of the desert of ice there was a message from life, from home, from all that home held for him. An answer came from far away, and he saw something black moving among the ice hummocks in the distance. He dashed on again, and soon the two men met. It was the English Arctic explorer, Frederick Jackson.

"I am damned glad to see you," he said.

"Thank you; I am glad too," replied Nansen.

"Have you a ship here?"

"No, my ship is not here."

"How many are there of you?"

"I have one companion at the ice edge."

Nansen had recognized Jackson at once and thought that Jackson also knew him, but it was not easy to recognize a European in this wild man. Suddenly Jackson, who had been staring at Nansen the whole time as they walked along, stopped short, looked him full in the face, and said quickly:

"Aren't you Nansen?"

"Yes, I am."

"By Jove, I am glad to see you."

And he seized Nansen's hand and shook it again while his dark eyes beamed with delight. There was a hail of questions and answers from both sides until they reached Jackson's camp. Jackson, who had been lying here for two years, had letters for Nansen. There was nothing but good news from home, and a feeling of infinite peace and restfulness descended upon Nansen's soul after all the strain of these three long years.

Jackson believed that the *Fram* and the other eleven men must have met disaster, for he thought he had noticed a sad expression on Nansen's face when he first mentioned the ship, and he quietly warned his men not to ask. But his mind was soon disabused of that error. The *Fram*—ah, she had indeed been a subject of conversation between the two Norwegians in their hut. Nansen had calculated that the *Fram* would come out of the ice between Spitzbergen and Greenland and would arrive home in August or September. The *Fram* and Sverdrup would make it without fail!

His delight in the enjoyment of all the good things of civilization was certainly not less this time than it had been after the Greenland expedition. The two black, shaggy, tattered, greasy savages were photographed at once. After all, rags and tatters are picturesque when worn by brave men.

When Nansen and Johansen stood stripped on the scales, Nansen weighed 92 kilograms, 10 kilograms more than when he left the *Fram*, and Johansen weighed 75 kilograms, having gained 6. This was a different story from previous experiences of life in the arctic climate.

Nansen once said that the secret of arctic exploration was to adapt one's self sensibly to conditions. All his polar work is a demonstration of this arctic sense, and all later arctic exploration which has been based on the principles of the Nansen school has been more or less successful.

NORWAY'S WELCOME

ON JULY 26 Jackson's steamer, the *Windward*, arrived and at once Jackson came in beaming with delight to tell Nansen that all was well at home, but that nothing had been heard of the *Fram*. On August 7 the *Windward* was homeward bound.

I quote from the diary written on board the *Windward*: August 9. "We are rocking on the long swells of the open sea, the blue sea as far as the eye can reach! Above the horizon far to the north one can see a reflection from the ice, the last greeting from that world which has been our home, and witnessed our joys and sorrows for three long years. How wonderful that all that should be lying behind us, while before us—it is like a beautiful dream, our thoughts sail on golden clouds."

After five days a dark line was seen one evening on the horizon—it was Norway. "I stood petrified gazing and gazing into the night . . ." he writes. On the morning of August 13 the *Windward* glided into Vardö harbor. Before the anchor was dropped, Nansen and Johansen were in the boat hurrying to the telegraph station. Nansen laid a huge bundle of telegrams on the counter, many of them over a thousand words long, and said he would like to have them sent as soon as possible. When the manager of the telegraph office saw the signature, a tremor passed over his face and he greeted the two men with emotion. The telegrams would take some time. Night and day for severals days Nansen's name was ticked out over the whole world to hundreds of millions of people. There were telegrams from Nansen to his wife and from Johansen to his mother, from all their companions on the *Fram* to those nearest to them, telegrams to the King, to the Government, to the donors, to the newspapers, to the whole world. The telegraph operators and all their reserve staff have never had such a job before or since. In a trice the whole town of Vardö was on its feet, and flags waved from every flagstaff and mast. Wherever the two explorers showed themselves, they drew a great crowd of people after them.

Nansen learned that Professor Mohn, the good friend who had been so intimately connected with the expedition, was at the hotel. He went there at once and crashed into his room. Mohn was lying on the sofa reading, with a long pipe in his mouth. He started up as though he had seen a ghost. "Thank God you're still alive!" he cried.

At Hammerfest, by a strange coincidence, they met Nansen's English friend, Sir George Baden-Powell, who was lying there with his fine yacht, the *Otaria*. He had just returned from a scientific expedition to Nova Zembla and had intended now to skirt up along the edge of the ice to look for the *Fram*. He at once put his yacht at Nansen's disposal. In the evening Nansen's wife and his secretary arrived.

After a brilliant fête in Norway's northernmost town, the town of arctic seamen, they all went on board the comfortable yacht.

Telegrams continued to pour in.

But what of the *Fram?* With dread Nansen envisaged the possibility of the autumn passing with no news of her.

On the morning of August 20, while he was dressing, Sir George knocked at the door of his cabin and announced that there was a man with a telegram. It was the manager himself, who "thought the message would interest Nansen."

Nansen tore it open, and read:

"Skjærvö, Aug. 20, 1896. 9 a.m. *Fram* arrived here to-day in good condition. All well on board. Leaving at once for Tromsö. Welcome home.

"OTTO SVERDRUP."

This was surely the greatest triumph of Nansen's Genius. He felt as though he would choke, and all he could say was, "The *Fram* has arrived!" Baden-Powell gave a leap of joy, Johansen's face shone like the sun, the secretary ran up and down in excitement, and the manager of the telegraph office stood in the midst of them enjoying the effect he had produced. Nansen disappeared into the cabin and shouted to his wife, "The *Fram* has arrived!"

Nansen read the telegram over many times before he could be sure that it was not all a dream.

When the *Otaria* glided into Tromsö harbor, there lay the *Fram,* strong and broad and weatherbeaten. As soon as the anchor dropped, the *Otaria* was boarded by the *Fram's* sturdy crew. "The meeting which followed I shall not attempt to describe," wrote Nansen. "I do not think any of us knew anything clearly, except that we were all together again, we were in Norway, and the expedition had fulfilled its task."

The *Fram* had continued her drift the last year according to schedule. When Nansen and Johansen set off she lay at 84° 4′ north latitude and 102° east longitude, in ice 25 feet thick. In October the *Fram* reached her highest latitude 85° 57′ where she withstood several violent attacks of ice-pressure. These, however, did not cause any uneasiness. Besides, excellent equipment had been prepared for crossing the ice and sailing if the *Fram* should go down. All the scientific observations went on as before. It could not be denied, however, that the third polar night weighed heavily at times. There was less work to occupy them, less hunting and less fresh meat, and their two companions were away. The stimulus of Nansen's personality was lacking; but as the light returned and the drift bore westward and south-

ward and homeward, the spirits of all revived. Some welcome
bears furnished adventure, fresh meat, and renewed appetite.
During the last 28 days of hard forcing through 450 kilometers
of pack-ice the men were in fine fettle. At last they were free
from the ice and bound for home, the problem solved exactly
in the time Nansen had calculated.

On August 13 the *Fram* ploughed out into the open sea.
It was the very day that Nansen and Johansen sprang ashore
on the wharf at Vardö.

Meeting a sealer, the *Fram* men shouted: "Have Nansen
and Johansen arrived yet?" The answer "No" dampened their
spirits. They had felt so sure that the two were already home.
They decided now to hurry to Tromsö, obtain more exact information, and go immediately to Franz Josef Land to search
for them.

At 2 o'clock in the morning of August 20 the *Fram*
anchored at Skjærvö and Sverdrup went ashore at once and
roused the telegraph agent.

When Sverdrup told him of the sealers' discouraging answer the telegraph agent said: "But I can give you information
about Nansen. He arrived at Vardö on August 13 and is now at
Hammerfest. He is probably starting for Tromsö to-day."

"Has Nansen arrived? I must tell the others at once!" and
Sverdrup vanished out of the door. Shortly afterwards two
thundering reports from the *Fram* got all the inhabitants of
Skjærvö out of their beds. The telegraph office had a busy day.

The State sent tugboats and thus they went south. It was a
triumphal march, a series of fêtes, along the whole coast of
Norway. "Wherever we passed, the heart of the Norwegian
people went out to us, from the steamers crowded with towns-
folk in holiday attire and from the poorest fisherman alone in
his boat among the skerries. It seemed almost as if old Mother
Norway were proud of us, as if she pressed us into a close and
warm embrace, and thanked us for what we had done. And
what was it, after all? We had only done our duty; we had

simply accomplished the task we had undertaken, and it was we who owed her thanks for the right to sail under her flag. . . . I realized to the full, for the first time, how near this land and this people lay to my heart. If we had sent a single gleam of sunshine over their lives, these three years had not been wasted.

"One felt all the vitality and vigor throbbing in this people, and saw as in a vision its great and rich future, when all its imprisoned forces should be unfettered and set free."

It is characteristic that Nansen, according to reports from the many banquets where he was honored, should have answered by paying homage to the Fatherland. If one reads the papers from those stirring days in August and September of that year, one cannot but be struck by the tremendous excitement into which the whole people was thrown by Nansen's exploit. It was not merely reserved for a few groups in the nation to feel, as Professor W. C. Brögger expressed it, "the wonderful elevating force which the achievement of a single man may be for a whole people, indeed for the whole of mankind." No, as Björnson wrote about an older exploit,

"Where two travellers in the hills meet
They must talk about the venture—"

and *"Glory prods us all to labor."* Norway grew from this exploit.

We shall mention only a few of the numerous receptions: that in Trondheim Cathedral was particularly affecting. It must have thrilled Nansen strangely when the organ, played by Lindemann, pealed forth the wedding march that had been composed for his wedding. Reissiger's "Autumn Prayer" and Grieg's "Landfall" for chorus, organ, and strings made a deep impression on the men of the *Fram* expedition and on all those who were present.

The fête in Bergen, the arena of Nansen's scientific labors

for five rich years of his youth, was, of course, unsurpassable. Men like Michelsen and Grieg, Armauer Hansen, Brunchorst and Gerhard Gran were guarantee enough that it was as festive as the old Hansa town could make it. But Nansen's dear friend, Dr. Danielsen, had died in 1894.

On September 9 the *Fram* steamed up the fjord to Oslo, going a little out of her way to greet the builder of the *Fram*, Colin Archer. The speech of thanks that Nansen made in honor of the old master came from a full heart and touched all who heard it.

The celebration in the capital lasted for five whole days.

All the steamers that city and fjord could muster met the *Fram* far out in the channel. Warships and torpedo-boats led the way, while 130 steamers, decked with flags and black with people, closed in behind the *Fram* in two rows. No prince has ever approached Norway's capital with a prouder company in his wake. And on that day the city was not merely the capital of the country, it was the heart of Norway, beating with pride and joy in the Oslo boy, Fridtjof Nansen, and his sturdy companions. There were thousands of visitors and a great many foreigners. The streets and wharfs and the walls of Akershus were crowded with people.

Then all the men-of-war saluted with thirteen guns apiece and the old fortress of Akershus followed with thirteen peals of thunder which echoed from the hills around.

A boat rowed by young sailors put off from the *Fram*. Tall and straight and calm, Nansen stood in the boat as it glided in to the wharf where honored guests are received and there he landed with his twelve men. Luther's hymn rose from a great chorus: "A mighty fortress is our God," and then the national anthem, "Yes, we love the land that towers," was sung by thousands with bared heads. It was an impressive moment which no one who was there will ever forget.

To the chairman's speech of welcome Nansen answered in a loud, clear voice: "Fellow countrymen! It is a difficult task to convey to you the feelings which animate my comrades and myself. I remember well the day we sailed from home. The fjord lay in heavy rain. Our hearts were heavy at parting. The responsibility was heavy. We felt that Norway's young fortunes were on board with us; we felt that if we failed, we failed our country. But I was certain that my men would do their duty to the last drop of blood that was in them. I tell you that finer men than I had have never set out for the North. I thank you from the bottom of my heart for your welcome, a welcome such as has rarely been extended to Norwegians before. I thank the city of Christiania. We have but done our duty. Therefore the welcome is tenfold more precious. Long live the city! May she often send out such a company as she gave me!"

Under a triumphal arch which was completely covered with white-clad gymnasts and sportsmen—looking like one of the bird cliffs of the North—the procession of carriages drove through the gaily decorated streets of the city to the University where they were welcomed on behalf of Alma Mater by the rector.

The following words from Nansen's reply are worthy of emphasis: "It is perfectly true that I have felt myself on my expedition to be an emissary and advance guard of scientific research. Now that I am home again at the seat of knowledge, words fail to express my feelings."

Then the student athletes stepped forward and with the words, "Comrades, let us deck with wreaths the heroes from the desolate snow-fields," hung a garland about the neck of each of the thirteen. The garlanded heroes then drove up to the castle, followed right to the gates of the royal dwelling by the shouts and cheers from a sea of people. And the sea did not subside, but every once in a while rose in thunder so that Nansen and Sverdrup had to appear on the balcony time after time.

King Oscar made a poetic speech expressing the feelings of the Norwegian people and their gratitude, which, he said, would outlive the moment and endure through the ages as long as Dovre Mountain stands.

In the evening the city was ablaze with bonfires and torches and throngs of people.

The next day homage was paid the *Fram* by a procession of children, 20,000 girls and boys with flags. Björn Björnson was the leader of the gay procession. They represented Norway's future which would grow from the seed of Nansen's exploit— their youthful exultation was a pledge of that.

The same day the city gave a great festive banquet for the *Fram* expedition and 500 invited guests. The Scientific Society of Paris, the Royal Geographical Society of London, and the University of Leipzig were represented. The poet Björnstjerne Björnson was present. Professor Mohn made the speech in honor of Nansen, dwelling on the true scientist's faculty for working with Nature in complete sympathy, and Professor W. C. Brögger announced the establishment of a Nansen Fund for the advancement of science, to which a quarter of a million had already been subscribed. The Fund at this writing is seven millions.

On Saturday there was a gala presentation at the theater, and on Sunday a popular celebration at the Fæstningsplass with two rostra. Every inch of the huge space was filled. Björnson spoke. He began by referring jestingly to all the bear meat the explorers had been forced to eat. "But as I am now about to address them, I have a feeling that if at the present moment they were offered a choice between still another oration and some polar bear meat, they would avidly seize the bear meat." This time, however, it was Björnson who was purveying the speech, and the bear meat had to yield. He showed the expedition in the light of the idea behind it, and in relation to the people from which it had sprung and upon which it would, in turn, have its effect. "For it is true that the work, the faith, and the self-control that a people wins in silence comes to light some day in a great deed, and then the great deed is just the same as though the whole people had attained its majority."

He put the question to the young people whether they had not gained greater respect for self-control and endurance, whether they had not felt their courage grow and would hereafter set themselves a higher goal. He believed that, when this warmth of purpose was carried over into their lives, Norway's national strength would be greatly augmented. He believed that Nansen, through this expedition, had said to the youth of his country: "Set yourselves higher goals, and try to reach them; put all your strength into attaining these goals, but do not set goals that are beyond your strength!"

The first evening after his home-coming Nansen stood down by the shore at his home at Svartebukta. The noise of the celebration sounded faintly, the woods stood silent and dark, and out on the headland the last smouldering embers of a bonfire glowed. The deep peace of an autumn evening sank down over his weary spirit. At his feet the waves rippled and whispered: "Now you are home!"

He recalled again that rainy morning in June when he walked down to this same shore, and his heart "wept for thankfulness." The ice and all the moonlit nights with all their yearning yonder in the North seemed like a distant dream, a dream that had come and passed away. . . . "But what would life be worth without its dreams!"

He had had the adventure of the ice—through all his days the great adventure of his life. Now it was a dream, an ever more distant dream from another world at the edge of the infinite, but it had put a deep mark on his mind for all time, deeper than the world ever suspected, deeper than he himself knew that evening as he stood, weary of fêtes, on the shore at Svartebukta while the waves lapping the familiar shore whispered, "Now you are home!"

He did not know what a task it would be to adjust himself to being home again.

HOME AGAIN

IN THE stone hut on Franz Josef Land Nansen seems to have taken all the rest he allowed himself after his strenuous exertions on the ice. Already in 1897, *Farthest North,* a big work in two volumes, appeared. This was followed during the next five years by the preparation and publication of the scientific results of the *Fram* expedition in six weighty tomes: *The Norwegian North Polar Expedition 1893-96, Scientific Results,* published 1900-05. Besides this he made lecture tours on two continents, where he was hailed as the man who had performed "the greatest human exploit of the nineteenth century."

Nansen's form of ambition, however, was rather to do things than to collect all the laurels in the world. He often recalled what the good Peder Henriksen said as they stood in to Trondheim fjord with the *Fram*—facing another town, another celebration, more physical and emotional satiety. "I say, Nansen," said Peder, "this is all very well, but there's too much *racket.* I am thinking of the arctic; we had a fine time up there."

There was loneliness, silence, and grandeur. He longed to be there once more, "to climb up on a hummock again to spy out the way—that is real excitement. There's a life of action for you."

Few of the sons of men have experienced such a triumphal progress as Nansen's at his age. There were moments on the way that he never forgot. One of them was the time in Nidaros Cathedral at Trondheim when the mighty work of Grieg and

Björnson welcomed him, and another was a similar moment in London when the chorus from *Judas Maccabaeus* sounded as though it had been written for the occasion. These were among the greatest moments of his life, but his head was not lifted up in pride by them; rather the hero's head was bowed in

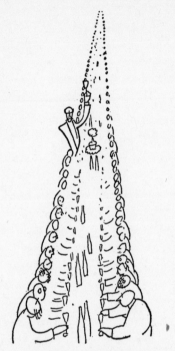

NANSEN SPEAKING AT A FESTIVE DINNER
IN MUNICH
Drawing by Olaf Gulbransson

humility and thankfulness that he should be the one chosen to carry out a deed which actually created a new spiritual atmosphere.

But it is not the easiest thing in the world to step down from the summit of life; after feeling the foaming crests of the breakers under the flying kayak, to glide into calm waters.

His friend Erik Werenskiold tells us that "after the *Fram* expedition he was quite a different man from before. His ex-

pression became profoundly serious, almost imperturbably
calm, as though frozen, without a smile. The first time that he
went out to a large party, he said: 'What am I to do amongst
all these people? What are they to me?' The contrast between
the loneliness up in the ice desert, where the question was always
to be or not to be, and everyday life with its everlasting trifles
and banalities was too great. Little by little, however, he began
to thaw and recovered again his old radiant countenance and his
joy in life, delighted in the society of his friends, built his new
house, and so on."

From his lecture tour he writes: "I am travelling out in
a great, empty desert and life is desolate." He feels his "soul
washed out, pillaged, trampled on by strange people, so that
one is forced to run away and hide in order to find one's self
again."

Of his travels in Europe and America, of the various experiences and festivities, we do not see a sign in these entries
for November 1897; they reflect only his own sad, empty heart.

"Am I worn out with suffering, privation, and longing? I
am less and less able to disentangle the threads in my own heart
—I gaze hopelessly into emptiness. And I sit here and look out
into the night as we travel over the prairies of Canada, but I
find no answer. . . ."

In America, he relates, many people assured him that his
book was a source of great delight to them. A lady gave him a
letter in which she stated that he had saved her in the darkest
moment of her life. She had been exceedingly unhappy and described to him what she had gone through. Then she chanced to
read his book, a new life was revealed to her, and the vision
had helped her over the crisis. "I do not know quite how," says
Nansen, "but I suppose it must be true." "Is it not sad that one
should be able to help others and yet be so helpless? It is the
irony of fate, to pour out wine when one has lost the power to
drink."

These years, in spite of travels and work, are really a life riding at anchor. A nature not created for sedentary calm is seeking restlessly within itself for the solution to its own riddle, for the goal of its existence, for the purpose of life. It is a winged creature caged.

Here is a note from his diary written at Brandbusæter in September 1898: "This same question always confronts one as soon as one takes time to stop and look around. Is it happiness that makes life worth living?—happiness, which is like drops in a sea of longing, like falling stars in the night that make it still darker. An unquenchable thirst for what we can never attain, a thirst that one day dies but is never slaked. It is that which gives life content, but not meaning. It is a chase which stops at the threshold of Nirvana—where everything is high and serene, and all human suffering sinks back into the lap of the universe."

"Has life too high a goal?—that which has no goal. Woe to him who has begun the chase, for he can never give it up!"

"But the peaks have been reached; they were so low. The vast expanse seems small and the snow-fields no longer gleam, the mountain tarn is not high nor lonely, and the white swans— they are flown.

"But once more, yet once more the wings can be stretched for one more flight, and then with all their strength beyond the vast expanse, beyond the peaks and snow-fields—thither none will follow!

"Ah, courageous dreamer!"

The mood of these pages of his diary, from the years immediately after he has come to rest after the *Fram* expedition, is related to those pages written in June, 1894, on board the *Fram* with their gloomy casting up of accounts with himself.

His melancholy is turned inwards to a contemplation of the vacuity of his soul. But this very melancholy was pregnant with new growth, and such is the case this time too, as a page from his diary written at Sörkje in July 1899 shows: "What a joy it is to create! It seems as though my work had never gone ahead so rapidly as now. New thoughts and visions crowd my

mind. All that I have been pondering over so long has suddenly
taken clear form. It is as though I had been walking in a mist
unable to find my way out; then suddenly the mist has lifted a
little and at once I see a landmark. The mist gradually clears
and my view becomes wider and wider almost more quickly
than I can follow it, and then suddenly the whole expanse lies
before me sunlit and bright, and broad visions open out in the
western sky. Now every step forward leads nearer the goal, and
it is good to travel towards it!"

He has found for himself a spot deep in the woods and
mountains where no jarring note from without can reach him, a
place "where I pillow my head on the bosom of existence. The
clamping irons of the will are slacked. I find complete repose
in my moods just as I did when I was a child and the woods
were my paradise. Here in this spot of God's earth I have chosen
my kingdom, beside the mountain lake, encircled by the dark,
solemn forest of evergreens with the birch trees in amongst
them and the bare rocks up above. Here I have Velebuhei on
the west and Aakelifjell on the south and behind me on the east
lies the beautiful Synhövd. There is nothing cramped about it,
nor is it too spacious. From the low, forest-clad crest on the
other side of the lake yonder I know that one can see out across
the slopes and forests down into Telemark with Tinnsjö and
Gausta and Lifjellene, but I do not long for that. I do not long
for any place on earth.

"For here it is peaceful and mild, and yet sober. Without
my being conscious of it, my soul has melted more and more into
this scenery. It opens up and closes me in.

"No neighbors—woods and mountains on all sides. Far
away in the ridge on the other side of the lake there is a glow
in the woods. I know that it must be from a Telemark sæter, but
I see only the roof of the house; and sometimes on quiet evenings I hear the sound of an axe chopping in the forest in that
direction. And on one rare occasion it happened that I saw a
bonfire on the shore down at Lauvodden on the other side of

the lake—Telemark men engaged in illegal fishing. But good Lord, there are fish enough in the lake for us both!"

Here in the mountains and woods, living a life of hunting and fishing, like Antaeus he got back his courage to face life, although the demons of melancholy with their consuming broodings in the depths of the ego would follow him here too.

"Let me climb the heights, let me have ski under my feet!" —and the demons were tossed into the snow drifts. When Nansen came back from his hikes he was a new man. It was from his own experience that he said in his rectorial address at the university in Edinburgh in 1926: "The call of the wild, vibrating under all our actions, making life deeper and higher and nobler."

"No one has known Fridtjof Nansen who has not met him out in the open," says his friend and companion on many mountain trips in recent years, Professor Jacob Worm-Müller. "There he was quite another man—simple and yet full of nuances: a child with open, confiding, kind blue eyes, a frolicsome boy scout who enjoyed every hour of the day with jest and mirth, and yet a man fearless and independent, modest and self-confident, honorable, upright, and pure-minded.

"Although he might reach the hut tired and worn out and haggard, after only a day or two he was as buoyant as a youth and full of life.

"I accompanied him to the mountains this year for the last time. He was more tired than ever before, but still as full of rapture and delight as a boy at seeing the mountains again. I fancy I still see him on ski, standing looking across Rondane, the tall commanding figure, with the broadbrimmed hat on his head, the close brown leather jacket outlining his athletic body, erect and rugged like an image of our country as we imagine it to ourselves when we most long for it. . . ."

He needed no hint from Rousseau; he understood Nature without an interpreter, as Wergeland did.

FRIDTJOF NANSEN
Painting by Erik Werenskiold

Nature gave them what they sought—strength and peace. As in Wergeland's poetry, so in Nansen's travel books, and especially in *Sporting Days in Wild Norway,* one can open them and read with delight many an expression of the beautiful longing and will to live of a rich and powerful but struggling soul.

One July day in 1900, in the fog north of Iceland, he wrote in his diary: "I sail on through the mists while the sea swells to meet me bringing a message and a greeting from the unseen beyond, I know not where, bringing longings, I know not toward what. I only guess that there is something to be longed for in the spaces beyond, on the other side of the mists where the day is sunlight and shines on glistening peaks."

But in the diary, too, there is a passage before this luminous outburst which is not in *Sporting Days in Wild Norway,* a passage where the fog is not only around him, but within him. It is an attack of the old, dark self-analysis, but he characterizes it himself as a "sick mood" and denies this mood the right to remain in possession of the field.

Belief in the sun helps the sun to overcome the mists.

In several of the bright sketches in *Sporting Days in Wild Norway* we see the sun in a cloudless sky, but in the diaries we see the sun's struggle preceding the victory. We surmise that in a nature so full of contradictions as his there must have been many a hard struggle between sun and lurid mists.

A strangely compounded nature, full of contradictions, was his, watchful of and attentive to the inmost movements of the soul—a brooder, a dreamer, and at the same time an unequalled man of action.

He was none the less great for this. On the contrary, he knew himself and, with his strong will, he always had himself under control. He knew, too, where his own salvation lay: in the life of the outdoors and of action, in the service of science, and beyond that, wherever there was need of a manly deed.

And his whole life was one great and rich development in the course of which he became less and less preoccupied with himself and sank all his powers in his work, a work which became more and more a work to help mankind, to array the world about him in the service of brotherly love. In this service he found without brooding the true content and meaning in life.

To this chapter, which tells of the man who succeeded in steering his ship out of the backwater and raising up the standard of the *Fram* again, we shall add some remarks from his great address as Lord Rector of St. Andrews University in Scotland in 1926.

He was then 65 years of age, an elderly man—an old man he never became. He had sailed under the banner *Fram*—Forward, but now he could allow himself to look backward a moment, to take a comprehensive view of the whole voyage of his life, and to tell the young students about his expeditions, about his life, and his experiences, and extract from them the wisdom of life which in his kind heart he did not begrudge his young successors.

"The first great thing in life is to find yourself, and for that you need solitude and contemplation, at least sometimes. I tell you deliverance will not come from the rushing, noisy centres of civilization. It will come from the lonely places! The great reformers in history have come from the wilderness. . . .

"There are many people who do not get time even to think over what they themselves hold to be the purpose of their lives. What is the purpose of yours? . . .

"Are you out for happiness? Well, many people are. But believe me, my friends, you need not look for it. The great thing is *to do your best,* and to be *independent* of all other 'necessities.' Dear me, how perfectly unnecessary many of these 'necessities' really are. . . . Mind you, by making your baggage-train longer you clip your wings."

He wishes to make the young students "understand how things that might seem impossible can be done when you have to do them, and how a life you may think hard is easily lived when you make a goal to work for. You may think it was hard to live a long winter dug in, on nothing but bear meat; but I can assure you it was a happy time, for we had the spring and the home-coming to look forward to."

He gave them this advice: "Check Master Irresponsible, and consider well before you move. Make your preparations carefully; they can never be too careful—the road is long. No guesswork, no approximations. But when you strike out, then throw your whole self into the enterprise. Set all your sails. No wavering, for self-confidence is the first secret of success—don't check your boat when you are tacking.

"We pass many cross-roads on our way through life, and the test of a man is how he behaves at each cross-road. Some people cannot decide, they waver, wishing to keep all ways open, and always looking back they end by getting nowhere. The traveller of the right mettle may consider well, but then he takes one road and sticks to that; and he always arrives somewhere. For him the only road is then the road ahead of him, and there is no way back.

"I have always thought that the much-praised *line of retreat* is a snare for people who wish to reach their goal.

"Let me tell you one secret of such so-called successes as there have been in my life, and here I believe I give you really good advice. It was to burn my boats and demolish the bridges behind me. Then one loses no time in looking behind, when one should have quite enough to do in looking ahead—then there is no choice for you or your men but *forward*. You have to do or die!"

"Oh, youth, youth! what a glorious word! Unknown realms ahead of you, hidden behind the mists of the morning. As you move on, new islands appear, mountain-summits shoot up through the clearing mists, one behind another, waiting for you to climb; dense new forests unfold for you to explore; free boundless plains for you to traverse. You are foot-loose and heart-free to sail beyond the sunset and to roam the universe.

"What a joyous thing to see the day dawning and to know

that you are bound on a voyage to new realms. Your soul bounds upward on beams of light to the vault of heaven.

"You laugh at the risks and smile at the dangers, youth's buoyant faith and self-trust is in command. The storm cannot reach you.

"And lo! far ahead, above the mist and the scud, rises your Land of Beyond! We all have a Land of Beyond to seek in life—what more can we ask? Our part is to find the trail that leads to it. A long trail, a hard trail, maybe; but the call comes to us and we have to go.

"Rooted deep in the nature of every one of us is the spirit of adventure, the call of the wild—vibrating under all our actions, making life deeper and higher and nobler.

" 'Have you known the Great White Silence? . . .

Have you broken trail on snowshoes, mushed your huskies up the river,

Dared the unknown, led the way, and clutched the prize? . . .

Have you suffered, starved and triumphed, grovelled down yet grasped at glory,

'Done things' just for the doing, letting babblers tell the story, . . .

Have you seen . . .

The simple things, the true things, the silent men who do things—

Then listen to the Wild—it's calling you.

Let us probe the silent places, let us seek what luck beside us;

Let us journey to a lonely land I know.

There's a whisper on the night-wind, there's a star agleam to guide us,

And the Wild is calling, calling . . . let us go!' "

THE FURTHER HISTORY OF THE *FRAM*

THE *FRAM* started on another arctic expedition, that of Otto Sverdrup, northwest of Greenland, in 1898—1902. Some changes were made in the vessel for this trip, the deck being raised so that there was more room below, a larger and more comfortable saloon.

The plan to force a passage along the north coast of Greenland in order to chart it exactly had to be given up on account of the impossible state of the ice. The *Fram* was caught fast northwest of Greenland, and ski expeditions were sent out with the ship as headquarters. In this way Sverdrup discovered and mapped 300,000 square kilometers of new land. *New Land*, too, is the title of the remarkable work in which Sverdrup describes this second great expedition of the *Fram*.

In 1910 it was Roald Amundsen who stood on the bridge of the *Fram*. His plan was to drift, in from five to seven years, through the vast unknown regions on the other side of the Pole.

Included in this plan was an oceanographical cruise in the Atlantic Ocean west of Scotland and Ireland, which was carried out with the *Fram* in June, 1910, before her final departure from Norway.

In April 1909 Peary had planted the Stars and Stripes at the North Pole. Consequently the interest of the public was not centred in Amundsen's undertaking which now had "merely" scientific interest. Amundsen could not, therefore, procure enough money for the prolonged expedition, so he turned the *Fram* southward towards the Antarctic.

While he and his brilliant ski-runners headed for the South Pole, the *Fram* went on an oceanographical excursion, cruising along two lines between South America and Africa in 1911, under the leadership of Captain Thorwald Nilsen. In January 1912 they picked up the South Pole adventurers at the barrier. The South Pole expedition was a great success and had been financially advantageous, so that the *Fram's* northerly mission, west around Cape Horn, across the Pacific and into Bering Strait, to drift from there across the broadest part of the Arctic Ocean, a five year drift, could now be undertaken.

The Panama Canal was just about to be opened and the *Fram* was offered the honor of being the first ship to sail through the canal. The *Fram* anchored in the roadstead at Colon on October 4, but here the polar ship suffered serious injury from the tropical waters. Rot got into her timbers, and after waiting in vain for three months, she was forced to go home. It was discovered that the decay had gone so far that it would not pay to repair her. She was laid up, but no care was taken of her. She was left to herself and to certain destruction, ungratefully treated by her owner, the Norwegian Government.

Her brilliant career was over. Farthest north and farthest south, she had been commanded by Nansen, by Sverdrup, by Amundsen. She might well be called "one of the most wonderful ships in history."

The credit for rescuing the *Fram* so that she could be preserved for an indefinite time belongs to Otto Sverdrup who with the help of the whaling magnate, Lars Christensen, and a committee in England under J. Howard Whitehouse, got the rescue work under way.

In the summer of 1930 she made her last trip round the coast to the exhibition at Trondheim. Thousands visited her, and a great deal of money was taken in for the resumption of the work. The plan is to haul her up on land and build a house for her, not as a dismantled hull, but just as she was and is, with masts and crow's nest and all the rest of it.

On October 12 the *Fram* made her last voyage up the Oslo Fjord followed by an escorting cortège of steamers and motor boats. There was a mournful tinge over the *Fram*. Her rescuer, Otto Sverdrup, was not with her. He was lying in his home at Sandvika with the anchor weighed for his last voyage; but from his window he could see his beloved *Fram* out in the Fjord.

The other two are also gone; our hearts are still bleeding from Nansen's death. But Wisting was on board, the man from the two Poles, the true friend of Amundsen and the *Fram*.

Now perhaps we shall build the *Fram* and all her memories into a house with walls and roof, with the *Fram's* standard waving over the house, in the free air, visible from afar, the standard of our country and our people.

NEW POLAR PLANS

For my purpose holds
To sail beyond the sunset and the baths
Of all the western stars until I die.

TENNYSON

IN THE introduction to his book *In Northern Mists*, Nansen writes on the "Why" of polar expeditions:

"In the beginning the world appeared to man like a fairy tale; everything that lay beyond the circle of familiar experience was a shifting cloudland of the fancy, a playground for all the fabled beings of mythology; but in the farthest distance, towards the west and north, was the region of darkness and mists, where sea, land, and sky were merged into a congealed mass—and at the end of all gaped the immeasurable mouth of the abyss, the awful void of space.

"Out of this fairy world, in course of time, the calm and sober lines of the Northern landscape appeared. With unspeakable labor the eye of man has forced its way gradually towards the north, over mountains and forests, and tundra, onward through the mists along the vacant shores of the polar sea—the vast stillness, where so much struggle and suffering, so many bitter failures, so many proud victories have vanished without a trace, muffled beneath the mantle of snow.

"When our thoughts go back through the ages in a waking dream, an endless procession passes before us—like a single mighty epic of the human mind's power of devotion to an idea, right or wrong—a procession of struggling, frost-covered figures in heavy clothes, some erect and powerful, others weak and bent so that they can scarcely drag themselves along before the sledges, many of them emaciated and dying of hunger, cold, and scurvy; but all looking out before them towards the unknown, beyond the sunset, where the goal of their struggle is to be found. . . .

"What were they seeking in the ice and cold?

"From first to last the history of polar exploration is a single mighty manifestation of the power of the unknown over the mind of man, perhaps greater and more evident here than in any other phase of human life. Nowhere else have we won our way more slowly, nowhere else has every new step cost so much trouble, so many privations and sufferings, and certainly nowhere have the resulting discoveries promised fewer material advantages—and nevertheless, new forces have always been found ready to carry the attack farther, to stretch once more the limits of the world. . . .

"Ever since the Norsemen's earliest voyages, arctic expeditions have certainly brought material advantages to the human race, such as rich fisheries, whaling, and sealing, and so on; they have produced scientific results in the knowledge of hitherto unknown regions and conditions; but they have given us far more than this: they have tempered the human will for the conquest of difficulties; they have furnished a school of manliness and self-conquest in the midst of the slackness of varying ages and have held up noble ideals before the rising generation; they have fed the imagination, have given fairy tales to the child, and raised the thoughts of its elders above their daily toil. . . .

"It is not until we come far down into the full daylight of history that we find men setting out with the conscious purpose of exploring the unknown for its own sake. With those early hunters, it was doubtless new ground and new game that drew them on, but they too were attracted, consciously or unconsciously, by the spirit of adventure and the unknown—so deep in the soul of man does this divine force lie, the mainspring, perhaps, of the greatest of our actions. In every part of the world and in every age it has driven man forward on the path of evolution, and as long as the human ear can hear the breaking of waves over deep seas, so long will the fascination of the unknown carry the human mind forward and upward."

MANY people were surprised, of course, that Nansen did not continue his career as polar explorer, and indeed a continuation was planned. He tells of this in a letter of April 4, 1913, to Sir Clements Markham, the former president of the Royal Geographical Society of London. The letter is, as a matter of fact, an answer to a letter from Markham in which the latter explains why he considered that Amundsen's South Polar expedition was not fair play towards Scott.

Scott and Amundsen set off at the same time by different routes for the South Pole, Amundsen with the Norwegian equipment and methods perfected by Nansen and himself, Scott with ponies and motor sledges. Amundsen reached the goal first. Scott and four companions perished on the way back.

Scott did not believe, according to his diary, that his equipment was the cause; but, as Nansen writes to Markham, had Scott followed his earnest advice to use dogs and not ponies and motor sledges, "we should still have had him in our midst." Delayed by his equipment, he was overtaken by winter on the return journey. Eleven English miles from the rescue depot these heroic men sat in their tent in a snowstorm lasting eleven days, waiting for death.

Amundsen, too, had given Scott the same advice and had offered him half of his dogs.

Nansen undertook to reply to the bitter attack which was launched against Amundsen. He maintained that none of the unknown regions of the earth is the monopoly of any single person or nation. The more expeditions there are, the greater will be the results. He deplores the fact that there was no opportunity for cooperation in the laying of the plans. Amundsen had to restrict himself to telegraphing from Madeira about his plan to Scott, who was then in New Zealand. Amundsen must be ac-

quitted of the blame of making a "secret landing." Amundsen's
South Polar expedition was no more unfair play than the expeditions which set out from England, Scotland, Germany, and
Sweden for the South Pole although they knew that Nansen had
been making preparations for his antarctic trip for several years.

Incidentally, we may add here what happened in 1926.
Amundsen had six competitors. Byrd and Bennett reached the
North Pole first, and Amundsen led the cheering.

Something might have been said against Amundsen, Nansen thinks, if he had stolen his plan from Scott; but his plan
was Norwegian in idea, in equipment, and in method, and of
earlier date than Scott's expedition to the Antarctic.

In order to help his English friend to an understanding of
his point of view, Nansen then tells him the story of his own
plans.

From his expedition across Greenland, it was clear to Nansen that it would be a comparatively easy matter to investigate,
with Norwegian ski and Nansen sledges, the interior of the unknown Antarctic which, he was convinced, was covered with ice
and snow very much like Greenland. He longed to try it, but
first he had to get the North Polar expedition off his hands. He
told the Scotch naturalist, John Murray, who came to Norway
in 1893 to see the *Fram* off, that it was his intention to go to the
South Pole when he came back. On board the *Fram* he frequently discussed the antarctic expedition with Sverdrup, and
the last thing Sverdrup asked when they separated in March
1895 was whether Nansen would begin the South Polar expedition before he, Sverdrup, came back with the *Fram*. During the
winter in the hut on Franz Josef Land, there was plenty of time
to think out the plan in every detail, and when he came home
the plan was ready. He worked hard to get the scientific reports
of the *Fram* expedition off his hands in order to start his new
expedition as soon as possible. At the Royal Geographical Society in London in 1898, he set forth his views on antarctic ex-

ploration and stated that a Norwegian expedition was in preparation.

On various other occasions he spoke of his new project, as for example, with the members of Jackson's expedition, and he had requests from many who wanted to go with him.

In the meantime the aforementioned expeditions were begun while he himself was tied down with international oceanic research work and was obliged on this account to promise the Norwegian Government to postpone his South Polar expedition. After having given four years to this work and got it running smoothly, he turned again to his preparations, but then the political crisis in the relation between Norway and Sweden arose, and again the Fatherland claimed him. After 1905 he promised the Government to act as minister to London, but only for one year—because he had other plans. During his term as minister he worked further on his preparations and intended to start in 1907 or 1908.

In January 1907 Nansen was at home for a visit. One day Amundsen arrived at Polhögda. Nansen had stressed in a lecture the importance of continuing the exploration of the Arctic Ocean. Amundsen now laid before him a plan to go through Bering Strait in a small vessel, then take to the ice, live there in a tent or hut and let himself drift along. Nansen, however, thought it would be difficult to attain further results by this means of travel. A vessel like the Fram was needed, but he was planning to use the Fram himself to go to the South Pole. Amundsen asked if he might accompany him there, and afterwards have the Fram for his arctic drift. Nansen thought it would be unwise to spend so many years in the ice.

After having considered this a moment, however, it seemed to Nansen that it would be fairer if he gave up the Fram and his own expedition for the sake of the younger man. The North Polar expedition, too, was of much greater importance. Amundsen was the right man for it, and if he did not have a chance to make the expedition now, it might perhaps never be carried out at all; so Nansen promised that when Amundsen returned from America in the fall, he should have his final answer.

Nansen felt that it would be hard to give up this expedition for which he had been preparing so long, and which he had hoped would be his masterpiece when he would profit to the full from his experiences.

And it may be added here that both men realized that, as far as Nansen was concerned, it was not a question of postponement, but of renunciation for all time. As he himself expresses it in his letter to Markham, he *renounced* his trip to the South Pole.

But Nansen was unable to make up his mind until the last moment, that September day in 1907, when word was brought to him in the tower that Amundsen was sitting in the hall. On the way down he stopped to speak with his wife in one of the rooms off the gallery surrounding the hall.

"I know what will happen," said Eva, "you are going to leave me again."

Nansen looked at her, and without a word turned and went down into the hall.

"You shall have the *Fram*."

When Nansen went down to the hall after his meeting with Eva—his indecision or No turned into a Yes—he noticed the look of suspense in Amundsen's face as he sat waiting there. He realized then too what a refusal would mean to Amundsen now: it would block the only way that was open to him, whereas he himself, as he said to Amundsen, had tasks enough.

On June 7, 1910, Nansen stood on the roof of the tower and watched the *Fram* sail out of the fjord with Amundsen on the commander's bridge. Eva had died in December 1907. Now the *Fram* was leaving, and he himself was left behind.

"The bitterest hour of my life."

It was many years after that day that he confided this to his son. It agrees with the letter to Markham in 1913 where he

194 THE SAGA OF FRIDTJOF NANSEN

writes that it was "with bleeding heart" that he renounced the South Pole plan.

Moments like the June day on the roof of the tower could undoubtedly be felt as bitter, but in his large mind such hours were not allowed to become more than rare "shadows of seconds."

When Amundsen had been promised the *Fram* he set to work to prepare for her third expedition to the Arctic. Nansen helped him with this, and a committee was formed with Nansen as its chairman. At his advice Amundsen went to Bergen and studied oceanic research under Professor Björn Helland-Hansen's guidance in 1907. Various results from the first *Fram* expedition had to be verified by the more exact means of research that had been made available largely through Nansen's improvements in instruments and methods. With this excellent assistance from Nansen and Helland-Hansen, Amundsen was able to draw up a plan which attracted great attention.

Equipment for a seven year drift was very expensive, and there were difficulties. Then in 1909 Peary reached the North Pole, and that removed the sensational element so essential to interest the public. Many promised contributions were not forthcoming and the creditors began to press for payment, demanding that their bills be settled before the *Fram* left land. Amundsen was afraid that the American creditors would put the *Fram* under arrest as soon as she showed herself in American waters. The plan was that the *Fram* should sail round Cape Horn and up along the west coast to Bering Strait. What was he to do? He at once decided upon a new plan: via the South Pole to the North Pole.

Feeling that he alone should bear the responsibility for this, he did not mention anything about the change of plan to the committee or to Nansen.

When the letter from Funchal reached Nansen through Helland-Hansen, he was rather upset. "If only he had told me, I could have helped him in so many ways." He questioned Hel-

land-Hansen closely regarding Amundsen's outfit for the South
Pole. Fortunately Amundsen ran his master a close second in
the art of preparation. Nansen understood Amundsen's motive
for changing the plan, but could see no purpose in concealing
it. Nansen did not believe that any obstacles would have been
put in Amundsen's way, but Amundsen did not feel so sure of
that. He thought people would regard his plan as foolhardy,
and that the creditors especially would not consider that it increased the security of their claim. When the *Fram* set her bows
southwards from Funchal, neither committee nor creditors could
turn her helm.

One July day in 1912 Amundsen again stood in Nansen's
hall. The expedition was over—"a victory of the human intellect, the result of ingenious preparation and brilliant execution"
was how Nansen characterized it.

All his life Amundsen cherished a great admiration for
Nansen. In a radio lecture just before he set out with the *Norge*
in 1926, he said: "That inspired explorer, that clear-thinking
and far-seeing scientist and sportsman brought about a complete
revolution in the planning and execution of polar expeditions.
. . . His dazzling methods have been a standard for all polar expeditions. Personally all my work up to the flight in 1925 has
been based on his. When I think of the twenty-three years I have
labored in the polar regions, my thoughts turn back again and
again to the man who in my earliest youth stood for my highest
ideal, and who later gave me his priceless support—Fridtjof
Nansen."

At the national celebration at Akershus the same year, on
Amundsen's birthday, it was indeed an experience to see these
two greatest polar explorers of all time side by side, white-haired,
but youthfully erect and taut. What a lifetime of achievement
lay behind these men! To Nansen's impressive address Amundsen replied with words from a full heart directed to Nansen. He
reminded him of the first time he came to see him when "Nansen

arose with a big, broad smile, and from that moment he has helped me and stood by me. As I stand here this evening it is with a feeling of the deepest gratitude to you who showed me the way. Had you turned your back on me that time, I should never have done it. I should never have succeeded."

Nansen found plenty of jobs to do, but through all the work that occupied him, the unsolved riddles of the North Polar sea murmured importunately in his soul.

The great white silence, the white patches on the map, the vast expanses—they were always calling to him.

The *Maud* which succeeded the *Fram* got no opportunity on her two year drift (1922-24) to solve the problems in the proposed area.

The bold, sporting flights to the Pole have left the great scientific problems unsolved. But the same technique which made them possible, also gave Nansen his opportunity. An international society for the exploration of the Arctic by air-ship was formed with Nansen as president and editor of the society's periodical *Arktis*.

In October 1925 he published here and in several large newspapers abroad a long article: "The Exploration of the Unknown Regions about the North Pole." In this he stated the problems to be solved and described the plan for an expedition directly across the Arctic Ocean and back along the unknown coasts. Fifteen scientists were to go along under his leadership.

He promised to write the book about the expedition to help defray its expenses, personally undertook to guarantee a part of the expenses for which there was as yet no definite provision, and did a great deal of work in connection with the scientific preparations for the trip. He conducted the business of the Society in Berlin, Leningrad, and America, and saw to the construction of mooring-masts in Norway and Alaska. The airship *Graf Zeppelin* was built. Nansen clambered about in her interior like an acrobat in order to get to know her in detail.

In the meantime difficulties arose. The sensational interest among the general public was an important economic factor this time too. This interest is never related to the scientific importance of an expedition, but exclusively to the sporting element in it, its news value. The various sporting flights detracted from the interest in Nansen's scientific expedition. The trip had to be postponed from 1929 to the following year, and even if Nansen had been ready then, it would have had to be still further postponed.

Nansen had looked forward to this trip. He had longed to see the desolate snow-fields again, to be reminded of the *Fram* expedition, of the dash for the Pole on ski, to recall the youthful years of toil and struggle, of creative joy and happiness, and now to travel through the air, high above the ice hummocks, to make the whole trip there and back in one week, "No harm can possibly come to us. Of course we shall take dogs and sledges in case of emergency, but the whole thing is now civilized and arranged and specialized. It is a fine thing, of course, but the romance is gone. It will never return. The *Fram* will never come back."

From experiencing that "never," from experiencing it up there, his Genius spared him.

IN THE SERVICE OF SCIENCE

FROM the excursion in the *Viking* in 1882 until the Greenland expedition in 1888, Nansen's field of work was the animal life of the ocean. Here he won his spurs as a scientist, a gold medal, and his doctorate. During the *Fram* expedition his field became the ocean itself.

Oceanography, the science of the ocean, is a young branch of knowledge dating from the seventies of the last century. Nansen's contribution was epoch-making. "It will occupy an extraordinarily prominent position in the scientific history of all times," says one of the world's leading oceanographers, Professor Björn Helland-Hansen, mentioned in the preceding chapter.

The ocean is the womb and cradle of life here on earth. Life began in the ocean; from the ocean it rose up and conquered the land and the air. The ocean has an important bearing on all the conditions of life; we all live at its mercy. It is the great heat reservoir of the earth, the great regulator. It determines atmospheric conditions, the distribution of temperature, and many changes in wind and weather. It supplies moisture for the land, and conditions the growth of the soil, of all the life of the earth. Without the ocean man at least could not exist. Besides this, there are all the riches that men draw up from the sea. And aside from all material considerations, what a marvellous thing the ocean is for the eye and mind of man! The sea awakens longings, swells wings and brown sails, urges men on to deeds of daring.

It is natural and necessary for men to learn to know the ocean, the heart and circulatory system of the great organism of life on our earth.

At one time the name, Oceanus, was itself the symbol of the great, terrifying unknown surrounding the circle of the earth-dwellers. Man was a landlubber; his path ended at the sea-shore. Then with primitive craft he began to creep along the shore. It was a long time before he ventured to let the land slip out of sight and give himself up to the might of the sea. It was still longer before the seafarers began to measure the surface of the ocean, and much longer before they sought to force their way deep down into the sea to solve the riddles of its depths. Not before the nineteenth century was the veil slowly lifted.

Even yet the ocean is the least known part of our earth.

When we know Nansen's mind and nature and have followed him where the sea bore him, we can easily understand that the riddles of the sea would attract him, that oceanography was just the science for him. It was particularly inviting since oceanography was a young science and the area of the unknown so great; for, as he said in an introductory lecture to his students, "The most important thing in all research is not simply the results, the final truths established. It is the research itself, the struggle to win them. The attraction is not so much in knowing the facts as in conjecturing and seeking for them."

Oceanic research, with its changes from the work of investigation and draughting in the laboratory and at the writing table to the fresh sea cruises, gave him just the rhythm of work that suited him, as his diaries show.

After his return from the Pole he became professor of his old subject, zoology, with no lecturing as long as the work on the scientific results of the *Fram* expedition lasted.

He himself worked on the oceanographical part of it, and it was in this field that the greatest results of the expedition lay.

I quote Professor Björn Helland-Hansen: "Already during the expedition he had made observations which led to the posing of problems and the forming of working hypotheses of great general importance for oceanic research; he examined them more thoroughly and made new discoveries in the course of the investigations. As a matter of fact, many, if not most, of the questions which he later handled in so splendid a manner occurred to him during the arrangement and preparation of the *Fram* observations."

Nansen began his lectures in oceanography in 1900, and in 1908 he changed the name of his chair to oceanography.

The political activity around 1905 and the years of his position as minister in London, 1906-08, took much time from his scientific research. During these years, too, he was busy with preparations for a projected antarctic expedition.

Of the two divisions of oceanography, the physical and the biological, Nansen took what might be called the root of the subject, physical oceanography, the study of the ocean itself, its form, its depth, and the conditions at the bottom, its temperature and salinity; the movements of the ocean, its circulation, the currents, their courses and deviations, the forces which set them in motion, the laws which govern them and their effect on atmospheric conditions, on fishing, agriculture, and so on.

In his scientific account of the oceanography of the Arctic Ocean, Nansen deplores the fact that the methods and instruments which were then available were not so exact as is necessary to study the ocean. "I have now learned," he says, "that future investigations in physical oceanography will be of little or no value if they are not made with a much higher degree of precision than has hitherto been the case."

The instruments he had with him on the *Fram* were the best that could be procured at that time. He now examined them for all imaginable defects and put a great deal of work into improving his equipment and methods. He later invented new water-bottles for obtaining reliable samples of water from any depth whatsoever. Nansen's reversing water-bottle is now the one in most common use. The temperature of the ocean is determined by means of reversing thermometers or by measuring the temperature of samples drawn up in an insulated water-bottle according to the principle of the Swedish scientist, Professor Otto Petterson. Nansen made great improvements in both of these methods. It is largely owing to Nansen that the temperature can now be determined at any depth whatever to 1/100 of a degree. He devised and perfected also other instruments and methods for oceanic research.

Another task of the greatest importance was the formation of an international organization for oceanic research. The ocean is large, the problems are legion, the work is costly. Nansen took an energetic and able part in the building up of such an organization, and was for many years a member of the International Bureau of Oceanic Research. A central laboratory, the task of which was to improve the methods of oceanic research, was established at Oslo in 1902 with Nansen as head and the Swedish scientist, Dr. Walfrid Ekman, as his chief assistant.

With their new instruments and improved methods, they began in 1900 the research expeditions in the Norwegian Sea which were continued for many years under the leadership of Dr. Johan Hjort, then Director of Fisheries.

The Norwegian Government built and outfitted a steamship for oceanic research, the *Michael Sars,* named after Norway's earliest marine biologist, Nansen's father-in-law. Nansen was along on the first excursion in 1900 and began at this time his collaboration with the oceanographer, Professor Björn Helland-Hansen, a collaboration that lasted for thirty years.

Nansen published in 1901 a preliminary report of the results of this first investigation of the Norwegian Sea with modern methods: *Some Oceanographical Results of the Expedition with the* Michael Sars, *Headed by Dr. Johan Hjort in the Summer of 1900.*

After a series of excursions to the Norwegian Sea, Nansen and Björn Helland-Hansen published a large book: *The Norwegian Sea,* in 1909, a work which aroused a great deal of attention. This work is "the first charting of ocean currents within a definite region by the new methods." It is called "the main pillar in our knowledge of the economy of the ocean—of the physical basis of plant and animal life, for human exploitation of the wealth of the ocean."

The years from 1900 to 1910, says the oceanographer J. Sömme, are reckoned as the golden age in the history of oceanic research. It was a period of creative development in which Norway was a centre for oceanic research with a number of its leading figures: Nansen, Helland-Hansen, Hjort, and H. H. Gran.

Björn Helland-Hansen declares that Nansen's work in improving the technique and methods of oceanic research and his rigid insistence on precision have had a fundamental influence on the later development of oceanography. His demands for accuracy often seemed exaggerated, but he has been justified. Recent investigations have shown that the conditions in the ocean are quite other than was believed from earlier investigations with inexact methods.

Professor Werner Werenskiold writes about Nansen's scientific work that it is "characterized by a wealth of ideas and a vigorous and consistent carrying out of the line of thought, combined with a sure feeling for the inherent physical relations of natural phenomena." During the *Fram* expedition Nansen was struck by the fact that the ice drifted to the right of the wind direction. He suspected that this deviation of the drift to the right of the wind was due to the earth's rotation; carrying this line of reasoning further he arrived at the conclusion that the wind-driven currents in the ocean must constantly alter their direction from the surface downwards, so that at a certain depth they will be at right angles to the direction of the wind and, still further down, directly opposite to it. He got Dr. W. Ekman to treat the problem mathematically. Ekman found a number of formulas which agreed with Nansen's conclusions. Oceanographers and physicists in all countries protested and pointed out that it was wrong; but Ekman's theory of wind currents, "Ekman's spiral," is now in every oceanographical text-book. Nansen's conclusions were correct and they have led to a completely new conception of wind-driven currents in the ocean.

Mention has already been made in the account of the *Fram* expedition of the dead water which the *Fram* encountered off the coast of Siberia, in places where a thin layer of fresh water lay on top of the salt water. Nansen found the explanation of this phenomenon.

From the measurements of temperature made on the *Fram* expedition he discovered that apparently there must be powerful undercurrents, with a height of from 40 to 50 meters and more, which flow along in the depths without making themselves felt at the surface. There is a lower and heavier layer of water which surges up and down in an overlying lighter layer. It is this slight difference in weight that causes the great height of these waves. If they were to come up into the air, the difference in weight would quickly lower the wave height to normal.

With the improved methods it was now possible to follow and study the currents with much more accuracy. In the Norwegian Sea great eddies were found about which nothing had been known before, but which threw light on many biological and other phenomena. It appeared, too, that the Gulf Stream is subject to great annual variations which may cause corresponding changes in the atmosphere and temperatures in adjacent countries. Since a variation of one degree in one cubic meter of water gives the same variation in 3000 cubic meters of air, it is easy to understand how a slight change in the masses of water in the Gulf Stream can have great influence on the weather and temperature in the northern countries. From the heat of the Gulf Stream in the southern part of the Norwegian Sea in the early summer, it should be possible to draw conclusions regarding the weather in Norway for the coming winter. Where the arctic currents with their load of food-stuffs and dormant germs of life, which do not develop in the cold and darkness, meet with the warmer currents, the plankton life blossoms forth as food for Crustacea and fish which in turn are food for seals and whales; and finally the greediest beasts of prey in the world arrive to fish and net and hunt to the tune of millions of dollars. The study of ocean currents, then, is of the greatest importance for the fishing industry.

Before the World War put a stop to oceanographical excursions, Nansen went on several in the Norwegian Sea and the Atlantic Ocean from the Azores to Svalbard (Spitzbergen). Besides this he worked up the material from several other excursions and published it in three works: *Northern Waters: Captain Roald Amundsen's Oceanographic Observations in the Arctic Seas in 1901; The Sea West of Spitsbergen: The Oceanographic Observations of the Isachsen Spitsbergen Expedition in 1910;* and *The Oceanographic Investigations with the* Fram *in the North Atlantic 1910 and the South Atlantic 1911.* The two latter were written in collaboration with Björn Helland-Hansen.

Later the two authors returned to the question of the relation between the temperature of the air and the ocean and the variations in solar radiation. They published a work on the former in German in 1917, which appeared in expanded form in English in the United States in 1920: *Temperature Variations in the North Atlantic Ocean and in the Atmosphere. Introductory Studies on the Causes of Climatological Variations.*

By working with a mass of material they finally reached the conclusion that changes in the temperature of the ocean and the atmosphere depend essentially upon variations in solar radiation. The heat of the sun produces the winds. Variations in the heat of the sun change the winds and hence the ocean currents. Thus the air becomes warmer in many parts of the world and colder in other parts. The authors believe that "a continued study of these conditions will, it is hoped, yield such results that it will be possible in time to predict the weather not only for a few days, but also for a considerable length of time—weeks and months in advance."

Of Nansen's oceanographical writings we shall mention further: *The Waters of the Northeastern North-Atlantic: Investigations Made During the Cruise of the* Frithjof *of the Norwegian Royal Navy in July 1910;* and *Spitsbergen Waters: Oceanographic Observations during the Cruise of the* Veslemöy *to Spitsbergen in 1912.*

He wrote a large book on the latter expedition in 1920: *A Trip to Spitsbergen.* In this book he has woven an excellently written travel description in with the scientific material and has illustrated it with his own masterly drawings.

In other fields of science, too, besides physical oceanography, Nansen has made important contributions. He also studied the land formations of the earth.

As early as the Greenland expedition he paid attention to the changes which the surface of the land and the relation between the sea and land must have undergone. On the *Fram* expedition he noted the flat, broad platforms or ledges which stretch out underneath the water along the coasts in the northern polar regions. This platform, "the Shelf," off the coasts of Svalbard, Siberia, and Norway, he studied for many years. Along the coast of Siberia it stretches out like a submarine socle for many miles into the ocean. Its depth is not more than 100 meters until with unexpected abruptness it plunges down to a depth of three or four thousand meters.

In the scientific account of the *Fram* expedition he discussed thoroughly the question of the history of the development of these socles upon which the continents rest. He believed they were old ocean levels.

Along our coast the reefs and skerries with their islands and islets and the old shore-lines form a surface which also indicates an old sea level.

These problems he has treated further in works dating from 1922 and 1928: *The Strandflat and Isostasy* and *The Earth's Crust, its Surface Forms, and Isostatic Adjustment.* "Here he touches on significant and interesting things in connection with the rising and sinking of the land during and after the ice age. The land was weighed down by the ice, but bulged up again when the ice melted. Then, too, there was so much water bound up as ice during the ice age that on account of this the sea was considerably lower. Conversely, when the land ice melts during a warm period, the sea rises for the same reason. When the surface of the land is dug out by frost, rivers, or glaciers, the land becomes lighter and the upper part of the earth's crust rises. Thus it may come about that the mountain tops grow higher and higher, out of all reason, while the valleys are dug out to such an extent that the whole country becomes lighter and rises up in the air." (W. Werenskiold.)

Nansen made an important contribution in still another field with a big scientific work. An English friend, Dr. J. Scott Keltie of London, requested him to write the history of the discovery of the arctic regions for an extensive series of books on geography. Nansen thought that he was familiar enough with the subject and that it would not require much time, but when he came to explore this untilled field where there was so much to be done, he found a task which gripped his mind so strongly that in order to satisfy himself he had to write a big work.

In Northern Mists appeared in 1911. It deals with the exploration of the arctic regions from the earliest times to about 1500. He did not get down to the north polar voyages proper.

He pictures how the conceptions of the North loom up and change from age to age, and live on in myths and illusions. "We obtain a peculiar insight into the way in which the human mind works in its struggle to subdue the earth and the universe."

To clear his way through the myths and legends to the solid bedrock of fact was a great and difficult task; and the more extensive his studies became, the more riddles he perceived luring him on farther and farther.

On many points he arrived at results which were in conflict with currently accepted views. This made it necessary to give not merely the bare results, but also a great part of the investigations themselves. A great sensation was created by his statement that the story of the Vinland voyages, the saga about Leif Ericson and Thorfinn Karlsefni, is so embroidered with legend and fairy tale that little that is trustworthy remains. The discussion of this matter is not yet closed.

The book is written with the scientist's passion for truth regardless of any treasured national beliefs. A tremendous amount of work went into this book. The bibliography mentions several hundred works in many languages. It is the permanent foundation for all future research in the history of polar exploration.

The edition of this huge work was not large; there was no plethora of subscribers. But those who have browsed about among Nansen's works are no longer terrified by his erudition. They have discovered that the learned author is a capital story teller, an artist, a poet. The work is illustrated by the author's own drawings, saga-like in their simplicity, monumental in line and mood.

This work occupies a central position in Nansen's literary production. Even if he did not quite reach the goal he originally set for himself, his book covers the largest and most difficult part of the work. It has cleared the way and built the propylaea; and it contains the man himself, scientist and artist.

Fridtjof Nansen has also written other historical studies in the field of natural science, on changes in climate within the historical era, partly in connection with the colonization of Greenland and the condition of life there.

His popular travel books, too, from his many journeys, both the scientific expeditions to Greenland, the Arctic Ocean, and Svalbard, and those which he made in later years, with essentially other aims, through Siberia, Russia, Armenia, and the Caucasus, are rich in observations with penetrating elucidations and explanations.

After the Siberian trip he was, says Professor S. Torup, very much occupied with the great number of interesting problems bound up with geographical and meteorological conditions in Siberia. He said that he had approached the Russian authorities regarding a systematic examination of the formation of tundra and other questions; but then the War, the Revolution, and the League of Nations work came and put a stop to it.

His last great plan, to explore the yet unknown regions of the Arctic Ocean by air-ship, he was not allowed to carry out. All the preparations were made, however; he gave an account of the plan as early as 1925. But, as W. Werenskiold says, "he has done enough. In several fields no investigator can afford to neglect Nansen's work; his many original ideas, his acuteness, his strict logic, and his thorough examination of all problems have created works which will endure in science."

His scientific achievements become still more impressive when we know how time after time he was obliged to interrupt his research for months and years to solve other kinds of problems in the service of the Fatherland and of the League of Nations.[1]

* * *

The following description of the first research excursion with the *Michael Sars* is from *Sporting Days in Wild Norway:* "A Cruise to Iceland and Jan Mayen."

Christiania, July, 1900. "By dint of much perseverance, Dr. Johan Hjort has at length induced the Norwegian State to build a special steamship for ocean research. It seems high time, considering the vital importance of oceanic conditions and their variations for our country as a whole and for its fisheries in particular.

"The vessel has been christened *Michael Sars* after our great pioneer in the field of oceanic research, and she is about to start on her first journey. Hjort has invited me to join the expedition

---

[1] The account in this chapter is based on articles by Professor Björn Helland-Hansen and Professor W. Werenskiold and on Fridtjof Nansen's manuscripts and notes for lectures at the University from 1902 to 1920.

in order to carry on physical investigations together with Björn Helland-Hansen. He himself will undertake the animal life and fishery research, and Haakon H. Gran the investigations of plant life. . . .

"To-morrow we must put to sea again. First we have planned a 'profile' with a number of stations for taking observations at different depths across the sea in the direction of Iceland; then we think of sailing to Jan Mayen, and after that back to Lofoten. The distribution of living organisms in the sea and the fishing conditions are Hjort's and Gran's subjects of study, while Helland-Hansen and I will try more particularly to obtain some information about the relation between warm and cold currents and water masses.

"We have all of us invented new apparatus, instruments, and methods for investigating the living creatures of the deep, and the physical and chemical properties of the ocean. We have great expectations of this expedition—we are rather inclined to think that it may inaugurate a new epoch in oceanic research."

At sea between Norway and Iceland. July 26.

"Life has at times its compensations. We have gained the first victory of our expedition. Last night our drift-net was full of herring, bright, glittering 'large-herring.' We also caught a coalfish and two big codfish, right out in the ocean.

"Hjort is radiantly proud of this confirmation of his theories. He had come to the conclusion that the various kinds of fish which supply our important fishing industry are not confined to the banks and the coast, but are distributed over the whole sea, even far out in the ocean—in fact, wherever there are livable conditions. His opinion had been strengthened by the stories of bottlenose-whalers who had seen quantities of fish out in the open sea.

"Here, then, we have absolute proof. At one blow the field whence the fisheries derive their rich harvest has been many times enlarged, and the reserves of fish in the ocean seem more inexhaustible than we had ever ventured to believe.

"I shall be interested to see whether we meet with rose-fish (*Sebastes norvegicos*) west of Jan Mayen, where in 1882 I found the stomach of a bladdernose seal simply stuffed with fresh rosefish which he must have caught immediately before. That was far out in the deep sea, too. And think of all the fish I found inside the Greenland sharks that we caught in Denmark Strait, between Iceland and Greenland!

"We used to regard the cod and the rosefish and their like as living only at the bottom, and to distinguish them from the so-called pelagic fish which roam far and wide about the ocean, such, for instance, as the mackerel. But now it seems as though they will all have to be classed as pelagic.

"The sea is calm. Long steel-grey rollers ripple the surface, lapping gently against the sides of the ship; the sun's fiery ball is sinking amid a purple glow. Silent-winged mallemucks (*Fulmarus glaciales*) flit to and fro across the shining water, crossing and recrossing the path of sunlight as though in search of something they can never find. But surely that is what we all do!

"Now I must get some rest. In a few hours the trawl will be taken up and then we shall have a whole night's work taking temperatures and obtaining water samples. So to sleep, as one can sleep only at sea."

One evening "when the sounding line was being hauled up, my newly invented water bucket came at full speed straight for the block. The line broke and the precious instrument with its costly thermometer disappeared into the deep. For a moment my heart seemed to stop beating—months of labor had gone into the making of that instrument."

But another evening they had good luck. "Ever since leaving Jan Mayen, night and day, we have been on the look out for jelly-fish. At last we have seen the first of them. We must put out the big drag-net while we have supper.

"Gran is investigating the surface plankton. Great jubilation!—he suddenly discovers a quantity of *Ceratium tripos* (a diatom that produces phosphorescence); this means either coastal water or water from the banks, as the presence of jelly-fish would lead one to expect.

"What will the drag-net reveal? It is drawn in. Excitement runs high. But when it comes up full of jelly-fish surrounded by large quantities of young fish there is no end to the delight on board. Gran dances about the deck and bursts into song; the captain runs out of his cabin with nothing on but a shirt and refuses to believe the news until he is presented with a whole plateful of lively young fish.

"Even Jacob, whose head is tied up in a big cloth on account of a gumboil, must needs come and gaze at the drag-net that had brought us such wonderful luck: real young codfish right out at sea between Norway and Jan Mayen, 600 kilometers from land. Our delight infected every one on board. We had advanced a step further in the knowledge of the animal life of the ocean."

In the beginning of August they reached the ice in Denmark Strait between Greenland and Iceland, Nansen's old battleground on the *Viking* cruise. He stood and gazed out over the huge floes with their hummocks and level stretches in the sinister solitude of the Arctic Sea, untrodden and unseen. The others wanted to go out on the ice, but Nansen had no desire to go; he had nothing to do there.

"Yet somehow, as I stood gazing out at the expanse, I began to feel a strange longing to be there once more—out there was the life of real adventure and action."

Then one evening in August he finds himself bound for home again, home again to his Norwegian mountains after nights and days in the fairy-like light of the midnight sun.

"How refreshing it was to return to dark nights again. The outline of the hills stood out black against the shadowy sky. A little gold from the moon shone through a cloud above a gap in the south. Far below roared the river with its rapids and inky pools among the fir-woods. I could just see a boat—no doubt they were out fishing in the night.

"I love this dark night that descends so gently, covering up all that is trivial until you see only the large, simple outlines—and the stars above."

NANSEN AS REVEALED IN HIS DIARIES

DETAILED and carefully composed diary notes are the basis for Nansen's books on travel from the first trip in the *Viking* in 1882 to the last through Armenia and the Caucasus in 1925.

Sporting Life in Wild Norway, first published in 1916, occupies a place of its own. It is a bouquet plucked from many diaries and from several years, from hunting, fishing, sailing, and skiing trips. Both *Sporting Life in Wild Norway* and the *Fram* book have their peculiar interest; they admit us to intimacy with the man himself. The excerpts which have been made for this biography from unprinted parts of his diaries deepen still more our impression of him, of his richly emotional inner life.

Nansen's nature spanned many octaves. It was full of moods, variable like the sea, sunshine alternating with cloudy weather, storm with calm, buoyancy with melancholy. In quoting fragments torn out here and there from the diaries, it is easy to get a distorted picture by using exclusively either the crests or the troughs of the waves, forgetting that Nansen was the whole wave. The course of the wave itself is the significant thing; its movement always reflects the moment, at the same time as it portrays the sea which sustains the movement.

It is especially these unpublished parts of the diaries which disclose his tendency to reflect, brood, and dream, a strange propensity for a nature so active and energetic; but his life shows that at the same time he had the urge of a superabundant strength both to do things and to wrest its secrets from the universe.

We remember the dreamy pauses between the first and second sock in his boyhood years. "Look at old slow-poke," the others said, "you'll never amount to anything, the way you dawdle along." In his early youth the urge to do things sometimes exhibited itself in his attempting the most impossible feats. One time, for instance, he tried to jump over a fence as high as a man, taking off from a soft field. He was left hanging on the fence. This impulse to leap barriers later took on a more sensible form, with a more correct estimation of the difficulty and of his own abilities; but the urge to push further back the boundaries of the impossible was always there. Both the Greenland expedition and the polar expedition were impossible and foolhardy in the eyes of the authorities, but what was impossible and foolhardy for others was the mark of genius in Nansen's plans. This time the "slow-poke" cleared the fence.

His highest form of activity was to be on the run towards the fences, the boundaries, towards the impossible. This impulse to leap barriers, common to science, religion, and art, to all creative activities, to all forms of the poetic impulse, is not satisfied by results, by accepted formulas and dogmas, but only by new fences, new barriers, new chasms, new strain, new effort.

Ibsen's *Brand* must have affected the young Nansen. The Ibsenesque cleft between desire and strength, between will and possibility, was a fundamental problem in his own mind. The agony of impotence and the joy of great visions often alternate in his diary. Now the boat lies quietly rolling on the old swells after a storm, now she sheers off, with swelling sail, towards new seas. At the edge of the chasms he spent many a weary evening in his tent with his true companions: dreams, reflection, and melancholy, and there was no limit to what melancholy might dictate for the diary; but the next morning, when camp was broken, he was again the essence of will and strength, vigorously toiling under the banner "Forward."

It is not particularly strange that the philosopher of religion who created the expression which characterizes the original impulse of religion as "the impulse to overleap the barriers"—Bishop Eivind Berggrav—should acknowledge that it was under the influence of Nansen's words and of his personality, that the idea and the expression came to him.

The entries in Nansen's diaries, aside from the travel diaries, are less concerned with what he is doing from day to day than with his thoughts and moods. He is constantly grappling with life's deepest problem; he fixes his Jacob's ladder firmly in the earth on which he lives, but the other end of the ladder does not seek the support upon which religion and the Church rest it.[1]

"I am always travelling towards something vague which I never reach. What I am engaged on, whether it be an expedition across the Arctic or work on a scientific problem, is and will always be something temporary, something that must be cleared out of the way first in order to get to the reality which is life. And so it will go on until one day I drop, I like the others. The reality has never been attained."

"As usual when this thought comes over me, everything I am working for sinks into sheer nothingness, and the work itself becomes a desert.

"Life is just a series of moments between two eternities, and yet we can afford to waste it in finding out what it is instead of living it!" (November 23, 1902).

[1] For Nansen's philosophy of life see his article in *Samtiden* 1908: "Science and Morality," and an article, which is in a sense his testament, in the American *Forum* for December 1929: "What I Believe." See also Professor S. Torup's article in *Samtiden*, 1930: "Fridtjof Nansen's Philosophy of Life."

In *Kirke og Kultur* 1930 Bishop Berggrav wrote: "... His honest conviction led him to place himself outside the Norwegian State Church. It seems as though the depths of his temperament had instead sought compensation in practising the sacrificial service of love on a gigantic scale.... Thomas à Kempis spoke of a Christus incognito. And right now the note is sounding from Canterbury that the Church's sign of recognition must not be first and foremost the word of the Church, but the temper and acts of Christian love. We cannot conceal the fact that in Nansen we are faced with the greatest contribution of love in our generation, but that the man himself had found that he must stand without the Church. This does not give us call for regret over Nansen, but rather for a sober examination of ourselves."

We know without the diaries what Nature was for him. It was more than the object of his scientific research; and the diaries bring us closer to his personal relation to Nature.

From two diaries for the years 1900-05, I have brought together a series of observations, not more detached than will allow us to follow the course of the wave through a period of years. Between the points represented by these dates we are able to see a large stretch of the sea of Fridtjof Nansen's life.

July 13, 1900. "The vast empty space envelops me again, the terror. Everything is sunk in a heap of trivialities—Fatherland and duties, life and death, what does it all amount to?

"My great discovery is that I have found hell, but there is no fire there. It is the land of clammy fogs. When the last vanity of man is gone, then life is a hell of fogs, empty space.

"Up man, you are sick. Fight or die for all that is beautiful. Remember, it is beauty that has value; remember your old kingdoms of beauty where everything was cool crystal, shining in the colors of the rainbow. No one could rob you of them. A man is filled with his own realm of beauty independent of others."

Two days later he is making tracks along the Otta River. (See *Sporting Days in Wild Norway.*) The city with its turmoil and inanity is far behind. "It puts fresh life in one to watch that mighty will as it goes singing its way triumphant through the valley it once hollowed out, unchecked by any obstacle. It shapes its own course, does its work, and runs quietly into the sea. And along its banks the lissom birch is fain to grow."

July 16, 1900. Grotli. "Once more I stand amid the mountains and the snows. The sun has just gone down, and the glacier is shining with a deep carmine glow under the crest of the mountain. Down there the lake and the level stretches around it are veiled in the cold shadow of evening.

"No sooner do I see the glaciers than my faith in life revives and that other feeling seems sickly lethargy. What is this magic power? When from the valley I caught sight of them this time, when I saw the dark ravines, the sheer ramparts of rock, the white patches of glacier, stern and harsh and hard, I felt their desolateness more strongly than ever before, and something within me seemed to say: 'Ugh, why do you go up there?' I felt the charm of the rich fields and smiling birch-groves; but then I stood and looked at the glaciers lying bluish-white and cold now that the sunset glow had left them, and I had to ask myself if I were not really most at home here. Here I can stand up erect and free."

July 17, 1900. Geiranger. "Rain and mist have blotted out the mountains; there is nothing to be seen; yet it feels good to be alive. I am after all a strange creature. I am always most cheerful in rain and storm. Is it that the damp air bedews my inner drought? At any rate it is all gone now."

These pages are from an ocean research cruise in the Norwegian Sea on the *Michael Sars*. They are sailing north towards the place where they are to work, and in the meantime there is nothing to do.

"What a good thing this laziness is for one! A man should not always work and always give of himself. He finally becomes quite empty."

July 26, 1900. "After the first victory of our expedition." "The sea is calm, the waves are rolling and gleaming in the last rays of the sinking sun. Wonderful weather. It entices one to rest. How I should like to seek out some of my old familiar authors! But I have none of them here, just new ones. These are said to be good, but I am tired of being perpetually on expeditions of exploration into the unknown. I would so gladly go back to old familiar places and lay my head softly down to rest in the glow of the evening sun with the shining waves lapping against the sides of the ship, and let myself be lulled to sleep by familiar melodies. That is the sunshine of life."

On July 29, 1900, he takes himself to task for his diary writing—"this self-analysis which yet has never the courage and perspicacity to come to grips with the actual realities that nevertheless lie at the bottom and come up again at every crossroad. You are small, man, you who once in your youth dreamed yourself great, and that does not grieve you. But it is hard to give up the demand that life should work out in accordance with a system and purpose, a problem to be posed and solved. Not a trip through the mists of chance—but still that is what life is and will continue to be."

August 4, 1900. Iceland. "Think of those rides in there along the lovely fjord, over the level plateaux and up the green valleys, of the brisk pace, the infectious mirth, the glittering snow-mountains and the sparkling sea away beyond. Life seemed young and free and easy. One had a feeling that here one could settle down for the rest of one's days. And then those splendid, kind-hearted folk, bred to a life of liberty!

"After three days there I had the same feeling as when I went away after a winter in Greenland. I left behind me a part of myself, the free child of nature in me."

October 1, 1900. Sörkje. "Our goals are what we make them. They are all equally qualified to fill life if only we are completely filled by them. Is it the struggle towards a goal that makes man happy? Is not the Eskimo's goal, his struggle with nature, just as great for him, and does it not satisfy him just as fully as it satisfies a Newton to discover the laws of gravity or as it would satisfy a scholar today to solve the riddle of existence itself? Does the Eskimo not experience just as great satisfaction from overcoming his difficulties, from reaching his goal, from feeling himself superior in the struggle, as the civilized man does in reaching his? Yes, the greatness of the goal depends on ourselves and on our valuation of it.

"... Out yonder the moon glides behind Velebufjell; it shines through the fir-trees in the black water, a cold strip of silver reaching in towards the shore. The wooded slope lies black on the other side with the substance of another life, of the life we should but do not live. A few dark silver-rimmed clouds hover near the half-moon; everything is dark, but so wonderfully remote from all this unsteadily vacillating, hurrying, fretting pettiness—spacious, simple, full of balance and beauty. Space with all that it holds, immutable for millenniums, where all human goals sink into dust—ah, Life, how beautiful thou art!

Sunday, January 6, 1901. "Eva is singing Kjerulf and Welhaven in there. What is it in these two that gives the effect of such marvellous coolness and purity? It is like a bath in which the soul is completely rested and led back to the lost realms of beauty. Superbly calm, no inflaming chase, no nauseating yearning, no nervous tempo too hurried to be intense.

Just listen to 'The River Course,' how it

Ceases its noise and takes its time.

I came by the river one summer day
To the grasslands broad and fair
Where the pulsing waters more gently play
For him who would linger there. . . .

Mine is the song and the minor key
Of the waves and the aspen leaves
And my soul is thrall to their minstrelsy
In the path that the ripple weaves. . . .

Oh, golden time—so crystal clear and free from ardor! Listen to 'Tirilltove':

A bird flew over the fir-clad slope,
It was singing forgotten songs.

". . . But the wood and the mountain lake had whispered their doleful sentiment into my mind for the first time, and now I shall never forget it!"

"Have you forgotten it in the obliterating chase? Where is the inner I, the old self of childhood's great sad forests? The modern soul has no time to follow the course of the waters, to hearken to the sad thoughts of wood and mountain lake."

September 29, 1903. "I am becoming more and more of a hunter. I am constantly thinking now of new trips to woods and mountains, of lying out at night in barns on the sæter, of roving about in the woods all day and sitting beside the fireplace in the solitary sæter shanty in the evening, chatting with Andres about forests and hunting while the autumn evening and the starry heaven envelop the sæter fields and woods outside. . . . I let the days glide past in carefree peace, with no miserly desire to fill them with visible profit—just with the moods of life in nature which come and go, a little wearily sometimes when we are tramping through bogs, over fallen trees and boulders in the dusk of evening, and then pleasantly when we stretch out by the fire after a good or a bad hunt and stare at the embers and let our dreams follow their trackless ways. So I could go on. I do not miss the world, and it misses me still less.

"The colors of autumn are all gone. How very quickly they passed this year! It seems to me as though it were only a few days since all the slopes were gilded and the mountain was a mass of red gold. Now the leaves are fallen—only on a birch or two over in Velebuhei is there a touch of yellow left. The leaves fell silently and yet so quickly; there was no storm to sweep them away. Peacefully resigned they sifted down with a gentle rustling sound as one walked through the woods or listened for the lynx. The forest stream was so thickly covered with yellow leaves that one could step into the deep pools without noticing that it was the brook. And before one realized it there stood the birches, naked, with their twisted branches stretching up into the autumn air waiting for the winter. . . . The hillside is dark and forlorn without the play of color—just fir woods and the dark brown bank. The sæter fields are withered and yellow, and the mountain is a desolate shade of dark brown. No more gaiety— all the joyous riot of color is gone. The earth is ready to receive the snow which the sky, radiant with clear sunlight day after day, persistently withholds from it."

October 5, 1903. "Winter was upon us, white and silent. We had to pack up in haste and make our way down the valley. . . . It was good-bye once more to the free life in the heights. I had to descend to the din, to the hair-splitting, to so much that goes against the grain—down, below, where briers entangle the feet.

"It was hard to leave when I should so much have liked to stay and watch the winter closing in, spacious, white, and pure, with no pettiness. . . ."

"What is it that makes life worth living?

"Is it the animal well-being that reaches its climax in the hunter's life when, tired and wet and hungry, one comes in, gets food and rest and dry clothes, and is free to stretch out by the fire, and yet the moment one hears a lynx, is on one's feet, gun in hand, running away from food and warmth and rest as though one had never a thought for such things?

"Is it life in nature? How many live without feeling the need of it! Is it those moments when we can give ourselves up to the ecstasy that high art can bring us? Many do not know it, but choose perhaps something else instead. If you ask the lover, he will answer love, but love seldom lasts forever. Ask a woman, and she will say love and motherhood, but how many have to live without those things and still desire to live. Ask a man and he will perhaps answer work. But work for what? just for the sake of working?

"It is perhaps, after all, this whole game that we call life that makes it worth living. It is the capacity for joy and sorrow—work, thirst, rest, toil, love, wild life, art.

"But the enemies of life are not care, not privation, not distress—they are its staunchest allies. Its enemies are the grey, clammy fogs without shadow and without light.

"Let us go, then, so that it may be still better to come back to this mountain world where the pale birches grow and where the fir-tree stands silent and solemn, and where the mountain blushes morning and evening."

April 16, 1904. "I was obliged to write a few polite words to an enthusiastic young Dutchman and would gladly have wished him something good in life, but what? In my haste I found nothing better to say than to hope that his youthful enthusiasm for everything that was good and worth a struggle might last for life, along whatever path he might travel!

"Perhaps that was after all the best thing I could have wished him on his way. What better possession could he have?"

During July and August 1904 Nansen was on an ocean cruise on the *Veslemöy*. July 22, 1904. Frierfjorden and Porsgrunn. "I work all day long, and then there is no place in the daytime for dreams and thoughts, just for the quest to solve the unsolved riddles of the deep. When I cease from work and look up, it is night; mountain and islands and sea are dreaming in the tranquil summer night. A few stars shine pallidly high up in the heavens. Jupiter stands bright and yellow in the east and for a while the golden strip of the half moon is mirrored in the silky blue water out towards the deep blue mountains. All the business of the day is far, far away. It is a different world, and again the soul is filled with thoughts and dreams of all the things that are not of the day and that cannot be expressed in words.

"Here, man, is thy home, but there thou art also at home. It is as though thou wert formed of two beings from two different spheres. The one is satisfied merely with the work and activity of the day. The other craves something else, something that is to be found somewhere in the west in the cloud kingdoms of the sunset, or in the dreamy splendor of the moon, or farther away in the trembling stars."

In September he is again in the mountains, grouse hunting all day long—then home to the sæter lea in the evening. "These evening moods are incomparably happy: the eye can feast in pleasant contentment on the cows and pigs that have come home and are gathered in the close; one's thoughts seek no distant goal, and the conflicting contradictions have ceased their tumult. The air is so clear and still that one can hear voices and cow bells from across the valley as though they were quite near."

September 10, 1904. "I sit here and laugh. Long ago the sun sank down behind the ridge over us. The twilight deepened, slowly dragging itself up over the slope from the black wooded valley down below, and the stars twinkled out in the blue canopy high above. Now the flames rise briskly from our fire, licking round the pot in which we are cooking the newly shot birds, and throwing a flickering light with dark shadows on the trees round about and above us. We sit and slash into the legs of the birds with white teeth, not allowing them time to be more than half-cooked. And as I look at these faces and these fingers, black from not having been washed for several days, and gaze into the fire, I laugh to myself until I chuckle. Why? I think how thin is this varnish that we call civilization. We strive generation after generation, society after society, to get away from Nature, to heap up refinements and unnecessary habits of living, to attain to the 'higher' forms of existence. Given a day or two like these, full of toil and with little food, and in less than an hour, in a minute, we throw it all overboard and dive head first back into Nature's unfathomable depths. What a liberating thought! What is the difference between us as we sit or lie here, dirty, wet through, ravenous as wolves, tearing with teeth and claws at our half-gnawed drumsticks, and those men clad in skins of animals who roved through these same forests and sat beside the same bonfire thousands of years ago? They killed their game with stones and sticks, it is true, and we shot ours with powder and lead; they kindled their fire with two sticks of wood and a bow, and we had matches; but their fire was just as good as ours, and their game perhaps better over the fire than ours in the pot; and if we are less tired, less wet, less hungry, we devour our chunks of meat just as greedily, and find enjoyment just as intense in resting and warming our tired limbs beside a fire of sticks. This is the independence of Nature thou hast attained, thou noble creature man! Or do we pursue our prey with less greediness? If it be only a bird, do we not tremble inwardly with the excitement of the chase every second that we wait for it to take wing. Or when the big elk bursting through the thicket comes crashing towards us, do we not feel as though our hearts had stopped beating in our breasts? Every muscle turns to steel. We hold our breath so as not to be heard, and when the magnificent, big animal with his mighty antlers comes out between the branches and stares at us—where is the civilized man then? Oh, ye blessed, ever refreshing, primitive feelings!"

August 27, 1905. On the way to Sörkje.

". . . Those who live in voluntary sadness, Dante buried deep in Inferno. They are in love with sorrow, and prefer to see shadows. As though it were not joy enough just to live and see the sun rise in the morning, see blushing clouds and green fields. Our first duty towards ourselves and others is to be happy and contented; but what a difficult duty that is for many, not least for me!

"I see valleys and mountains, woods and green meadows, fields where the golden grain stands ready to be cut. This glorious land is mine—I want to live, to give it of my best powers which I feel are still lying unused, waiting for an opportunity. I see farther ahead a new world to be built, and I want to build it."

September 1, 1905. Sörkje. He sends a telegram to his student comrades celebrating the twenty-fifth anniversary of their matriculation.

"Let us drink to Norway's Spring, in the faith that our greatest lifework still lies before us when we shall help to build the future of a free Norway in league with the courageous spirit and strength which will now grow in our people.

"Twenty-five years ago we met. Life with all its possibilities lay before us like an unknown land hidden by the clearing mists of morning. We were the new discoverers who were to go through this promised land, each on his own path. Oh, what a beautiful time that was! We had faith and courage and great dreams of all that we should find and attain. And now twenty-five years later, when from widely separated paths we meet in the midst of this land and pause to look back, what have we to say to one another about the journey? How many of us have found what we expected and hoped for? How many hopes and illusions lie crushed along the way! Oh, we have all learned how difficult the art of living is—with a modern man's education and requirements.

"We have lived in a difficult age. The old values have been destroyed, and the new are not yet created. The old wise ordering of the world with a planned evolution towards higher forms and an assured goal, that system with its definite responsibility and free will has fallen to pieces. The solid foundation we built tottered under our feet. The theory that 'energy is constant' had insinuated itself into our whole interpretation of the world and our view of life; and when we perceived that intention and purpose are human utility concepts, it seemed as though our whole structure had sunk into ruins. Our ideals became wan wraiths, our faith in life was undermined. It all seemed an empty and comfortless game of strength, a chaos in which one thing only was certain: eternal change; but whence, whither? Like the wind.

"We had learned merely to fix our glance far ahead on a chimæra, Evolution. We had forgotten the prerogative of life, and we had forgotten the words of our Master to behold the fowls of the air and consider the lilies of the field.

"We were running the risk of becoming a doubting generation without faith and without ideals.

"But now Spring is coming in Norway. The time of action is at hand again. A young, vigorous generation with an understanding of the prerogative of life, with faith in itself and in the future of the country will grow up and, untrammelled by old forms and superstitions, will build new dwellings for mankind. .... Let us all fight for the intellectual Spring that is now coming."

September 3, 1905. "Oh, there is a whole world of new ideas weltering and fermenting within me, seeking form and longing to burst forth. It gives me no peace and I cannot escape it, but will it ever be anything more than a world of dreams? What do I want? I want to expand, to create, to work. I want to give the coming generation some of that world which is fermenting within me. I want to help them throw overboard all 'corpses in the cargo' and paint life for them in all its power and fulness, to show them Nature's healthy, purifying beauty, the child's superiority to the grown-up with his 'worm-eaten reflectiveness.' "

NANSEN IN 1905

THE UNION between Sweden and Norway was not without flaws from the start. On the part of Norway it had not come about quite voluntarily. Nor was Sweden entirely satisfied. For many years King Carl Johan continued to suggest changes in the Norwegian Constitution.

The Act of Union, which contained the terms, gave Norway equal status with Sweden. The conduct of the foreign affairs of both was placed in the hands of the King of the united countries. But a year after the triumph of parliamentarism in Norway, the Swedes made a change in their own constitution, whereby the King's power to manage the foreign affairs of Norway was automatically transferred to the Swedish Foreign Minister. This change in the Swedish Constitution in 1885 was the source of a twenty years' strife in the Union. One Union committee after another was wrecked by the different interpretations of the Act of Union.

The Norwegian Constitution, as accepted at Eidsvold, May 17, 1814, contains instructions covering the appointment of Norwegian consuls; but during the period of the Union a partnership developed and the management of the Consular service came under the Swedish Foreign Minister. Meanwhile, as Norway's shipping trade grew to be one of the greatest in the world, three times as great as that of Sweden, the Norwegian demand for consuls exclusively responsible to Norwegian authority also grew.

The inconveniences of the partnership increased when the commercial interests of the two countries began to conflict. Sweden embarked upon a policy of high tariffs, while Norway continued almost a Free Trade country. The commercial treaties made conjointly had now to be replaced by separate treaties. When Sweden terminated the Free Trade agreement between Sweden and Norway, the vital nerve in the commercial and industrial co-operation of the two countries was severed. The many conflicts of interest which now arose did not strengthen the Union.

From the Norwegian point of view dissolution of the partnership was the only way out.

The Consular question entered into Norwegian politics in 1891. A Norwegian committee unanimously agreed that Norway should demand full control of her Consular service. Repeated resolutions of the Storthing were brought to nought when the King, in response to Swedish public opinion, refused to act upon them. This led to a cabinet crisis in 1892, and a similar crisis again in 1893. A new Government was formed, and again a deadlock resulted. In Sweden there was a strong movement in favor of compulsory revision and a resort to arms. Norway had never considered war as a means of settling accounts between the two sister nations, and the country was practically unarmed. In order to prevent a breach, the Storthing opened negotiations with Sweden on both questions: the conduct of Foreign Affairs and the establishment of a Consular service. A committee on these questions sat for several years, but the negotiations were wrecked on the Norwegian demand for a separate Consular service.

In 1902 a new committee was appointed. The question of Foreign affairs was laid aside, and the negotiations dealt solely with the Consular service. The Committee agreed unanimously that it was possible to appoint separate Norwegian Consuls exclusively responsible to Norwegian authority. This led to an agreement, the so-called Communiqué of March 24, 1903, signed by the Swedish Premier Boström and the Norwegian Premier Blehr. The document was officially sanctioned by the King in December on the advice of the Governments of both countries, who were authorized at the same time to continue negotiations thus defined. Boström took matters into his own hands and put forward in 1904 a suggestion which conflicted with the previous agreement. Boström revived the claim that the separate consuls should be subordinated to the Swedish Foreign Minister. This move tore up the whole foundation necessary for the negotiations, and they were broken off in February 1905.

Boström's attempt to treat Norway as a dependency united the Norwegian people with one will. As Nansen wrote: "The affair has become a parting of the ways towards independence or towards self-abandonment."

The Hagerup Government, which had followed that of Blehr, was succeeded by a ministry formed from the various parties under Christian Michelsen. Its program was to carry into effect Norway's constitutional right to her own Norwegian Consular service, and to maintain Norway's sovereignty as a free and independent kingdom.

What was to happen now? Negotiatory methods were no longer applicable. The case called for action, whether by the longer route of having the measure vetoed by the Crown through three sessions of the Storthing, which would require five or six years, or by the shorter course of precipitating a crisis on the question of the royal refusal of sanction. According to the Norwegian Constitution, any bill passed by three successive Storthings, elections being held every third year, became law without the King's sanction. Most of the people were completely bewildered. Gerhard Gran, the editor of *Samtiden* sent a "What now?" out to Nansen, and the reply came as follows:

"WHAT.NOW?

"As I see it, the central point in the present situation is this: We Norwegians have no doubt of Norway's right to her own consuls. This right is denied from the Swedish side. Consequently it has become necessary for us to assert our independence upon this point."

Olav Anton Thommessen, the editor of *Verdens Gang,* went out personally to visit Nansen asking the same question. His visit resulted in the four famous articles in *Verdens Gang* in February. They struck down with the force of lightning, clearing the air. More than the words of any other person they contributed to rapid consolidation and action. The first one, "The Way," appeared on February 12, and the others followed at intervals of a few days: "Men," "Courage," and "Recklessness."

I quote from "The Way": "There are certainly many of us who are reading with increasing amazement these days the debate as to ways and means in a question that involves nothing less than Norway's independence and honor. We hold the opinion that since the publication of the documents of the negotiations there can no longer be any doubt as to the way. Have we Norwegians forgotten that at least there has been a time, here in this country, when something else was worth more than even the boldest words, and that was action?

"Big words certainly do not improve the situation. For us, therefore, the resolution about the establishment of the Consular service represents the only way, the sole means by which the dignity of the nation can be asserted. There is talk of incurring the royal veto with such a law; but surely this cannot be well considered. It would seem to offer an indignity to the royal house. The King must be the first to defend the independence and honor of the nation. That is why he is King. His honor and the honor of the people are one and the same thing, except that he is the first to safeguard it.

"The severance of the Union is not under consideration. We must have our honor and our rights respected. The other problem belongs to the future. The matter at issue now is the Consular question."

A few days later the next article, "Courage," appeared:

"They seek to terrify us by saying that if we follow the direct route, the only one which we find straight and open, it will be serious for us—as though anyone doubted that. They try to frighten us by pointing out that we will stand isolated in Europe, perhaps for several years, that we may expect a Swedish invasion—as though we had not considered that and were not fully prepared for it.

"Fear—everyone knows all about that; but has anyone mentioned courage? Is there not such a thing as a people's having courage too? At any rate, there was such a thing at one time in Norway. But what is the use of it if we are not to act until all possibility of danger is eliminated?"

On February 23 the Students' Association held a meeting: there was a full house and feeling ran high. Nansen spoke in favor of immediate action.

When he concluded, Sigurd Bödtker shouted: "You have written that we need men: you are right, for you are a man; and you have the right to cry 'Courage,' for you have yourself shown courage. It is said that you cannot be a Prime Minister because you have declared yourself outside the State Church. But I beg you to remember the words of Henry IV: Paris is worth a mass. Take the helm, Fridtjof Nansen! At this moment *you* are Norway's flag." Loud applause sounded from the assembly.

Nansen was the first to whom Michelsen appealed, but he answered that he could serve his Fatherland in other ways.

Norway had no representative before the outside world. She had not had one in 1814, nor again in 1821 when a circular note to the Powers prepared them for the Swedish *coup d'état* in Norway. And now in 1905 public opinion abroad was uninformed about the relations between Norway and Sweden. Norway needed spokesmen. What Carsten Anker was for Norway in 1814, Nansen became in 1905, except that Nansen's voice was much more far-reaching and much more effective. His celebrated name and the confidence inspired by his personality opened the door for him once more. In England especially he dominated public opinion. What Nansen was for Norway in 1905 can not yet be fully revealed.

The Norwegian intelligence and propaganda service was well organized, and the Government used its people where they had most influence. We had Fritz Wedel [1] who, better than anyone, knew the statesmen and diplomats of Europe and who, full of ideas, swift and bold, was active wherever he was needed.

In Sweden, too, Michelsen sounded the situation through Wedel, Benjamin Vogt, W. C. Brögger, H. Koht and others who conferred with the Swedish leaders.

On March 25, Nansen published in the cosmopolitan London Times an account of the Union conflict, and the paper supported it with a sympathetic editorial. It was also taken up by Le Temps, in Paris, in the Kölnische Zeitung and in many other leading newspapers. On June 7 Nansen published a small book: Norway and the Union with Sweden. In this book he gives an account of the origin and development of the Union, so that the causes of the conflict are made clear and the Norwegian claim understandable. The book appeared in English, German, French, and Norwegian.

Through the educational work of Nansen and others, it began to dawn on Europe that Norway was not a subordinate country in the Union with the right to only a limited independence.

On March 6 the recommendations of the special committee were ready, and the shorter line of action was chosen in accordance with the spirit and determination expressed in Nansen's articles.

A storm of addresses descended upon the Storthing and the Government.

The Seventeenth of May this year stood not only for the memories of 1814, but was pregnant with the fulfilment of that

---

[1] Fredrik (Fritz) Hartvig Herman Wedel Jarlsberg, Norwegian diplomat, became Minister in Paris, Madrid, and Lisbon in 1906.—Translator.

which was about to happen, that which should not fail again.

Of course Nansen made the speech in honor of the day in Norway's capital. I quote from his address: "Is it not true that the joy, the fervent pride we felt within us in our country and our people has gained a greater sweep of wing to-day? ... It is a happy time we are living in, a period of emancipation; for do we not all feel that during these last months the Norwegian people has grown, that every Norwegian woman and man has learned to think larger thoughts, learned to lay a larger measure on himself and his country, learned to forget his own and all petty interests. . . . A people can only grow by taking up that cause which it can not honorably lay down, even though it lead to defeat. Let us remember that a worse misfortune than defeat may befall a people. Ten times worse are the voluntary humiliations of a vacillating and weak policy of which we ourselves and our descendants must feel ashamed. We cannot leave our children a worse heritage.

"There is talk of sacrifice, but there is no sacrifice in giving everything, one's last penny, one's life, for the freedom of one's country. A tiger will fight for its young as long as it can move a limb; and a people is surely not poorer spirited than a tiger. It will defend its independence and its hearth to the utmost of its abilities. Of this we are sure: come what may, we must and shall defend our independence and right of self-determination in our own affairs. On these rights we must now stand or fall.

"There have been times when it looked as though the measure of a man here in Norway had become petty, times when it looked as though we had become so humble, so little proud, that we were not ashamed to show ourselves small and to consider gain for person or party. But that was a mere semblance, as these times have shown.

"We lacked confidence in each other and perhaps most of all in ourselves. We were so used to never being able to agree about anything, so used to walking in the tread-mill of everyday trivialities, that we believed ourselves bereft of the power of making a great united effort; and it was undoubtedly this lack of confidence that made it seem for a short time as though we were wavering and looking irresolutely about us for men.

"The happiest experience we have ever had is certainly beyond all comparison the discovery of this power that our people have shown to think largely, to see past all the immediate demands of the day. Their purposeful determination to unite, regardless of party barriers, regardless of former views, has grown stronger and surer for every day; a mature calmness and strength of will has settled down upon the whole people and made us all confident. We have a Storthing upon whose unanimous firmness we can all rely, a Government in whose hands we can confidently repose our country's fate.

"We can say to them to-day, both Storthing and Government: Go to your work calmly and feel confident that the enthusiasm, the self-sacrificing spirit which now animates us is no evanescent intoxication. It will endure.

"All roads back or to the side are finally closed. Now there is but one way, and that is forward, forward perhaps through trials and tribulations, but forward to self-determination, to a free Norway. Let us believe that we are a people composed of Norwegian women and men who will accept nothing as a gift. We cannot receive our independence as an alms, as something we are begging for. . . . Let us believe that our tri-colored flag shall always wave freely on its staff every Seventeenth of May, as it does to-day, over a people with faith in itself and with faith in its future."

This speech reverberated far outside of Norway. "Now Nansen is at it again," they wrote in Sweden.

On May 18 and 25 the King refused his sanction to the Consular law, and the Ministry resigned.

On June 7 the Storthing declared that the Union with Sweden was dissolved, as a result of the King's having ceased to function as a Norwegian monarch.

The next day Nansen sent a telegram to the London

Standard in which he summed up what had happened and why: "It is our hope that the Swedish people will understand that this is the best solution, that the severance of the Union will meet with no protest from abroad. I may add that there is no ill-will towards Sweden, as is clearly evinced by our wish to see a prince of the house of Bernadotte on the Norwegian throne."

A general plebiscite taken on August 13 returned 368,208 votes for and 184 against the dissolution, a clear proof that the whole Norwegian people stood behind the Storthing and the Government. The vote had been demanded by Sweden, and the result strengthened Norway's position in the eyes of Europe.

During the Karlstad negotiations regarding the terms for the severance of the Union, Sweden's demand for the dismantling of the Norwegian fortifications on the frontier aroused great indignation in Norway, while the Norwegian counter claim for a neutral zone from the southern end of the frontier up as far as Kongsvinger was hard fare for the Swedes. The two delegations stood like "mountain against mountain" at Karlstad. Both countries mobilized.

At this tense moment a quiet word from Nansen was heard in *Verdens Gang* and *Morgenbladet:*

"WHAT WE WANT

"We have desired to maintain our right of self-determination in our own affairs. What we desire now above everything else is a peaceful settlement of the dissolution of the Union, and we are all agreed on two points. On the one hand we wish to assert Norway's independence and dignity with no haggling, and on the other hand we are anxious to negotiate conditions for a good and friendly relation with our neighbor nation in the future. We do not wish, in so far as it can be avoided, war and unrest on the peninsula, a political crime which would destroy for all time to come the possibility of understanding and friendship between the two peoples. This object must be kept clearly in view, especially now, on both sides of the frontier. Thanks to the statesmanlike sagacity of our leading men, our political conduct, in this period so crucial for our country, has so far won the unanimous recognition of Europe for its sober manliness. It has been on the one hand firmly determined, but on the other hand it has constantly found expression in the controlled moderation which comes from the consciousness of inner power.

"It is natural that since the referendum of August 13 we should feel stronger and more sure of ourselves than before. But our self-confidence must not be allowed to go to our heads. If we have gained in strength, it is all the easier for us to be conciliatory and make concessions. There is talk of humiliating terms for Norway, but have we completely forgotten, then, that we have set the great main condition, the dissolution of the Union?

"This condition, the demand of a unanimous people, the larger country, Sweden, has had to acquiesce in either willingly or unwillingly. This is the real state of affairs which we must be most careful to keep in mind. We are just as little desirous of inflicting humiliation as we are of suffering it. Such desires, aside from being bad politics, are the mark of inferior breeding. It is, therefore, reasonable and politic for us, so far as Norway's dignity and interests permit, to try to help Sweden by concessions and liberality, so that the dissolution of the Union may be carried through without the Swedish people's feeling itself humiliated."

Nansen's dispassionate and calm attitude helped his countrymen to keep their heads.

The offer of the Norwegian throne to the house of Bernadotte was not popular in Sweden, and already before King Oscar's official refusal, the ground was being sounded in Denmark with a view to Prince Carl's candidature. Nansen was in Copenhagen twice in July and August in connection with this arrangement, but the tale of what happened on these trips has not yet been told.

*　　　*　　　*

Up in the mountain at Synhövd, near Sörkje, a man was tramping round in search of grouse the first few days of September; broad mountains, deep woods, long valleys—a long day's journey—lay between him and the world and all sorts of crises.

But on September 7 a messenger came up in haste from the telephone down in the valley with an urgent message for the hunter at Sörkje. It was from Minister Sofus A. B. Arctander, requesting him to come to the city as soon as possible. Nansen rowed across Sörkje Lake, cycled in the pitch darkness the long way to Kongsberg, and was in Christiania the next forenoon. Michelsen arrived the same morning from the recess in the negotiations at Karlstad. He told Nansen of the course of events in Karlstad and of the sudden demand of the Swedes for the razing of all the fortresses except the old historical parts, and their insistence upon having an answer, yes or no, within two days. He asked Nansen to go to England at once, and Nansen left the evening of the same day.

The next day in Copenhagen he had a conference with the Danish Foreign Minister, Count Raben, the German Ambassador, and the English Minister. Nansen explained the situation to them at some length. Raben became very much excited, and said that Denmark could not possibly regard with equanimity the prospect of a war at her very doors. He proposed that the Danish Government should ask England, France, Germany and Russia to address urgent but amicable remonstrances to Stockholm against the Swedish demands taking such form as to make war unavoidable. The same evening the note was drafted by Raben and looked over by Nansen; the next day it was laid before the King and the Government and sent to the four Great Powers. The same evening Nansen went on to London.

Russia and France responded immediately to the suggestion, and sent their earnest remonstrances to Stockholm. Germany and England took their time. Germany contented herself with asking for "explanations," while the English Minister took a daily walk to the office of the Foreign Ministry and said that he took it for granted that everything would work out to a peaceful conclusion. According to Fritz Wedel the British Government at the same time pointed out through the Swedish Minister in London, Bildt, the necessity of a peaceful solution, apparently after Nansen had communicated to the English Government the substance of the Norwegian proposal according to Michelsen's telegram which, Nansen hinted, was the outcome of the suggestion of Sir Thomas Sanderson, permanent secretary in the Foreign Office.

On September 14 Michelsen telegraphed to Nansen from Karlstad: "Confidentially offered yesterday in return for a neutral zone in the European sense and arbitration raze Örje and Dingsrud and the new forts around Fredriksten and Kongsvinger. If not accepted willing to submit to arbitration all fortresses before the Hague tribunal or some other court of arbitration."

Nansen, who arrived in London September 10, got in touch with the most influential papers, the *Times,* the *Morning Post,* the *Westminster Gazette,* and these papers all came out in a short time with editorials after having conferred with Nansen. One day the editor of one of the leading papers came to Nansen with an article which was to appear in his paper. Nansen read it and said that if that article were accepted he must ask for permission to add some remarks, as it was incorrect throughout. The editor took a telegram blank and telegraphed to his paper: "Cut it out."

Neither the English press nor the Foreign Office seemed to have any idea of just how serious the Norwegian-Swedish situation was until Nansen arrived. They were not aware that Sweden had mobilized a large army and her entire fleet. Nansen telegraphed to Michelsen and obtained information from the Norwegian secret intelligence that Sweden had at least 60,000 men mobilized and her whole fleet, while the Norwegian mobilization consisted of a frontier guard of 4,000 men and some few ships. In the same telegram Michelsen stated that "we are willing to raze Őrje, Dingsrud, and the new fort at Fredriksten, but not Kongsvinger." That same evening Michelsen went back to resume negotiations.

Sir Thomas continued to believe that it was a far cry from war, and regarding Nansen's wish to get in touch with the Foreign Minister, he stated that it was difficult for the British Government to interfere, as the negotiations were, of course, secret. It would be necessary for something serious to happen first. To this Nansen replied that the British Government might easily come too late. We feared that the attack might come suddenly in order to prevent our mobilization, and without a declaration of war. We were, of course, simply insurrectionists, and not a recognized belligerent power. England must understand the difficulty of our position.

Nansen mentioned arbitration as a way out, if it were impossible to agree on the fortress question, and Sanderson was of the opinion that Sweden could hardly get around that. Nansen took up further the question of Prince Carl's candidature. England's help in this matter would be very significant as an indication of whether, in the event the choice fell on him, we could obtain future advantages by the renewal of the November Treaty, and whether we could count on England's guarantee of the neutral zone, neutral both in peace and war.

Sanderson promised that he would write to the Foreign Minister, Lord Lansdowne, regarding all these matters, and also that he would himself take them into consideration. Nansen telegraphed a part of Sanderson's conversation to Michelsen.

To "play out the English King" Nansen soon saw was not possible. There had just been a conflict between the Government and the King on this matter. The Government thought the King interfered too much and had declared that the Government could not be responsible if he insisted upon conducting foreign affairs in person.

Through Sanderson, Nansen was enabled to send a statement to the Foreign Secretary and he wrote also to Lord Rosebery. He received answers from them just when the tension in Karlstad was beginning to relax. Lansdowne explained why he had been unable to meet Nansen and why the English Government had not intervened against Sweden. "On the other hand they have been made fully aware of our views." He delayed his letter for twenty-four hours in the hope of being able to offer congratulations upon a happy settlement.

After Lansdowne's return from Ireland, Sanderson arranged a private dinner at his home where Nansen and Lansdowne were guests, and after dinner they had a lengthy conversation. That was on October 3. They discussed the most urgent topics: Prince Carl's candidature and the renewal of the November Treaty, the republican movement, the Karlstad agreement, and British recognition of Norway as a republic or as a kingdom.

Nansen telegraphed that night to Michelsen approximately as follows: "Prince Carl of Denmark will probably bring the November Treaty extended to guarantee Norway's absolute neutrality. More definite promises cannot be given before the matter is decided. Little more to be done here. Am leaving for home to-morrow unless you wire to the contrary."

On the gangway he got in touch with the press again. The result was new editorials. He wrote one himself and a new concluding chapter to his book *Norway and the Union with Sweden* which came out in a new edition in November 1905.

On October 5 he left for home.

The Karlstad agreement was ratified on October 9 in Norway and on October 13 in Sweden.

After the Karlstad settlement the question of the form of government arose again. The republican forces had made themselves felt quite strongly after June 7, and agitation for a republic began again after the Karlstad agreement. Michelsen considered that the monarchical form of government was still in force and that the Storthing by virtue of the Constitution had the right to choose a king. But there was a strong feeling among the people in favor of a popular vote, that the people

should be asked whether it would agree to allow the Storthing
to choose the king now or whether it wished to leave the decision open. There was dissension within the Government on
this point.

From Nansen's diary for October 18 we see that he imparted
to Michelsen the verbal and written communications he had
had with Lord Lansdowne. The latter had stated that so long
as we had unsettled conditions we could not count on concluding
binding treaties. The election of Prince Carl would be a decided
help in getting the November Treaty renewed. This treaty, the
only joint contract of political import concluded by Norway
and Sweden, was entered into in 1855 during the Crimean War
and signed by England and France. It was a guarantee against
Russia and consequently of great importance. By the choice of
Prince Carl, the sympathies of Great Britain for Norway would
be strengthened, and we could count on having the November
Treaty extended to guarantee the absolute integrity of Norway
against all powers.

On his return home Nansen was permitted to communicate
these opinions to the Storthing and the Government behind
closed doors. Nansen stated further that the republican agitation
had created an unfavorable impression abroad and weakened
the sympathy which would otherwise have been forthcoming
during the Union crisis. In Nansen's opinion a year's con-
tinuance of this state of affairs might have extremely unfortunate consequences for our country. These communications from
Nansen had great influence both in the Government and in the
Storthing in deciding them to proceed at once to the election
of the king without a popular vote.

Denmark was keeping a close watch on the Norwegian
press. Foreign Minister Raben and Prince Carl were of the opinion that it would be best to agree to a popular vote. In telegrams
to both, Nansen sought to reassure them regarding the republican agitation and persuade them to give up the idea of a referendum.

On October 20 Nansen was sent to Copenhagen as chief intermediary between the Norwegian Government and Prince Carl and the Danish royal house. All were easily persuaded to regard the popular vote as unnecessary, with one exception; but that one was Prince Carl. Nansen displayed all his most telling powers of persuasion in several interviews. He reproduces these conversations in their entirety in his diary, and adds:

"In the summer I had talked with a comparatively undeveloped youth; but now he had grown up into a mature man, and my respect for him increased as he warmed to the subject. I had come in the belief that it would be easy enough to persuade him and bring him to view the matter in a different light; but here I met indeed a man who had considered the proposition from several sides and who answered my objections very cleverly and with keen arguments. I told him that everything he said merely convinced me all the more completely that he was just the man for the throne of Norway. He cherished the liberal views which befitted a king of the Norsemen. He said, moreover, in the course of the conversation, that he thought the people had a right to voice its opinion on so important a question, and in this he believed he was more liberal than I."

Wedel thought he could easily manage the Prince, but he was no more successful.

Nansen tried again, in a different way, and the result was that on October 23 he was able to telegraph: "Prince Carl declares that he must hold by his wish for a referendum, but will not cause difficulties for the Norwegian Government if it is regarded as absolutely inadvisable in the interests of Norway. He would, however, be very much gratified if some method or other could be found which would at the same time satisfy the interests of Norway and his own personal wishes."

And Michelsen found the way. The Storthing could authorize the Government to offer the throne to Prince Carl on condition that the Norwegian people should give its assent by a popular vote. On October 30 the King was elected, and the vote taken on November 12 and 13 resulted in 259,563 for the monarchy and 69,264 against. Both Prince and Government could feel assured of the will of the people.

Nansen's last piece of work in connection with the election of the King was to take part, at Michelsen's request, in the campaign before the voting. From November 3 to 12, he travelled from Kristiansand in the south to Steinkjer in the north, making twelve speeches before large audiences.

At the Students' Association on October 10 after Nansen's speech on the situation the president, Mich. Hansson, made acknowledgment in a speech of thanks, which concluded with the words: "Nansen has cut his name an inch deeper in the Norwegian monolith."

In his diary for November 23, 1905, Nansen describes the dinner given by the citizens of Christiania for the Government. Nansen sat by the side of Björnson at the table. Björnson was very amicable, thanked Nansen for all he had done, and expressed his satisfaction with the final outcome. They discussed among other things monarchy and republic, and Nansen said in jest that he regretted now that he had helped to usher in the monarchy when he saw all the snobbery it had already stirred up in the newspapers. Björnson laughed and said to Professor Hagerup who was on his other side that Nansen was more courageous than he; Nansen said what he only dared to think. Then Nansen and Björnson discussed the various lines of action in Norwegian politics that summer. Björnson was forced to admit now that the policy which had been chosen was a good one in any case. Yes, Björnson thought it had worked out very well, but it might have gone much worse. Nansen thought that Björnson's policy would have been infinitely more uncertain; what would he have done if after a unanimous election it had been decided to terminate the Act of Union and Sweden had then said No? In that case it would certainly have been necessary for us to use force whether we wished to or not, for a whole people will not be coerced. Yes, but Sweden would not have said No, replied Björnson; of that he was sure. But Nansen was of the opinion that the events of the summer had shown that this assurance was rather slight to build on.

Shortly after this Michelsen made a speech, which was not on the program, in honor of Björnson as the man who had taken a distinguished part in what had happened. True, he had not approved of the tactical line of action, but to the younger generation he had been the leader above all others in our struggle for national independence.

During Michelsen's speech, a torch-light procession arrived. Fifteen hundred torches cast their red glare against the windows of the banquet hall. Michelsen and Lövland, Björnson and Nansen had to appear at the windows and were greeted with roaring cheers from the great masses of people who had come together to pay homage to them.

*　　*　　*

The Swedish writer, Ann Margret Holmgren, who has been in close touch with the political life and public opinion in both countries from 1905 up to the present day, writes to the author regarding the Swedish view of the dissolution of the Union and the men who led the movement on the Norwegian side: "It is certainly true that there was strong dissatisfaction with Nansen in Sweden in 1905. The great majority of Swedes were entirely opposed to the severance of the Union and saw in dissolution a future perspective of constant trouble. It was quite natural under the circumstances that anger should be directed against those who had taken an active part in and brought about the severance. And equally natural was it that the small number of Swedes who openly declared themselves on Norway's side, and who said that Norway was justified in her struggle for independence and her determination to sever the Union, should have been regarded almost as traitors to their country. But all that is forgotten now. No one mourns the Union any more; no one sees a misfortune in its dissolution—on the contrary; Norway and the Norwegians are now our best friends and extremely popular in Sweden. As a result of this, of course, the feeling of animosity which was at one time harbored against Nansen has disappeared.

"Anyone who has followed the press and the parliaments in the nineties both in Sweden and Norway, must be amazed at how quickly public opinion can be changed under favorable conditions. And how fortunate that in 1905 we had such wise rulers and such a good King and Queen that war could be avoided. It came about as both Björnson and Ellen Key prophesied: A peaceful separation would make us better friends than we had ever been."

This Swedish testimonial coincides with what Michelsen said: "The day is not far distant when we will both understand that the dissolution of the Union was an historical necessity, and in the long run in the interests of both peoples." This view is confirmed in 1930 by the Norwegian historian Jacob Worm-Müller, who sums up what we won as "what is to-day the happiness of our peninsula, our understanding and friendship with the splendid Swedish people."

Kjölen is no longer a mountain of ice, and the Swedish shadow from 1905 has completely disappeared from Nansen's picture.

AT THE COURT OF ST. JAMES'S

THE NORWEGIAN State had further use for Nansen. He allowed himself to be persuaded to accept the position of Norway's first Minister to the Court of St. James's, and for over two years, 1906-08, he filled this important post.

The most considerable matter with which he had to deal as Minister in London was the negotiations with the English Government relative to the treaty which was signed in Christiania on November 2, 1907, called the Integrity Treaty. In the early part of the summer of 1906 the Legation in London, as well as those in Paris, Berlin, and St. Petersburg received instructions to tackle this matter.

It might seem strange that, after having regained their national independence and the political recognition of it abroad through a policy carried out by level-headed leaders on both sides with no breach of the peace between the sister peoples, they should now seek the guarantee of the Great Powers for this newly won independence.

On the other hand, one can well understand the reasons which led Prime Minister Michelsen and Foreign Minister Lövland to pursue this line of action. It was essentially because of the old, now obsolete November Treaty of 1855. This treaty, entered into conjointly by Norway and Sweden during the Crimean War, and signed by England and France, was a guarantee which breathed a spirit of mistrust towards our great neighboring empire, Russia. After the events of 1905, this treaty was

in need of revision. We wished to have it extended to guarantee
Norway's absolute integrity against all powers, with Russia as
one of the signatories. We wished to create a frank, neighborly
relation with Russia as with the other Great Powers. This motive, together with the strong Norwegian popular feeling in
favor of the peaceful settlement of all international disputes and
the desire to hold aloof from any conflict among the Great
Powers, was, according to the opinion of Minister J. Irgens, expressed in a letter to the author, the real motive behind Michelsen and Lövland in their attempt to have Norway's territorial
integrity guaranteed by the Great Powers. Since the World War,
which has entirely altered the political situation abroad, Norway
has abrogated the treaty.

Nansen was not particularly enthusiastic about the idea
embodied in this treaty, but it was, of course, the Government's
order and, as Irgens writes, "with his indomitable energy, his
great political insight, and his ability to speak at the right time
and place, he, more than any other person, pushed the matter
through."

Irgens stood very close to Nansen during the London years;
he was Secretary of the Legation, and in 1908 succeeded Nansen
as Minister. He states further: "I have the most affectionate
memories of him from that time, as my chief, as a friend, and as
a man. Although he held an excellent, indeed in many ways
unique, position in London both in respect of the English Government and public and, especially perhaps, of the scientific
circles in London, he did not wish to retain his diplomatic post.
After the conclusion of the Integrity Treaty, he regarded his
mission as accomplished and continued to act only until after
the official visit of the English King, Edward VII, to Oslo in
May 1908, after which he handed in his resignation.

"Nansen spoke and wrote English excellently. He had acquired an enormous vocabulary in the rich English language and
had a thorough acquaintance with and admiration for all the
great and inspired body of English literature. Nor was he con-

sidered as a real foreigner by the English, but rather as a very closely related friend from another country.

"In the midst of Nansen's life as a diplomat in London, it was always his scientific work that stood nearest his heart. On his huge writing table there was always a mass of literature on geography and natural science and rough drafts for new writings together with the business of the Legation." The daily routine he was able to leave to the Secretary of the Legation, who in many instances was given full powers. "I remember particularly that *In Northern Mists* was begun in the London period. He explained to me how the work was becoming bigger and bigger as he got deeper into the subject. His studies became more and more extensive, reaching all the way from the sporadic traces of exploration in antiquity up through the Middle Ages to the present time."

And Irgens mentions in closing that trait which was so highly characteristic of Nansen: "What has always impressed me most about Nansen's work, both as one of the boldest and bravest explorers that ever lived and as statesman, diplomat, and scientist, is his effort to penetrate to the depths of the problems by his own research. He took nothing for granted."

When he gave up his ministerial post in London in 1908, he again accepted a professorship in oceanography at the University. The years of his ministry in London were in many ways a useful school. He made many connections there and gained an insight into many things which were of use later in other tasks to which he was called by Norway and by the League of Nations.

In 1907, while in London, Nansen suffered a heavy blow. His wife became seriously ill and died before he could reach her. Her ashes rest under the rose-bushes in the garden at Polhögda. There are masses of rose-bushes in Nansen's garden—he loved roses. One of them knows that Eva's ashes rest under it. And it is the only one who knows.

Every year during the London period he came home for a

hunting trip to the mountains. Nansen in ambassadorial attire in London high-life and Nansen in hunting costume in the mountains at Sörkje were two very different men. Certainly he himself thought that the latter was the real Nansen. In an entry in his diary in London, February 20, 1907, he writes: "I only long to break these chains, I long for the woods and my free mountains. I cannot be tamed!"

IN WASHINGTON

NORWAY cannot provide itself with breadstuffs. We import about twice as much grain as we ourselves produce. Before the War we got most of it from Russia, Roumania, and Germany—and just 8 percent from the United States; but by 1916 we were getting 99 percent of all our grain imports from America. We also bring in millions of kroner worth of other products, both foodstuffs and raw materials for manufacturing. During the War we had plenty of money and bought all we needed, and more.

But when the United States entered the War in 1917, we found out that it is possible to sit up to one's neck in minted gold and yet starve. During the third year of the War imported goods could no longer be procured for money. Trade between countries became more and more a barter. The sellers no longer asked for money but for produce, and Norway was now in a difficult position.

Nansen's wide-awake eyes had early foreseen this and in January 1917, in the magazine *Samtiden,* he spoke his mind. He explained the situation and did not conceal the fact that he thought those who were managing the affairs of the country had shown little foresight.

What Nansen prophesied came to pass. At the beginning of April 1917 Norway received the first warning of the difficulties that would arise upon America's entry into the War. Our Minister in Washington, H. H. Bryn, informed us on April

8, 1917, that America's production would be more than ever
sequestrated by America and her allies. He recommended that
Norway ban the export of all foodstuffs; otherwise we should not
be able to get any from America. This was impracticable by
reason of the agreement with Germany which had been forcibly
brought about by her submarine campaign. On May 9 the Nor-
wegian-American Chamber of Commerce in New York sent an
urgent call to the Norwegian Government to send a commission
to the United States with full power to deal with trade relations.
On June 11 Bryn telegraphed that the United States was organizing a very thoroughgoing control of her export trade.

After carefully discussing the details with Nansen, Throne
Holst, Chr. Vogt, and other proposed members, the Government
named on June 22 a large and representative Commission
charged with the task of entering into negotiations with the
American Government to ensure Norway's supplies, particularly of foodstuffs. The chairman of the Commission was, of
course, Fridtjof Nansen, who had early seen clearly and pointed
out how matters were shaping, and whose name, especially in
the Anglo-Saxon world, opened all doors to him. Nansen asked
and obtained the rank which conformed to his enormously important task, being made Minister Plenipotentiary on Special
Mission.

The other members of the Commission were Joh. Baumann,
wholesale merchant, Oslo; C. Borgen, manufacturer, Stavanger;
T. Meling, shipowner, Stavanger; Director Throne Holst, Oslo;
A. Utne, managing agent, Bergen; and Chr. Vogt, lawyer, Oslo.
Wilhelm Morgenstierne, Secretary in the Department of For-
eign Affairs, was made secretary of the Commission.

After several weeks of preparatory work, collecting statistical material, and conferring with the Government and with business men, the Commission sailed from Oslo on the *Hellig Olav*
on July 13 and arrived in Washington towards the end of July.
Any misgivings about leaving Norway on a Friday and the thirteenth of the month were not shared by Nansen. He was of the

opinion that such days had hitherto rather brought him good luck than otherwise.

While the Commission was at sea, the situation had altered further in an unfavorable direction for neutral countries. On July 15 the American Government had placed an embargo on all exports, and it was intimated that no licenses would be granted to Norway before a general agreement had been reached. The Commission was, therefore, confronted with a difficult situation when immediately after its arrival it entered into negotiations with the government institution to which it was referred, namely the Exports Administrative Board, later known as the War Trade Board.

Nansen had prepared himself for his task with his usual thoroughness and had acquired detailed information about goods and prices, consumption and requirements. Before leaving he had, by consulting with his friend Professor Torup, extended further his knowledge of everything relating to calories and the nutritive value of foodstuffs. He found excellent support in his colleagues on the Commission, who were, of course, all outstanding specialists in their own fields. Nansen was fully armed, therefore, to meet the Board and able to give exact information on every question.

In spite of all the goodwill of the American people towards Norway and their admiration for Nansen personally, it was uphill work for a long time. The weeks passed seemingly without arriving any nearer a solution. In the meantime Norwegian shipping was feeling the difficulties more and more. By the American requisitory orders of August 3, all ships under construction in American dockyards were requisitioned by the Shipping Board, and this hit the Norwegians harder than any other nation. Ships putting in at American harbors, too, met with increasing hardships. It was required that a neutral ship, in order to secure bunker coal, should engage to return to an American port after every trip. In this way the Shipping Board obtained a hold on our ships and could dictate its own terms for every trip with respect to the place of destination, cargo, etc. These questions monopolized the attention of Nansen and Meling, the expert shipping man of the Commission.

In Norway people were now beginning to perceive the actual seriousness of the situation. Famine was no longer merely a distant possibility. In the latter part of August the Commissioner of Food Supplies announced that there was grain enough in the country to last for two and a half months. The coming harvest would furnish enough for another two and a half months. This meant that before February new supplies would have to be procured from without. Just at this time Nansen telegraphed to the Government that Norway must not expect to get grain from America, that is to say from the Allies, without first going on rations. In responsible quarters in Norway, however, they seemed reluctant to take this step. "The measure of the belly" must prevail, as a politician said. Sweden had already gone on rations in December 1916. Nansen thought it very detrimental to the work of the Commission that Norway did not do likewise. He pointed out that it was not easy to convince the Americans that the need was so great when the Norwegians were not willing to make this sacrifice.

While the negotiations for a general agreement were practically at a standstill, the Commission succeeded in obtaining various concessions in special matters. Thus shortly after his arrival Nansen got license "No. 1"—the first of the millions of licenses issued by the War Trade Board—for provisions for Roald Amundsen's *Maud* expedition. Later he obtained a license for 400 tons of ghee which would soon be needed by the Norwegian State railways. Of great importance, too, was the trade which came about through the Belgian Relief and which was endorsed by the American authorities. Norway received 68,000 tons of grain in return for placing a certain number of vessels at the disposal of the Relief organization. This eased the situation somewhat, but it was not enough to carry the country through until the next harvest could be garnered. Nansen frequently emphasized that it was chiefly owing to Baumann that this arrangement was made.

During the fall the situation became steadily worse. Great Britain cancelled her departmental agreements and not only our food supply but also that part of our industrial life which required raw products from without was seriously threatened. Uneasiness began to spread through large sections of the population. The Government found it necessary now for the first time during the War years to permit the Storthing to discuss before open doors the whole situation with respect to foreign affairs and commercial policy. This occurred in November and December, and the result was that the demand which Nansen had put forward in August for rationing "without delay" was finally complied with.

The Norwegian Commission consisted, as was mentioned before, of seven men plus a secretary. Over against this strong Commission the Americans had only two negotiators, supported at various meetings by an expert in the subject under discussion. Under these circumstances it was made clear from the American side after the first meeting that only the same number of Norwegian delegates should meet at the conference table. Thus it came about that it was Nansen and Baumann, together with the secretary, Morgenstierne, who participated in the conferences. In addition Meling, the shipowner, sometimes with Nansen and sometimes alone, dealt with certain problems within his own special sphere. To the other members of the commission fell mainly the important task of giving the negotiators expert information and arranging the statistical material. At length, however, they found it rather unsatisfactory not to be able to participate directly in the negotiations, and having gradually accomplished all that there was for them to do, the members of the Commission sailed for home. One member left early in October and the others on November 17.

At this juncture the prospects for arriving at an agreement were not very promising. Our export of fish to Germany seemed to be a special stumbling block. It was difficult to make the Americans understand the justice of Nansen's strong argument that putting a stop to this export would be equivalent to breaking with Germany. The negotiations came temporarily to a standstill on this question, and did not advance again until Nansen suggested the possibility of limiting the export of fish definitely to 48,000 tons a year. Then new difficulties arose. At the conference on November 27 a proposal was put forward from the American side which indicated a further stiffening of the demands, and the situation looked very dark to Nansen. It was demanded among other things that Norway should not export anything at all to Germany, except the amount of fish specified, not even the four substances, molybdenum, ferro silicon, calcium carbide, and calcium nitrate. The Norwegian Government maintained that it could not stop the export of these articles without serious consequences. Again the negotiations came to a standstill, and the weeks passed.

Telegrams exchanged between Nansen and Foreign Minister Ihlen show that Nansen did not have quite the cooperation he wanted. He deplores the fact that he has received no information on vital points as, for example, Germany's attitude, and the matter of rationing "which we understand is to be introduced at home." The explanation is probably, according to Dr. Wilhelm Keilhau's book *Norway and the World War*, that the Government wished to retain all decisions in its own hands and considered it proper that it alone should have full knowledge of the situation.

Towards the end of January 1918, the Norwegian Government sent new proposals for an agreement, but these were not acceptable to the American negotiators. When the negotiations were nevertheless successfully steered into a more promising channel, it was owing, first and foremost, to Nansen's firm stand. It was now well on in 1918, and Nansen began to be impatient. The only remaining member of the Commission, Baumann, was

obliged to go home to Norway in March, and Nansen and Morgenstierne were alone in the work.

Nansen was now determined to have a settlement. He telegraphed home and asked for authority to sign an agreement
when a favorable moment should arise and the Americans were
somewhat amenable. He believed that he might safely take the
responsibility upon himself; but the Government was reluctant
to grant him such unconditional authority.

In the meantime the spectre of famine had begun to rear
its head in Norway. The scarcity of commodities was daily becoming more galling; the people found the rations small and
the "native flour" bad. Nor was butter of whale fat any treat.

Nansen now set himself with all his strength to reach the
solution which his countrymen were awaiting with suspense and
not without anxiety for the future. He displayed all his energy,
his excellent abilities as negotiator, his rare powers of persuasion.
Early and late he was astir. He was convinced that while the
only course hitherto had been to let matters mature with dogged
endurance and constant pressure, the time had now come to
strike a blow. Even if the present proposal did not meet the
Norwegian demands on all points, it nevertheless embodied
essential concessions, and Nansen was convinced that it was time
to close the bargain. His experiences during these nine months
of negotiations had taught him that the situation and atmosphere were subject to abrupt fluctuations and it was impossible
to turn one's eyes away from the fact that the attitude of the
Americans, perhaps under pressure from other sources, might
again stiffen. He sent one telegram home after another—and
waited. But the Norwegian Government was in a difficult position and had many things to take into account, especially its
relations with Germany. Nansen's answer had to wait. Then it
was that Nansen, at a meeting with the War Trade Board on the
afternoon of April 30, signed the agreement on his own responsibility after having obtained some further concessions from the
American side. He telegraphed word of this at once to the Gov-

ernment, but owing to the tardy telegraph connections during the War, it took an unconscionably long time for the telegram to reach its destination. And thus arose the peculiar, not to say comic, situation, that the Norwegian Storthing sat the following day, May 1, and discussed what stand they should take on the American proposal, and that the Government then sent Nansen a qualified authority to sign. This telegram reached Nansen on May 2, two days after the signing.

The American Agreement materialized through Nansen's resolute conduct. Subsequent events showed conclusively that Nansen's clear-sightedness at this time had again benefited his country.

The situation became more straitened again. The other neutral countries, after Nansen had obtained his agreement, met with great difficulties, and it was a long time before they were able to make any arrangement with the United States.

In return for various counter concessions Norway was assured by this treaty for the duration of the War a yearly supply of 300,000 tons of breadstuffs, 200,000 tons of oil-cake and maize, 14,500 tons of coffee, 50,000 tons of sugar, 76,000 tons of mineral oil, and 250,000 tons of iron and steel. Fortunately peace was made half a year later, but at the time when Nansen signed this agreement, for which he had fought for over nine months, he saved Norway from approaching famine.

That there had been great difficulties to overcome is clear from the account given here, and it is confirmed by an American business man who writes the following in *Morgenbladet* for March 9, 1918:

"Here in this country we understand the difficulties with which the Norwegian Commission has had to contend. It has done all that was possible. . . . It is interesting to see how the feeling towards Norway has altered here, thanks to the work of the Commission in enlightening the people about the true state of affairs in Norway. Last year few business firms would sell goods to Norway, because they believed that Norway stood in close relation to Germany. Now the business situation is shaping quite favorably for Norway. . . . From the Norwegian newspapers I see that the people over there have no conception of the difficulties which the Commission has had to overcome. But here we understand."

It is characteristic of Nansen's generosity that so often in the course of the negotiations in Washington he insisted upon sharing the honor with his co-workers. In a letter to Foreign Minister Ihlen, praising highly both Baumann's exceptional qualities as a negotiator and Morgenstierne's great efficiency and tireless energy, he writes among other things: "On the whole I must say that I cannot well imagine two more able and prudent men to work with than Baumann and Morgenstierne. Norway is indeed fortunate in having these two men here, and what they cannot accomplish can certainly not be accomplished by anyone else."

But these two men declared that it was Nansen's genius which brought to port the first agreement between a neutral state and the United States, an agreement which became the pattern for all those to follow. The present Consul-General in New York, Wilhelm Morgenstierne, who stood in such close relation to the negotiators, writes at the request of the author: "By his superior skill in negotiation, by the frankness and sincerity which radiated from his whole person, Nansen succeeded not merely in convincing the American negotiators on the merits of the case, but also in winning to an unusual degree their confidence and their hearts. Nansen's American Agreement was a victory for a type of diplomacy which is not always called by that name, but which, nevertheless, represents that form of international negotiation which leads farthest and which will be that of the future."

This year, too, which Nansen himself considered a step aside and a precious year lost from his real work, provided him with experience and information and connections which were extremely useful to him when he became organizer of the great relief work after the World War.

Chr. Vogt, one of the members of Nansen's Commission, tells a couple of Nansen stories from those days: "One Sunday morning the American papers were burning with fiery indignation on the occasion of the revelation of the Swedish Legation as a medium for German telegrams. There were threats of forcing Sweden to become involved in the War. Nansen then went to Secretary Lansing and told him a little more about Sweden than the Americans, or at least their Press, seemed to know, and the next day the State Department in Washington had seen to it that the tone of the Press was considerably dampened."

"One evening the members of the Commission were guests of the Norwegian colony in Brooklyn. The auditorium of the Academy of Music was packed with thousands who had come to hear Nansen tell about Norway during the War. In evening dress wearing the Order of St. Olav, Fridtjof Nansen entered a reserved loge. Tall and magnificent he stood there alone, and as the enthusiasm of the thousands for Norway's greatest son surged up to him, he answered with a little embarrassed smile and a glance from his strong eyes as open and fearless as a seventeen-year-old boy's. It was as though Norway's flag itself were unfurled before the assembly. It was a splendid personification of the country's ideal."

Then came the homeward journey.

The Seventeenth of May that year found the *Bergensfjord* with Nansen on board far out on the Atlantic; but the weather was so foul that the Seventeenth was moved forward to Whitsuntide. By that time the weather was fine and Norway's national holiday was celebrated with speech and song, with athletic contests, games and fun.

A big man, six feet tall and about 55 years of age, was one of the keenest and gayest participants. One of the passengers took a snapshot of him in the sack-race across the deck. A sack-race lasting for months in Washington with both Norwegian and American sacks around his legs did not seem to have sapped his strength, but rather to have created a desire for perfect freedom to make use of it again. He lined up for the tussle in the national sport of *revkrok*.[1] Thirty-six years ago on board the *Viking* he had swung round every last man of the *Viking's* crew of 61. His first victim on this occasion was a huge fellow from Oslo, taller and heavier even than Nansen. He was whirled round in a second amidst general rejoicing.

"Then," relates my informant, "we heard of a heavyweight wrestler on his way to the Olympic Games who was training on the foredeck. He was brought in, and Nansen dispatched him just as quickly. The wrestler sat there for a while wondering just what had happened to him and then he asked leave to try again. This time it was a real struggle. The wrestler set a stiff neck or bridge as it is called in wrestling language, but slowly and surely he was turned over with both legs in the air amidst endless shouting from the spectators."

[1] Something like the American Indians' leg wrestle.—Translator.

NANSEN IN NORWEGIAN POLITICS

NANSEN was never a party man in politics, and above all not a fair-weather politician; but the people knew they could call on him in an emergency, when the need was not for party guarantees but for a man.

In 1913 Nansen and Michelsen had the political barometer under observation and exchanged letters about it, but no action was taken at that time. The World War broke out. Nansen was a close observer of the Government's guidance of the Ship of State. As told in the preceding chapter, his article published in *Samtiden* for January, 1917, criticizing sharply the Government's management of the country's supply of food and other essential commodities, led to the appointment of the Commission with Nansen at its head to save Norway from famine.

There are times when a single issue is all-important and when to deal with it successfully there must be a united people and a strong leadership. When the War was over, the worst was yet to come—the ravages it had made everywhere. Nansen saw the necessity now of concentrating the best talents of the country on this one thing needful, economic reconstruction. It would be necessary to bring together the ablest men, regardless of party, to form a Government which could take control with a strong hand.

The people looked to Michelsen and Nansen. Michelsen came to Oslo in 1919, but it was not possible to unite the parties. Again, on the change of government in 1926, a number of

the outstanding men of various party affiliations appealed to the
leaders of the four bourgeois parties to form a coalition ministry under Nansen with financial reconstruction as the sole
program. Nansen was willing, although his time and strength
were already heavily taxed. There was an increasingly strong
public opinion behind the proposal for a Nansen non-party
ministry, but there was not time to give it proper expression,
and the plan for a coalition again failed to materialize, as it had
in 1919.

There was a call for Nansen again in 1927 at the election
for the Storthing in Akershus. The bourgeois parties were
anxious for co-operation, but it proved difficult to agree on the
candidates for the first assured places. In order to prevent the
Right and the Liberal Left parties going to the polls each with
its own list, the party leaders agreed to try to get Nansen to run
on a list common for the two parties. As there was need for
haste, a delegation was sent to wait upon Nansen, who was hunting far up in Telemark. They met him in the mountains in the
evening on his way back to the hut, his gun over his shoulder
and his dog at his heels. He was in the best of spirits at being
in the mountains again. Geneva had often kept him away from
them. Rolf Thommessen, editor of *Tidens Tegn,* came straight
to the point, and after a dinner of grouse the delegates continued to make a strong appeal to Nansen. It would stimulate
the bourgeois parties to have the leading man of the country as
a rallying banner. Nansen listened with interest. Their plans
harmonized with his own ideas in 1919 and 1926; but he declined. He reminded them of his age: he was too old for a three-
year guest rôle in the Storthing. It was the post of leader of a
national coalition Government that had interested him; it was
only as the future premier that he could consider a period in
the Storthing. But the experience of 1926 forbade a fresh
attempt. He felt now that in the years still left to him he would
prefer to devote his strength to his scientific work. He had still
much to do there. "But, gentlemen, let it stand over until to-

morrow; I do not believe that I can, but you shall have my final answer before you leave to-morrow." They had a merry evening by the fire-place, Nansen entertaining them with his story teller's art. The next morning came the decisive refusal. But that the envoys might not have had their trip entirely for nothing, each of them was given a substantial bunch of grouse. If the result of the errand was a disappointment, both Munthe-Kaas and Thommessen testify that the grouse were excellent and that the visit with Fridtjof Nansen there in his own kingdom fully repaid them for the long journey.

THERE was hope for an enterprise when Nansen put his name to it. Institutions and societies sought him out and were happy merely to get permission to use his name.

He lent his name and gave his assistance in the organization and development of the new patriotic association, *Fedrelandslaget,* founded in 1925 after a conference at Gamlehaugen between Michelsen and Nansen lasting for three whole days. Michelsen presided at the opening meeting in Bergen and Nansen at a similar meeting in Oslo. In the program of Fedrelandslaget these two men met again on the same platform: a concentration of all the bourgeois forces on economic reconstruction. They hoped to win over the whole nation and enlist all classes in this program.

I quote from Nansen's speech: "We are suffering from the consequences of the greatest world conflagration that mankind has ever experienced, a universal catastrophe in which the passions and evil instincts of men were let loose and gave rise to all the horrors, all the evil and wickedness that could be expected. The curses of our age are suspicion, despondency, hatred, and envy. There is suspicion and hatred between peoples and between the classes within society, and on suspicion and hatred and envy no future can be built!"

The essential thing in Nansen's opinion was to create a

feeling of solidarity. "Nothing great and good can be furthered in the world without co-operation."

All progress must be built on the past. "Nothing in human life and development comes to pass by sudden leaps."

He could well understand that the younger generation, disappointed when the ideals men professed had failed at the first cockcrow, were turning to new forms, new ideals, and felt attracted to Communism as the antithesis of the capitalistic conception of society. "Communism is a beautiful doctrine in harmony with the first primitive Christianity, a doctrine the principle of which was to establish equality for all and which is based on many of the highest ideas to which we all subscribe, and which are among the main features of Christian moral teaching. But beautiful as the real communistic doctrine may be, the difficulty is that it is adapted only to a small and extremely primitive community. I have lived in such a community, that of the Eskimos. But no higher and more complex society can be built up and developed on such a genuine communistic foundation. Those who believe in Communism must have the right to work for it as long as they do not resort to unlawful means, but all attempts to use brute force, whether they come from above or below, must be opposed. Revolution may be inevitable in a country like Russia, but not in a country with full civil liberties, universal suffrage, and equal rights for all.

"Fedrelandslaget's program is," said Nansen, "to weld the Norwegian people, town and country, all classes together into a homogeneous nation with the feeling that we are all working for one great common goal—Norway, to make the lot of every citizen as easy and as free as possible."

With this end in view Nansen allied himself with Fedrelandslaget. He would not accept any office, but allowed himself to be elected to the administrative council and attended its meetings.

He made his greatest contribution as speaker at the gatherings of the association. The meetings became rousing ones when Nansen was present. In 1928 he spoke at Tunsberghus before an audience of 15,000. In 1929 he went on a propaganda expedition on the *Stella Polaris* from Bergen to Hammerfest. Everywhere there were throngs of people wanting to see and hear Nansen. He was the best propagandist for Fedrelandslaget. This expedition became a triumphal procession for Nansen himself which must have reminded him of that of the *Fram* expedition along the same coast thirty-three years before. No one could have suspected, to see this erect powerful figure with the supple, muscular movements, that his life was so near its close. But it was characteristic of him, that he was young all his life.

Nansen was president of the Norwegian Defence Association.

There are those to whom it seems entirely inconsistent that the great apostle of peace should be the spokesman for national defence in Norway. The fact of the matter is simply that it is not the defence system of the small nations which threatens the peace of the world, but very often the designs of the great on the small. So far no one has seen any steps worth mentioning towards the limitation of armaments on the part of the Great Powers. They are down on their knees in economic impotence, but with the sword lifted high. The small nations may preach the gospel of peace for the great, may help to disarm their minds, but the great must take the lead in realizing their words and promises and obligations by cutting down armaments. Only when the Great Powers show by their actions that they really understand how the stern law of necessity is contained in the commandment to love our neighbors, only then can the small nations allow their weapons to rust. Then and not before can we believe in Briand's words: "No more war!"

IN THE WAKE OF THE WORLD WAR

ON JUNE 28, 1914, the Archduke Ferdinand, heir to the throne of Austria-Hungary, was shot in Serajevo by a Serbian student. On July 28 Austria-Hungary declared war against Serbia. On July 31 Russia mobilized. On August 1 Germany mobilized and declared war on Russia and France. On August 4 came England's declaration of war on Germany followed on August 6 by Austria-Hungary's declaration of war on Russia. Millions of armed men marched towards the frontiers with banners and song and music, glowing with enthusiasm, every man a warrior for freedom and country.

Only a few Quakers interpreted the Christian teachings of their childhood otherwise. They refused to kill, but they went along to care for the sick and wounded. There were Quakers who won the order of merit for their devoted work in saving lives and were afterwards incarcerated for years.

Men were killed by the millions. Among the prisoners of war—over five million men on the Eastern Front alone—the ravages of death were even worse than in the trenches. Of from two to three million prisoners in Russia, more than a third died, and of the rest, hundreds of thousands were shattered for life. In the face of such accumulated wretchedness and misery, where the sufferings of the individual are lost in the mass, the sympathy of people at a distance is dull and passive. The war victors at Versailles seemed to have forgotten that the problem of war prisoners existed.

The prisoners in Russia, Siberia, and Turkestan, altogether 2,232,378 men, suffered most. Of these the Slavs were interned in Russia; the rest—the majority—in Siberia and Turkestan. Transports of prisoners were sent as many as 8,300 kilometers to regions where the temperature was as low as —60° C. The prisoners, jammed into cattle cars, were sent by rail, a three to four months' journey. On many trains the prisoners never got out of the cars; when the train arrived there was often nothing in the cars but a heap of corpses. In European Russia the camps contained from 2,000 to 10,000 prisoners. Some of the Siberian camps held as many as 35,000 men. They were generally housed in squalid hovels, often mere earthen huts, leaky, cold, and dirty. They had to sleep on wooden benches without mattresses or bedding. The food was wretched. Vermin abounded, and diseases: spotted typhus, cholera, plague, scurvy, rheumatic diseases, malaria, and tuberculosis.

A picture of Camp Totzkoye on the Samara River is sufficiently representative. In March 1915 the first transports arrived. Spotted typhus raged throughout the fall and winter. Medicine, straw, soap, wood, and water were all lacking. The small windows were covered with snow so that it was dark all day. The prisoners fought for the lower beds, for the fever-stricken could not climb to the third and fourth tiers. There were no latrines, and the dying were no longer able to drag themselves out into the snow. Every day the men's hands and feet froze painfully. If a man in his death agony fell from the upper tiers he was left lying on the stone floor until some one kicked him aside. The stench of the living mingled with the odor from the dead. The daily mortality rose to 350. Something like 2,500 corpses lay in a heap unburied, gnawed by rats and dogs. Towards spring they were flung 30 at a time on to a sledge. A rope was fastened round the load and a prisoner seated himself on top of the heap of corpses and drove off.

Those who would have sought death in the river were prevented by sentries from putting an end to their miseries so quickly.

In this camp 17,000 of the 25,000 prisoners died.[1]

Of the 200,000 prisoners in the twenty-five camps of Turkestan, 45,000 died. Seventy thousand prisoners were sent to work on the construction of the Murmansk railway. Eighteen hours of work a day was required. There was no accommodation for the sick. Once several car loads of sick men were sent to Kem, but they all froze to death on the way. After fourteen months 25,000 men were dead and 32,000 seriously ill.

The psychological effects of such captivity were no less awful than the physical wretchedness. Many became entirely apathetic. The brain no longer reacted to any sort of impression. Prisoners in this condition, when letters from home would finally reach them, were absolutely indifferent to them. Many prisoners went out of their minds, especially in places where there was no work. Those who kept their sanity acquired through their sufferings an attitude which is expressed in a letter from a prisoner: "We have lost faith in humanity."

Besides the prisoners of war proper, there were 330,000 civilians who belonged to the Central Powers but had been living in Russia. These were taken as they stood, women, children, and old people, scattered far and wide, sent to the most distant outposts without clothes or food. In 1915 and 1916 Germany and Austria-Hungary sought to help them; they devoted several hundred million marks to German and Austrian civilian prisoners, but during the latter part of the War, and after the collapse of the Central Powers, very little help was given.

Later on the Red Cross organizations set to work in some countries. Delegates were sent out to inspect a number of prison camps and dispense clothing, medicine, instruments, tools, and books. In several places the prisoners organized themselves, secured better quarters, and worked at handicrafts. Red Cross Conferences in Stockholm in 1915, 1916, and 1917 took up this

[1] From Brändström: *Among Prisoners of War.*

relief work, and the American Y. M. C. A. furnished similar help until the entry of the United States into the War in 1917. Thousands of disabled prisoners were exchanged. Denmark built camps costing four million kroner for partially disabled prisoners of war whose disablement was insufficient to qualify them for exchange. In Norway, too, some accommodations were made. Altogether two million prisoners were finally given work.

The Bolshevist Revolution brought about a quick change. Prisoners became "free citizens"; the prison doors were opened, and the sentries disappeared. There was rejoicing and hope of repatriation. But time passed. There was chaos and want. Hundreds of thousands of starving captives began to trek westwards. Ninety thousand of them joined the Bolshevists. The rest were interned.

After the Peace of Brest-Litovsk, the Central Powers sent twenty-five evacuation commissions out over the whole of European Russia, in May 1918, to regulate the repatriation of prisoners, but armed "internationalists"—Communists among the prisoners—forced the prison transports back. The attempt of the Soviet Government to curb the internationalists failed. The local soviets paid no attention to orders from Moscow. A great many prisoners escaped home in spite of this. After the Revolutions in Germany and Austria-Hungary, however, the work of repatriation had to cease, the evacuation commissions having been appointed by the previous governments. Over one million prisoners had been repatriated from European Russia.

When the Bolshevists advanced into Siberia in 1919, the prisoners expected freedom and repatriation; but they were disappointed. The Siberian soviets saw where they could make use of the prisoners and therefore refused to send them home; and the internationalist troops counted on gaining supporters from among the prisoners with whose help they should one day conquer their homelands for Bolshevism. They guarded the railway lines and seized those prisoners who attempted to flee.

The worst treatment the prisoners of war received in

Siberia was, however, from the counter-revolutionists, the White Guards. They allowed the prison camps to die out from hunger and disease. At no time did the prisoners suffer so much as in 1919. When the Russian Government got control of Siberia, it found that the most convenient way of handling the prisoner problem was to declare the captives "free citizens." In this way the authorities rid themselves of any obligations towards them.

For the hundreds of thousands of prisoners still in Siberia, Ural, and Turkestan existence became worse than ever, isolated as they now were. Those institutions in Europe that wished to help stood powerless before the difficulties with which, owing to the state of affairs in Russia, they were confronted.[1]

The International Red Cross then asked help of the newly founded League of Nations, and the latter appealed to Fridtjof Nansen.

*   *   *

The World War had affected Nansen deeply. To him it was the greatest confession of defeat of humanity, a degradation, devoid of meaning, an orgy of self-destruction in which nothing flourished but the lust for power, hatred, and stupidity—the bitter fruits of which mankind must eat for a generation. The smoke-clouds of war mingled in every breath he drew, even out in the forests of Norway or up on the mountain highlands far away from the world. The red horizon of the world conflagration was everywhere.

He quotes from his diary for June 1916, in *Sporting Days in Wild Norway*: "Nothing but this vast highland expanse in all directions, and the valleys look like narrow fissures in the great mountain plain. Deep down below winds the river of human life; how far away it seems up here! A man can breathe more freely, there is rest for eye and mind. . . .

---

[1] There were prisoners in such out of the way parts of Siberia that only after from ten to eleven years in captivity did they learn that the War was over. Some of them came home in 1930 after wandering about for fifteen months.

"But other, more distant, pictures arise. There are fortifications, trenches—piles of mutilated human flesh. No, there is no escape from that awful picture, not even here. It will not leave one in peace. Amid all this beauty one remembers the lamentations of millions of women who have lost everything, their friends, their husbands. One sees despairing mothers looking for their sons . . . bent, grey-headed fathers searching for the hope of the family.

"What a nightmare of insanity; and no one can stop it—no one. . . . The people of Europe, 'the torch-bearers of civilization,' are devouring one another, trampling civilization underfoot, laying Europe in ruins; and who will be the gainer? . . . And for what are they fighting? Power—only for power! . . . How could it be otherwise? A civilization that sets up power as its aim and ideal cannot possibly achieve progress for humanity. It must inevitably lead hither—towards destruction."

"It had to come. The civilization of Europe has failed—it was rotten to the core. Like the diseased tree in the forest, it fell as soon as the storm burst upon it.

"Civilization? What does it mean if it cannot tame the wild beast in us? If it does not lead us away from barbarism? That is its very essence; without that it is merely an empty shell. But the wild beast is raging in unrestrained joy: Fenris, the wolf, is at large, Garm is howling menacingly outside the Cave Gnipa.

"The greatest victory is the conquest of self. Surely this applies not only to the individual but also to nations and to all human society. We wage incessant warfare in order to master the powers of nature and make life secure; but man himself is still responsible for the greatest disasters and the deepest misery. Nor have we yet progressed so far that we can put a stop to it. What a terrible, a humiliating admission!"

"The heavy cowl of mist on Smiu-hammer grows darker, and the gap below has turned a bluish black; the mountain seems to frown.

"Can all my musings be true? It must be; for the combatants are Great Powers, and a Great Power can do whatever it declares to be right. In this world the majority decides what is right; a Great Power is always in the majority; therefore it is always right. And the small nations are wrong. . . .

"But no. I can make neither head nor tail of it. Rather let me pass on across these moss-carpeted stretches, where there is nothing to hinder one's footsteps. The eye searches the rolling plains and the mountainsides; reindeer were plentiful about here once, but now none is to be seen. There is not a sign of life anywhere. Man has stamped them out.

"What a wonderful creature is Man!—plundering, robbing, at war with the animals, at war with his fellows. A beast of prey wherever he is found. . . .

"No sooner does a man wear a uniform, a suit of clothes of particular cut and color, with, perhaps, a decoration, than he acquires the right to commit any outrage—to drop bombs from the air upon peaceful towns, upon hard-working citizens employed in their daily pursuits and unconscious of danger; to destroy home, property, livelihood. Furtively and without warning these uniformed men can send ships full of their fellow-creatures—hundreds of innocent men, women, and children—into the jaws of death. But if anyone who does not wear a uniform defends himself and shoots at the perpetrators of these outrages—that, of course, is a shameful crime. If he is caught he is tried, and shot or hanged in accordance with the law.

"It makes a man's blood boil. Yet the most respectable people see nothing wrong in it; at least they do not raise their voices in protest.

"Has the world no civilization but this to save it? Then let it rather bleed to death, let it end.

"And what of ourselves, of our Norwegian nation? . . . We shared the same greed of gain that lit the blaze of war; but we are living without the great emotions by which it is sustained. . . . Is it possible that this mad Berserk fury may yet result in something good—in a new era? . . . What though effete civilization crumble away? The loss is not irreparable. The same thing has happened before; and mankind has survived it.

"Spare your sorrow. Since the old races were ready to devour one another, it is well that they should give place to the new.

"It is not civilization but the old predatory instinct that has led the masses astray and swept them back into savagery by the power of suggestion. The telegraph, the telephone, the Press, all help in spreading this poison with lightning speed. And the multitude, bereft of independence of thought and judgment through the increasing pressure of modern life, is soon carried away.

"There must be a regeneration—a new era with new ideals —when spiritual values will again be the end and material values only a means, when the world will no longer be ruled by mediocrity and the mob. In that day the noble spirits will lead humanity upward to the heights; every spiritual discovery, every conquest in the world of the spirit will be greeted with the enthusiasm now accorded to material progress; and mankind will live a greater, simpler, more beautiful life.

"The ceaseless turmoil of cities, the nightmare of money-making, is dwarfing the race. It is from the deserts, from the solitudes, from the elemental depths of nature, that the new men have always come.

"O, the solemn strength of a night such as this! One seems to hear the great Hymn of the Universe itself; how lofty it is, how spacious, how pure, how untrammelled. . . .

"This is the world whence the men of the new era must spring—the men of strong, simple mould, cast in one piece, without the warped vision of a dual morality.

"In this silent grandeur of night must germinate the thoughts that will bring healing to the generation to come."

The man from the great expanses of Rondane, the man akin to the men from the deserts, from the solitudes, from the elemental depths of nature, received the call from the League of Nations to do the work of a Good Samaritan in the wake of the World War, and to do a still more far-reaching work: to disarm men's minds.

REPATRIATION OF WAR PRISONERS AND REFUGEES

IN THE spring of 1920, the year of the founding of the League of Nations, the Supreme Council of the World Conference sat in Paris and deliberated. The World War had thrown Europe and most of the rest of the world into chaos, want, and misery, and had sown the dragon's teeth of hate in a soil saturated with the blood of millions. The worst thing about a war, said the great Samaritan of the World War, is what comes after the war.

The Supreme Council headed by the "Big Four" sat and deliberated. The most immediate and greatest problems were of the sort for which neither the League of Nations nor any single government could possibly secure the necessary co-operation. The Council thought that the best way out was to get a single man to take charge of affairs, a man in whom all the world had faith and confidence.

England and the United States had a short time before selected Nansen to be arbitrator between them—a great honor. The arbitration commission, consisting of one Englishman and one American with Nansen as final arbitrator, was to deal with all questions concerning relations between the two countries which could possibly be conceived of as likely to lead to disputes between them.

Now Nansen was asked by telegram whether he would undertake to direct the work of repatriating prisoners of war.

Nansen declined. Such a work lay entirely outside his experience. Why should a professor be called upon to perform such a task? He was now deep in his scientific work and happy in being left undisturbed to devote all his time and all his energy to the great problems which lay in wait for him there. The work of repatriation would have to be done by others.

But the Council of the League of Nations believed that Nansen was the man they needed for this work. They answered that the work would not take more than a month or two of his time; if he would first devise a program and form an estimate of the expenses, the League would attend to the rest. Philip Noel Baker, the English professor, at that time attached to the Secretariat of the League of Nations, went to Lysaker and succeeded in persuading Nansen to accept. But Mr. Baker was unable to say how many prisoners there were, or whether the Soviet Government would give any assistance, or where he was to get ships, trains, clothing, food, and quarantine and disinfecting stations. Nor could he say where the money was to come from.

Nansen soon perceived that the problem undertaken on April 11, 1920, would not be solved in two months, but he hardly suspected then that it would be followed by one task after another, each one more arduous than the last, throughout many years, in fact throughout the rest of his life.

This was not the first service Nansen had rendered the League of Nations. In the League's hour of fate Nansen fought for the idea on which the League of Nations was founded and for the inclusion of the neutral states. In February 1919 he had gone to London for the Norwegian League of Nations Society, of which he was president, to strengthen the co-operation between it and the large English society, and to urge the necessity of including the neutral states in any League of Nations. Early in the spring of the same year he had travelled across the battlefields of the Western Front to Paris and there taken

FRIDTJOF NANSEN
Photographed at Sofia, 1922

part in the debates of the council which decided upon the place of the neutrals in the League of Nations.

At home in Norway, too, he had fought vigorously for Norway's adhesion to the League. His successful advocacy there influenced greatly the other Scandinavian countries, and in a measure the neutrals as a whole. Without the inclusion of the neutrals there could have been no League of Nations; for its object was partly to curb the designs of the great nations upon the small.

Nansen saw that a happy solution of the problem he had undertaken for the League of Nations was important for more than the prisoners of war. It was of the highest political significance for the League of Nations itself, for the great reconciliation of the nations, for an international effort to banish war. He saw the whole range of the problem and entered into it with all his strength. In Philip Noel Baker he found an excellent assistant, and in the Norwegian, Captain D. Finne, an able secretary.

Without a mediator the belligerent governments had trouble in entering into relations with one another, and were powerless to do anything about the prisoners. There were prisoners from twenty-six countries. In many of the countries from which the prisoners came the whole system of society was disrupted and there was no one to look after them. The prisoners had no money, nor had they the strength to undertake the long journey hundreds of miles to their homes. Most of the prisoners were from the first year of the War, from the battles on the Eastern Front. During the Revolution and the civil war the government had not had much thought for the prisoners. For four, five, and six years they had dragged out their lives in exile without connection with home and finally without any hope beyond that of deliverance through death.

The first essential was to arrange for co-operation among the many governments interested. The governments of the League of Nations and the governments which had prisoners to repatriate were at once willing to accept the help of the League of Nations and its High Commission. It was more diffi- cult to come to terms with the Soviet Government in Moscow. Without its help it was impossible to get hold of the prisoners in Siberia and Russia. The Soviet Government was hostile to the whole of Europe. Chicherin, the People's Commissary for Foreign Affairs, explained to Nansen that the Soviet Govern- ment did not recognize the League of Nations and consequently would not negotiate with Nansen. Nansen replied to this by ordering his train to be ready in two hours. That helped. Nansen then assisted the Russian over the dangerous point by suggesting that as regards Russia he should act not as the rep- resentative of the League of Nations but of the various govern- ments, and a satisfactory agreement was soon reached.

The Soviet was to send at least two trains a week to the western frontier, most of them to Narva, with prisoners from Russia and Siberia, and Nansen was to bring thither prisoners from Germany and Central Europe who would be transported by the same trains on their return journey. Concentration camps were established at the frontiers with quarantine and disinfec- tion institutions for delousing and bathing the prisoners and supplying them with clothing. In spite of the fact that the Rus- sians were at war with Poland at this time and needed all available railway supplies, they kept to their agreement and sometimes brought out more prisoners than they had promised. The governments of those countries which were to receive pris- oners from the east or give them transit had been worried lest the prisoners should carry dangerous diseases with them, and all those countries through which they were to pass helped to the best of their abilities in establishing camps, procuring trains, and generally assisting Nansen's staff in every way.

The most difficult and most arduous work, says Nansen, was here, as is usually the case, the getting of money for trans- port, camps, clothing, food, and so forth. Where was it to be found? The League of Nations had no money; neither had the countries to which the prisoners were to go. Nansen was informed that some of the money which certain governments had promised as a loan for the reconstruction of Central Europe still remained. He pointed out to the commission which had charge of this that bringing prisoners back into productive work was economic reconstruction, and the commission agreed. Nansen succeeded in persuading a number of governments to take the same view, and after lengthy negotiations he received the promise of a loan of adequate funds for the time being. The League of Nations thus effected for the first time an international loan for countries unable to secure credit for themselves. Those countries to which the prisoners were to be returned agreed to accept the loan and turn over to Nansen the money to cover the expenses, that is the cost of transport from the Russian frontier home.

But large sums were required for another purpose: to procure food, clothing, and medicine for the thousands of war prisoners who would be obliged to spend a seventh winter in Siberia, and for the Russian prisoners in Poland and Bulgaria. With Nansen as chairman a central organization was formed of representatives from the German, Austrian, and Russian Governments, the International Red Cross, and the Y. M. C. A. under the name of the Nansen Relief to co-operate with all the relief organizations. This Nansen Relief was under Nansen's personal direction with a head office in Berlin and a select committee.

In Russia and Siberia distribution stations were established with the help of the Russian Government. Trains with food and clothing were rushed direct to Siberia under the guarantee of the Russian Government. This Nansen Relief had nothing to do with the League of Nations; the money for its work was obtained through voluntary contributions. No foreign organization could enter Russia without Nansen to open the door.

Nansen mentions and praises especially the International Committee of the Red Cross. It collected the prisoners, took inventories, disinfected them, and gave them clothing, food, and other supplies. The secretary, E. Frick, was the driving force behind this great effort. He also mentions the German organization for the repatriation of prisoners under Schlesinger's efficient leadership. The Swedish Red Cross under Prince Carl gave great assistance at the camp at Narva, especially in supplying the prisoners with new underclothing after bathing and disinfection.

The first transports from Narva to Swinemünde began on May 19, and in November, at the first meeting of the League of Nations at Geneva, Nansen was able to announce that 150,000 prisoners had been sent home. He had hoped to repatriate all the prisoners before winter came, but for several reasons, chiefly because of the war between Poland and Russia which put obstacles in the way of land transport, 80,000 men were forced to spend still another winter in Siberia.

It had not been easy to get hold of the necessary ships. The English, who had taken the German fleet and had the ships lying in German ports, refused to turn them over for the transport of prisoners. They were to be sold. Nansen offered to have the ships repaired before returning them; he was then given two. After a further exchange of telegrams, the number was finally increased to fourteen. They were repaired in German drydocks and manned with German sailors. Nansen paid with English pounds, which weighed well in Germany, and the whole operation was thus effected very economically.

There were thousands of prisoners in the region about the Black Sea; to get them home was still more difficult. In Odessa and Novorossiysk, "cities of death" in an extinct land, 12,000 were collected after having gone through sufferings even worse than those of the prisoners in Siberia. They were taken to Trieste and thence to their homes.

In Eastern Siberia many prisoners, instead of trying to make their way westward, where they could join the regular transports, had attempted to work east to the Pacific Ocean, in the hope of getting home by that route, and 15,000 prisoners assembled in Vladivostok. The passage-money to bring them home would be 30 pounds sterling per prisoner. This was insuperable. Then Nansen appealed to the Americans. The Red Cross and other American organizations formed a Repatriation Committee and raised a million dollars. With this Nansen was able to hire ships which also carried cargoes for good pay, thus reducing the expenses considerably.

In the Balkans there were 25,000 Bulgarians in Greece and Jugoslavia. They, too, were brought home. Nansen effected also an exchange of 800 Bulgarians held by Greece as hostages and 500 Greek children whom the Bulgarians had taken. He contrived further that 1,000 Germans who had been prisoners for six or seven years in Siberia and were now held by the Greeks should be released and sent home.

All in all, during 1920 and 1921, about 437,000 prisoners were liberated after many years of exile and misery, and brought back to their own countries. The work had taken eighteen months and cost 400,000 pounds sterling, something less than one pound per man. The American contribution is not included in this, and Germany paid for her own prisoners.

And the results? Those that can be measured in figures and statistics will always be impressive, but if we could have followed each of the hundreds of thousands of prisoners to his expectant home, we should have beheld results infinitely more affecting. "There is not a country on the continent of Europe where wives and mothers have not wept in gratitude for the work which Nansen did," says Mr. Baker, his staunch colleague and friend, who followed Nansen's work and saw its results at close hand.

The repatriation of the prisoners of war was the first big undertaking of the League of Nations. The happy result was attained through the co-operation of many countries and governments, of nations which had just been at war with each other. This achievement gave hope that the League of Nations might become not only the healing Samaritan in the bloody tracks of war, but a great mobilization of all the powers and minds which regard war as shameful and unnecessary.

It was not without reason that the League and its Commission expressed their profound gratitude to Nansen and his associates for work well done.

EVEN BEFORE the work of repatriating prisoners was finished, Nansen had undertaken, in September 1921, a new and still more difficult task for the League of Nations. After the Russian Revolution in 1917 and after the counter-revolution, when Denikin's, Kolchak's, and Wrangel's armies were defeated, more than a million and a half Russian refugees were scattered over Europe and Asia.

From September 1921 until his death Nansen was occupied with the work of aiding these people, from 1924 until 1929 in co-operation with the International Labor Bureau in Geneva. The most strenuous effort was made from 1922 to 1924. Only some few refugees had obtained work; most of them were out of work and in great need, a problem and a burden to the countries in which they were living. The question was to find places where they could live and support themselves. It was a big task merely to search out where they were and get in touch with them in order to move them to the localities where they would best fit in.

Again it was necessary to organize a great collaboration among many countries and many institutions in America and Europe. Not all countries were eager to do this work. Many countries had issued a standing order not to allow any Russians to slip in. Only a few thousands went back to Russia; most of them were, of course, actively hostile to the Soviet authorities.

The Russian Government was not opposed to the return of the refugees, and it was easier to adapt them and place them in Russia than anywhere else. How the six thousand that returned home fared it is not easy to discover, as no examination of any such persons could take place except in the presence of a representative of the Government.

Let us look at some examples of the many strange cases that had to be dealt with: In Poland, where there were altogether too many refugees, a decree was issued stating that all who had crossed the border illegally from Russia, and who were not political refugees, must leave the country before a certain day. They were Russian Jews, all these refugees, and there were many thousands of them. Back to Russia they could not go; there they would be shot. Nor was there any other country to which they could move. They were driven across the frontier to Danzig, but they could not remain there. Thus they were driven across the border again, and so these poor people were tossed like a tennis ball, says Nansen, back and forth across the frontier. At his suggestion, the European Jews, through their organization in Paris, undertook to maintain them until an arrangement could be made. Several thousand refugees were collected in a camp outside of Danzig until they could finally be sent to America.

And again: Of Wrangel's defeated army—with women and children altogether 90,000 souls—which had fled from the Crimea to Constantinople, 10,000 were permitted to enter Bulgaria. Of these 7,000 later got permission to return to Russia. The Bulgarian Government became afraid of the Communist plague, and in the spring of 1925, 250 of them were put on board a fragile vessel, barely large enough for fifty, and with bad and scant provisions, launched on the Black Sea to sail to Odessa. But no agreement had been made to receive them there. The Russian Government sent them back on the Black Sea again. Whither? Not to Russia, not to Bulgaria could they go; there was nothing for it but to try Turkey. It was no pleasure trip; they were almost out of food and water and the ship was in danger of sinking. At last they reached Constantinople, and there was great joy on board. But they were not allowed to land. A tug came out to tow the *Triton* through the Bosporus into the Black Sea again. Now there was panic on board; many

Russians leaped into the sea. An English steamer came to their rescue, and the captain frightened the Turkish police into allowing the Russians to disembark. They were interned in an enclosed area on the bare ground. Here Nansen found them. He applied to the Russian Government which referred him to the Bulgarian. In the meantime the refugees were leading a frightful existence in their miserable camp. Death began to take its toll and would have made an end of most of them had not Miss Anna Mitchell at the League's office for refugees at Constantinople collected money from the American-European colony in the town—enough for a daily ration of a little bread and a cup of thin soup. When Nansen visited the camp on June 9, her funds were exhausted. The refugees' money, some seven hundred Turkish pounds, had been confiscated by the Turkish police.

The Bulgarian Government would not take the refugees back, the Turkish Government would not allow them to remain in Constantinople, and other countries also refused to accept them.

Nansen now used a sum of money placed at his disposal by the publisher Chr. Erichsen, of Copenhagen, to arrange for the temporary maintenance of the refugees. Afterwards the big American Near East Relief organization supported them for a couple of months on condition that a definitive settlement could be guaranteed within that time. He then induced France to take a number of them "who were good workers," and the Soviet Government in Moscow took the rest "on condition that the Bulgarian Government abstain in future from sending Russian refugees to Russia without making the necessary arrangements with Moscow."

These examples are only two among many which show what refugees might have to go through and what difficulties the leaders of the relief work had to contend with.

One problem was that the refugees had neither passports nor papers which other states would recognize. Nansen called together representatives from the various governments to a meeting at Geneva in July 1922. Thirty-one were represented, and they accepted Nansen's proposal for an identification certificate for each refugee which could be used as a passport. Fifty-two governments have recognized these certificates, which are stamped with Nansen's picture and known as "Nansen Passports." They may be obtained by Armenian, Chaldean, Turkish, and Syrian refugees. This is a new kind of passport for people who are no longer citizens of any State, citizens whom the World War has driven from home and country. Up to 1930 there have been several hundred thousand of these issued. They carry a stamp costing five francs in gold and may be renewed every year for the same amount. A large sum is taken in every year by this means for the support of unemployed and needy refugees.

Nansen started negotiations with all countries that he thought might be willing to accept refugees and give them employment. He persuaded the governments to appoint a representative or institution in their capitals to negotiate with himself or his representative. Besides this he got in touch with many charitable institutions and Red Cross associations. The situation in Constantinople, with the 90,000 refugees from Wrangel's army, was the most tragic. These refugees were in such a state of wretchedness and starvation that, although it was not part of his task, Nansen was obliged to set about collecting money for their maintenance at once. He obtained $25,000 from America for food for four months and transportation to other countries on condition that he himself raise $30,000. He got half of this from the American Red Cross and the rest from some other source. Altogether, the great-hearted Americans came to his assistance in many a pinch.

Constantinople was, after the city was occupied by the Allies in 1920, an aslyum for refugees, a stopping place on their flight from country to country, where at least they were safe. Constantinople has seen many tragedies but scarcely such an accumulation of human misery as there was during the three waves of refugees which washed in, one after the other, over the city, first of Russians, then of Turks, and finally of Greeks.

About 170,000 Russians, 75,000 Turks, and 155,000 Greeks and Armenians are figures which give some idea of the magnitude of the problem presented by Constantinople to the relief activities of the League of Nations and other organizations. During the year from September 1, 1922, until September 1, 1923, the League of Nations sent 20,000 refugees from Constantinople to forty-five countries, and the following year 6,000 refugees.

Nansen succeeded in placing thousands of children and students in Czecho-Slovakia. Bulgaria, which took thousands of adult refugees, took also 5,000 children and put them in Russian schools. Bulgaria took also 1,000 disabled men with families. A large number of Jews were settled in Palestine and in the United States. Jugoslavia took 55,000 refugees. From Egypt and Cyprus 5,000 were brought to Jugoslavia. The English Government, which had used enormous sums in the maintenance of these, voted 150,000 pounds sterling on condition that Nansen take all future responsibility for them, and that any possible surplus be divided equally between the British Government and Nansen's relief work. Nansen handled the transport of the refugees in three weeks for 70,000 pounds, thus gaining 40,000 pounds, a welcome addition to the fund for helping other refugees.

Nansen proposed that all the governments in the League of Nations take Russian students and maintain them at their universities. Czecho-Slovakia and France responded first and set a good example. Nansen was always careful to see to it that the children and young people should secure instruction and education. It was his opinion that the future depended on the ability and industry of the growing generation.

There are still at this writing thousands of Russians without work and in a difficult situation. In the fall of 1929 there were over a million refugees in Europe for whom no definite arrangement had been made, 180,000 without employment. Of these 40,000 were placed in Syria and 12,000 in the Caucasus. Thousands are settled every year in France. In 1930 there were in Western Europe 108,000 Russian and Armenian children, most of them in want. The work is to be continued by the High Commissioner for Refugees of the League of Nations, but not for more than ten years, as it is hoped that the refugees can either return to their native land, of which there is certainly little prospect, or become citizens of the countries in which they are living, or that the governments of these countries can procure work for them.

For the remainder of its period of activity this bureau will bear the name: The Nansen International Office for Refugees.

THE FIGHT AGAINST THE RUSSIAN FAMINE

IMMEDIATELY after the work of repatriation, and while the refugee work was still going on, an even greater and more difficult task followed: that of relieving the famine in Russia. When Nansen got this call, says Erik Werenskiold, he was depressed. "If I undertake this it means giving up my scientific work,—what I live for." Great scientific plans were ready to be launched, but could not come to anything if he undertook this new task. He was in despair. "If I know you rightly you will never have peace of mind if you refuse," said Werenskiold. As in 1920, he had no rest until he had accepted.

The Russian question was not new for Nansen. There were few men in Europe who had given it closer attention. When the Treaty of Versailles was made, he says, the Russian factor was entirely neglected. The authors overlooked, or gave the impression of overlooking, the many hundreds of thousands of prisoners who were still in Central and Western Europe. But if the Supreme Council followed the negative policy of the "sanitary cordon" and the "blockade," an explanation might be found in the attitude of the Soviet Government and in the obstinate disinclination for peace of the Russian émigrés and the anti-Bolsheviks.

Aware of the need in Russia, Nansen had conferred in the spring of 1919 with Mr. Herbert Hoover in Paris regarding what could be done to help the Russian people. They agreed to submit a proposal to the Supreme Council for the formation of an organization to supply Russia with food and other necessities. America was ready to accord the necessary credit. On April 3, 1919, Nansen sent a letter to each of the four members of the Supreme Council, President Wilson (the United States), Clémenceau (France), Lloyd George (England), and Orlando (Italy), suggesting the formation of a neutral organization to supply food to the Russians.

The Supreme Council answered on April 17 giving Nansen's proposal the warmest support: "It is shocking to humanity that millions of men, women, and children lack the food and the necessities which make life endurable." But there was a condition attached: that all hostilities in Russia should cease. Nansen was to send out this answer at once, but several of the governments of the members of the Supreme Council refused to allow the use of their wireless stations to transmit this message to Moscow. At the same time the Russian émigrés in Paris became extremely active in opposing Nansen's suggestion.

We must remember that at this time Soviet Russia was being attacked from all sides, encircled by her Russian enemies who were receiving support from the governments of Western Europe. In despair at the loss of precious time, Nansen left Paris for Norway intending, if necessary, to go to Russia himself with the telegram. Finally the telegram was sent by wireless from Berlin on May 4. Chicherin answered at once, thanking Nansen warmly, but absolutely refusing the condition of the Supreme Council. To agree to this would be to lay Soviet Russia open to the intervention policy of the counter-revolutionists and the Allied Powers. The Soviet was willing to enter into bona fide peace negotiations, but not under the disguise of a pretended humanitarian work. Chicherin suggested a conference abroad between representatives of the Soviet and Nansen and his colleagues to discuss these vital questions.

The Supreme Council, however, held to its condition, and thus the whole project had to be abandoned.

Nansen was always convinced that "if these negotiations

had attained their object, the state of affairs in Europe would have been entirely different from what we see to-day. The raising of the blockade, and Russia's renewed entry into relations with the outside world on a purely economic basis, at a time when she still possessed considerable supplies of raw materials, would have exerted a great influence on the restoration of the equilibrium of European production and consumption."

The misfortune was, however, that in 1919 and 1920 Russia was considered only from the political standpoint. The most eager manifestation of interest in Russia was in helping the counter-revolutionists to crush the Soviet. This effort failed of its object. Europe's placing Russia outside of the European federation did not tend to restore equilibrium in the economic life of Europe.

The effect of this blunder was felt when the spectre of famine seriously raised its head in the valley of the Volga and the Ukraine and, on top of all the misery following seven years of war, drained the strength of the people so that it would take the country many years to get on its feet again. The famine, to which Nansen had drawn attention as early as in the spring of 1919, became catastrophic in 1921 after the complete failure of the harvest in the most fertile district of Russia, the Volga valley and southern Ukraine. A region twice as large as France with about thirty-three million inhabitants was threatened with starvation. If relief were not brought and brought quickly, millions of people would die. The granary of Europe, the Volga valley, lay like a parched desert. Together with the famine, dysentery, intestinal inflammation, cholera, and spotted typhus raged. From 1918 to 1922 there were about thirty million cases of spotted typhus with a mortality of about thirty per cent. Homeless children by the millions fell victims to the scourge of tuberculosis and other diseases; among infants the mortality was eighty per cent.

Nansen's answer to the refusal of the Supreme Council was to arouse a mighty wave of sympathy throughout the world among men in whose hearts politics had not killed all human compassion. An international conference in Geneva on August 15, 1921, consisting of delegates from forty-eight Red Cross and charitable associations, appealed to Nansen and asked him to take charge of the relief for the famine-stricken Russians.

On August 27 Nansen was in Moscow and concluded an agreement with Chicherin regarding the administration of relief and the raising of an international government loan under control of an international organization and the governments of the Great Powers. The work was to be conducted from a Central Office in Geneva with a branch office in Berlin, which in turn was in touch with the office of the Nansen Mission in Moscow for Greater Russia and the Volga valley and a similar office in Kharkov for Ukraine and the Crimea. The office in Berlin was to have charge of the transport of foodstuffs to the Russian border, whence the transports in sealed cars were to be conveyed to the various places where the workers of the Nansen Mission would receive the cars, check up on the materials, and handle the distribution. Transport in Russia was to be taken care of by the Russians.

Herbert Hoover was at the head of the co-operating organization in the United States.

In one way it should not have been a very difficult task to satisfy the hunger in Russia. There was food enough in the world and means of transport and plenty of workers. In the United States the wheat was rotting in the fields for want of buyers, and in Argentina maize was being used as fuel. Thousands of vessels and thousands of workmen were idle in the harbors of the world. "The ships lay idle in many countries and thousands of men were unemployed. Some of the idle ships, with a small part of the unemployed men, could easily carry sufficient superfluous American corn to save the starving and dying millions," said Nansen.

But there were other things harder to find than food: one of them was an altruism strong enough to see beyond mere political expediency. Helping their imprisoned countrymen to come home to productive occupations, and freeing their own countries from the troublesome refugees, was a paying form of charity, but to save the peasants in Russia from dying—that was loving one's enemies, the Bolsheviks, and that command was not written in the hearts of the politicians.

At the Assembly of the League of Nations at Geneva on September 9, 1921 (on the twenty-fifth anniversary of the *Fram's* return from the Pole), and still more strongly on September 30, Nansen tried to awaken the nobler feelings of the politicians. It became apparent with appalling cheerlessness that certain politicians had no such feelings as far as Russia was concerned. Every day lessened the possibility of being able to bring help. Soon winter would close the best means of transportation in Russia, the rivers and canals, and millions would be doomed to death by starvation.

The ice of the Polar Sea was easier to overcome than the ice wall which Nansen met in Geneva. The strong man stood pale with emotion, the sonorous voice almost failed:

"Is it possible that Europe can sit quietly and do nothing? I cannot believe it. I feel convinced that the people of Europe will compel the governments to reverse their decisions. I believe that the greater number of those governments which are represented in this room to-day will join the ranks of the few who have already acted; for let me remind you that a number of the smaller governments are already giving help. If the others only sacrificed the cost of half a battalion of troops, they would be able to find the money. They cannot do it? Then let them say so frankly, but do not let them go on summoning committees and conferences, and discussing day after day and month after month, while people are dying of hunger.

"The mandate I received from the Conference for which I act is to go on appealing to the governments of the world. I shall go on and try to rouse the countries of Europe to avert the greatest horror in history, and I believe, whatever this

Assembly may decide, we shall be able to do something to alleviate the dire distress which exists. . . .

"In the name of humanity, in the name of everything noble and sacred to us, I appeal to you who have wives and children of your own, to consider what it means to see women and children perishing of starvation. In this place I appeal to the governments, to the peoples of Europe, to the whole world, for their help. Hasten to act before it is too late to repent."

The representative of Serbia, that country for whose sake Russia had gone to war, answered that it were better that the Russians should die than that the Russian Government should receive help. This was a direct, harsh, and honest answer to these words in Nansen's speech: "Is there any member of this Assembly who is prepared to say that, rather than help the Soviet Government, he will allow twenty million people to starve to death? I challenge this Association to answer that question."

Nansen's speech in Geneva will endure.

The correspondents of the great newspapers of the world sent accounts of the speech and told of its effect. Nansen spoke with all the thrilling power which he possessed when he was himself fascinated and filled and moved by his subject. Silent and cold, but deeply stirred behind the mask, the dignified assembly sat in the hall. When he concluded, the tightly packed galleries burst forth in a storm of wild applause. It was a man with his heart in the right place who had just spoken and at the same time a man of great clearness of vision.

The battle he had waged ended in defeat for the time being, but above the defeat shone a mirage of the "land of the future" which he saw and believed in—a belief which the League of Nations during those days had cruelly disappointed.

Time after time Nansen had appealed to the League of Nations to support his request for credit for the Russian Government to the amount of ten or five million pounds—half the cost of a battle-ship.

He was forced to see his attempts fail. No appeal could move the governments. The League of Nations' Commission 6 recommended that the proposal be rejected. It had no confidence in the Russian guarantee for transport and distribution of supplies, which Nansen had obtained. There was no one who did not have confidence in Nansen himself; he was above suspicion. But there were some who thought he was too unsuspecting and trusting. It is true that faith and confidence were outstanding features in Nansen's character. They went with his open and honest nature. Hence it was possible by the art of diplomacy to entangle his feet in a tight place. Nevertheless, he was also a man who looked before he leaped. He showed this in everything he undertook, in his choice of associates, in his planning and execution. The routes he selected were not always those on which people had reckoned, but they led to the goal.

"From the first moment Nansen had a statesman's vision of the task he had in hand," says Philip Noel Baker. He appealed to the League of Nations to guarantee a loan to be used to fight the famine in Russia—just such a loan as that which saved the Austrian Republic twelve months later. "Who at this distance of time would deny that he was right?" asks Baker.

Baker was with Nansen on a later occasion in the Greek Foreign Office when, in October 1922, he first proposed a League of Nations loan for the settlement in Greece of the refugees who had fled from Asia Minor. All the "practical politicians" denounced the scheme as wild and foolish; there could be no solution, they said, unless the refugees returned to Asia Minor. But Nansen stood firm, and calmly insisted that only his plan could possibly succeed, that within a generation it would make a new and greater Greece. Before a year was over the doubters were defeated and his scheme was carried through.

In 1921, however, when it was a question of Russia, the short-sighted policy prevailed—though not by an open and honorable refusal; the matter was referred to a conference in Brussels in October.

"It is a terrible race we are running with the Russian winter, which is already silently and persistently approaching from the north," Nansen had said. "Soon the waters of Russia will be frozen; soon the transportation will be stopped by the ice. Shall we allow the winter to silence forever those millions of voices which are crying out to us for help? There is still time, but there is not much time to lose."

It looked as though they wished to lose just that time.

The Brussels Conference in October set conditions: a committee of investigation must be sent to Russia, and Russia must recognize the debts of the Czarist Government. "The hunger of twenty or thirty million people is to be used to enforce a claim," wrote a Norwegian paper.

Pending this settlement, the governments called upon private organizations to support Nansen in his battle with the famine. But the race with the Russian winter ended in the way Nansen had foreseen. The waterways were frozen before help could reach all the famine-stricken. Between three and four million died a slow and agonizing death from starvation, and millions more of the deaths which were ascribed to disease could properly be put down to the account of the famine.

Nansen went again to Russia. In July 1921 he writes: "The famine in Russia is worse than words can describe. Millions of human beings are being tortured slowly to death by hunger and cold."

Nansen's Norwegian co-worker, Major Vidkun Quisling, relates that cart-loads of corpses were the first sight that met his eyes when he came out of the station at Kherson, his headquarters. Quisling, who was director of the relief work in Ukraine, arrived there in January 1922, but it was not until May 17 that the first consignments of supplies reached him.

In January 1922 Nansen travelled to the chief cities of Europe and America describing the need and showing slides from photographs he himself had taken, "an album of horrors." All the animals were eaten up, even dogs and cats. The thatched roofs from the farm buildings were ground into powder and eaten mixed with grass, moss, leaves, and bark. Crowds of peasants with their wives and children wandered about the country trying to find food. They flocked to the railway stations and there lay down in the streets and died. Nansen tells of a mother with three children who lay in the street for several days in a temperature of 25° below zero. But wherever people went the country was equally devoid of food, and the migration stopped of its own accord.

In towns and villages the inhabitants lay at home waiting for death, too weak to go and get the food which might save them. In many of them hunger finally drove out all human feelings and understanding. Parents in their frenzy killed their children to get food. In the churchyards the bodies were dug up and eaten. In Nansen's pictures we see churchyards where the corpses are no longer being buried; the naked bodies lie piled in great heaps. "Salted human flesh was sold in the open market-place," Nansen relates. "Hundreds of thousands have already succumbed, and millions will be wiped out if sufficient relief is not sent at once. Russia's enemies have spread reports that the relief which is sent does not reach the famine-stricken, but is consumed by employees of the Soviet Government and the Red Army. These are black lies, invented by human devils who for the sake of political intrigue think nothing of delivering millions up to hunger and misery."

Nansen gave his lecture in the Calmeyergaten Mission House in Oslo before 4,000, in one of Stockholm's largest churches, in Copenhagen, in many places in England and other European countries. He then went to America, to New York, Philadelphia, Chicago, and the Middle West. The largest auditoriums were packed and crowds stood outside. He did not use strong language. The horror of the facts themselves spoke through the pictures, a language that pierced the marrow of one's bones. The hearers wept; some went away because they could bear no more; others fainted. In conclusion Nansen said:

"I say now and I shall continue to say: never shall I forget the death agony in the eyes of those Russian children. Save Russia!"

On one occasion, as Nansen hurried to his automobile which carried him away to new work for the starving and dying millions, a newspaper man who reported the lecture condensed all his ideas and impressions, his respect and admiration for Nansen's humanitarian work in the words: "The church towers bow down in the night as he drives by."

Nansen's appeal to the humane part of humanity was answered in a way of which the world has never seen the equal. Nansen's own country was the first to send its help in the form of 700,000 kroner worth of cod liver oil and fish. Had the other countries given in the same proportion as Norway, there would have been plenty of food. Denmark followed suit. The Swedish Red Cross supported 10,000 needy. America undertook the maintenance of two and a half million children, a society in England 250,000. The Soviet itself relieved two and a quarter million people, supplying 600,000 tons of seed grain and 150 million gold roubles. From America came $60,000,000, twenty of it from the Government on condition that the Soviet give ten million toward the purchase of seed corn. The Quakers supported 65,000 children; the English Government sent 250,-000 pounds' worth of supplies; Holland, 4,000 tons of food. From France came six million francs, from Amsterdam two million marks' worth of medicine and food to the value of half a million guilders. Italian socialists gave two and a half million lire in food, and the Pope one million lire. An English newspaper sent twenty thousand pounds, and so on.

With this relief, which flowed in mostly from private and semi-official sources, a good ten million people were supported for many months through Nansen's and Hoover's organizations. Of Hoover's relief work Nansen says: "In the whole history of the world there is no humanitarian work that can be compared with the relief work organized by Hoover during and after the War, which had its climax here in Russia."

Nansen went to Russia several times, covering enormous stretches of territory, to observe conditions and organize the relief work.

Spotted typhus raged, and millions died of it. It is carried by lice. The mortality is high and the danger of infection is particularly great for older people and foreigners. Of Nansen's tiny company three became ill and two died of it. Nansen insisted that his workers wear smooth, tight leather clothes to which the lice could not cling and in which they could not find any crevice to creep in. And still there was danger of being bitten. Quisling was bitten in the neck, and it was with considerable suspense that he waited the ten to twelve days of incubation, but fortunately there was no infection.

All the stations of the Nansen Mission had lists of the number of people that could be supplied with food throughout the winter, but the news of the relief food spread far and wide to many more than were on the lists. If all were to be given food, none would be saved. All would perish in the course of the winter after a long-drawn-out struggle with death. It was not easy to harden one's self—to see emaciated mothers and children, to watch them die without being able to put forth a hand to help them.

What Nansen went through in Russia turned his hair white. Several years later he said: "The things I saw are a constant nightmare to me."

In 1922 Nansen was in Russia for the third time. In March of the same year he saw that it was time to renew his appeal to the League of Nations. The state of affairs in Russia and elsewhere in Europe had developed exactly as he had foretold. In Russia millions had starved to death, and there were still over twenty millions on the verge of starvation who could be saved if relief came soon. The famine with its trail of epidemics had become a menace to the whole of Europe. Moreover, if Russia, the great wheel, were to stop, there was danger for the whole economic machinery of Europe.

Nansen's proposal for a commission to investigate the famine, not for the sake of the famine-stricken, but on account of its significance for the whole world organism, received the support of the Norwegian Government. The League of Nations began to realize that there were more sides to the question than its hatred of the Soviet Government had hitherto allowed it to see, and began to collect information in order to judge of the situation. When the worst period of the famine was over, therefore, Nansen was not done with Russia. A fresh famine must be averted by helping the Russian people to help themselves.

In August 1922 he wrote about procuring agricultural machinery and seed-corn which should be paid for out of the next year's harvest. Direct relief for children, sick people, and invalids would, however, still be necessary. Nansen's organization undertook to co-operate with the Red Cross in Russia in providing drugs and medical instruments and combating the intestinal fevers which constituted a danger not only for Russia. Schools received books and educational materials. In co-operation with international organizations for European Student Relief, 30,000 students were provided with food while studying. Students and professors were furnished with books and instruments, and Russian institutions of learning were given access to the learning and intellectual resources of Western Europe.

A man with the background of Nansen could not but be thoroughly aware of the importance of science. Without her science Germany must have gone under completely. A nation which neglects research will soon cease to develop and lose out in competition. How a country stands and what its future possibilities are, can be gauged by the vitality shown in that country's scientific research and scholarly work in all fields. Consequently Nansen had to give his attention to Russian scholars to provide them with livable conditions and contacts with the world.

Altogether Nansen's campaign for Russia was on a wide front.

In connection with his work to save life in the famine districts and renew relations with Europe, a bureau of information was established with offices at Geneva and Moscow. The object was to gather reliable material about conditions in Russia. What was disseminated on the one hand by the Soviet Government and on the other by the Russian émigrés was not always very reliable.

In 1923 Nansen published a book entitled *Russia and Peace*. In the preface he says: "The more one sees of the unbounded incompetence and national self-righteousness everywhere so blatantly manifest to-day, the more clearly does one become convinced that the first condition for finding a way— if a way there be—out of Europe's present confusion and advancing disintegration must be the attainment of a better mutual knowledge and understanding between its various peoples.

"Another people's outlook, actions, and conditions generally, should be judged as far as possible by the norm of its own psychology, way of thinking, and preconceptions, and not by our own.... In this book the endeavor has been made to render, without prejudice, passion, or partisanship, a brief account of the existing social, and especially economic, conditions in this vast and unhappy country, in the light of my impressions and those of my collaborators during the years that we have worked there, and of the information that we have obtained from the sources which seemed to be most reliable."

Nansen gives us an idea of what Russia means in the world's domestic economy—that mighty country, with an area equal to half of Europe, with a population which in 1914 was estimated at 138 millions in the territory of the present Soviet Union. Although the World War and the Revolution took 22 millions of human lives, the population in 1926 had increased to 146.5 millions, and at the ordinary rate of increase it should now (1931) be about 160 millions.

Russia had a grain area amounting to 34 per cent of the cultivated land of the globe, with a grain production—in spite of primitive methods of agriculture—and a grain export several million tons greater than that of Canada, the United States, and the Argentine together. In 1913 Russia's grain export was over ten million tons; but in 1922 the crop was down to half, and in the famine districts a million and a half peasants had lost all their livestock.

"The revival of life on the limitless steppes, a resumption of the normal relations between the great agricultural population of the East and the over-industrialized peoples of Central and Western Europe will have an influence on international economic equilibrium which it is unnecessary to emphasize."

"Russia's importance in the world's domestic economy is not dependent on the shifting political systems. . . . All governments are transitory. The people and the soul of the people endure. Doubts may be entertained regarding the future of Western Europe and West European civilization; but there can hardly be room for doubt that the Russian people has a great future before it, and a great mission to fulfil in the further life of Europe and the world."

"Not yet has the soul of the Russian people been able to cast off the yoke of Western Europe and to achieve its free development; not yet has it found a way to express *its own* truth. But its time will come. When we read the literature of Russia, and perhaps even more when we listen to the national music of the Russian people, its strange charm, vibrant with the suppressed glow of passion, makes us conscious of the mighty, stirring echoes of melancholy from the limitless steppes, from the unknown depths of an alien existence; we seem to hear a soul still in bondage utter its eternal yearning for liberty, and deep down in that soul we recognize a world still unborn."

The world has produced a whole literature about Russia

since the Revolution, and still it is difficult to form an opinion which one dare rely upon as answering to the truth. The accounts differ so much according to the eyes that see, according to the basic view that interprets what the eyes see. Often the report is simply a weapon in the struggle for or against Bolshevism.

Nansen did not look at any issue through party spectacles. Consequently opinion about him in his own country varied. The Conservatives regarded him as a Bolshevik, the Bolsheviks as a Conservative. He was president of Fedrelandslaget which was opposed to all tyranny either from the right or the left. To the pacifists he was a militarist, and to the militarists he was a peace idiot with no sense of realities. To all of which his friend Erik Werenskiold answers somewhat caustically: "That a Norwegian should think independently is unthinkable for a Norwegian!"

Right from his youth Nansen evinced an unusual power to think independently without a trace of preconceived reverence for authorities.

He declares that he gradually gained a deep sympathy for the Russian people and faith in their abilities and their future. Like the soil of Russia, the Russian people were poorly cultivated but rich in latent power. Before we judge and condemn, he said, let us first learn to know and try to understand. He reciprocated the confidence of the Russian people by honestly stating his opinion of the blunders of the Soviet authorities. He showed here, as in other cases, that he saw things as they were and discovered the causes of conditions and the remedies for them, honestly and impartially.

The old idea of Russia, that Russia is outside the pale of humanity and that its mission in the world is to be a terrible example and warning for the other people of the earth—that idea comes from a point of view which was not Nansen's.

One of his colleagues for many years on the Commission for Refugees, Mr. T. F. Johnson, noted, on Nansen's death, something that was very characteristic of him. When asked what trait in Nansen's character had particularly impressed him, he answered: "His unique objectivity and impartiality. He always considered matters entirely apart from the political and other aspects and thought exclusively of the welfare of the persons with whom he had to do at the moment." It was, Mr. Johnson thinks, especially this quality that made possible the solution of the difficult problem of war prisoners. It won for him the confidence of the Soviet and made him "the only man outside of Russia whom the Russians trusted." [1]

During the famine the philanthropic organizations in England and America were at a loss; they could not gain admission to Russia. But Nansen solved the problem. He made himself their guarantee. The Russians trusted his intentions and his impartiality, and allowed the relief workers to enter as Nansen's representatives.

For him Russia was not "outside the pale of humanity."

Without good will and confidence no society can exist, no co-operation is possible between individuals or States.

So it came about that upon this one man was heaped one enormous task after the other till his heart broke under the burden.

"One has to go back to the age of Cæsar or Augustus to see similar world problems laid in the hands of a single individual," says his colleague, Major Quisling.

---

[1] He was once shadowed by spies. He was not in the least perturbed. "I have nothing to hide," he said.

REHABILITATION OF GREEK AND
ARMENIAN REFUGEES

THE GRECO-TURKISH war ended late in the summer of 1922 with a crushing defeat inflicted upon the Greeks. About a million and a half Greeks and Armenians fled in wild panic from Thrace and Asia Minor across to Greece.

The 300,000 from Eastern Thrace had time to take along with them their animals and wagons, tools, food, and money, but the much larger number, over a million from Asia Minor, took the plunge as they stood. Clad only in summer clothing, and mad with fear of the Turks, they left their homes and farms where the grain stood ripe in the fields and crossed to Greece or some other part of Europe on ships or in small boats. European Turkey was at that time in the hands of the Allies. The fugitives had been granted a respite of 48 days but, illiterate as they were, they made the mistake of thinking it was only 48 hours.

The League of Nations had just assembled in Geneva when this happened. One morning Nansen received a telegram from the Greek Government asking for his help. Nansen, on whom the formalities were not binding when it was a matter of saving life, asked the chairman at once for permission to make a pressing announcement. It was granted, and he mounted the tribune with the telegram and said that the League of Nations could not neglect this catastrophe. There was no time to be lost if one and a half million human lives were to be saved.

The forms had to be respected, but the matter was immediately referred to Commission 6. The Commission recommended putting the whole affair into Nansen's hands and beginning relief measures at once under the auspices of the League. The Assembly adopted this resolution the next evening, voting an appropriation of $18,000. Nansen then turned to the British Government which promised 55,000 pounds sterling on condition that other governments also help. In the course of the evening a large sum was raised, and during the night a quantity of food was bought and ships hired to transport it. Nansen left for Macedonia to meet the refugees, collect them, and settle them in barracks and tents for the time being. Then followed the still harder task of evolving a plan for a definitive arrangement. The Greek Government was, with good reason, afraid lest the refugees bring infectious diseases. A company of 27,000 Greeks from ports near Constantinople were dying at the rate of 500 per week from epidemics of typhus and smallpox. The Nansen Commission, aware of the danger that threatened, mobilized against it with the energetic co-operation of the Red Cross, the Near East Relief, and the All-British Appeal, and in a short time the death rate was lowered by ninety per cent to the normal rate, and the epidemics were checked. The Greek Government recovered from its fear.

In the beginning of October we find Nansen in Constantinople carrying on negotiations with an assembly of foreign relief societies, drawing up programs for relief work, organizing and getting things going. He concluded an agreement with the Turkish ambassador regarding the exchange of prisoners and of whole populations. A week later his automobile was racing through Thrace. Here he was met by the stream of refugees, "a whole nation on the highway." He saw people running insanely away from the ripe harvest in the field, and telegraphed to the Greek Government, which at once put a large sum at his disposal in order to stem the flood long enough for the fugitives to take some of the rich crop with them. This attempt was partially successful. The Thracian refugees were not entirely destitute when they reached Greece, whereas the million from Asia Minor rushed off without taking anything at all with them, not even their tools.

A migration of this nature and magnitude has scarcely a parallel in the history of the world. The misery of the fugitives was indescribable; hunger and disease made an end of 300,000. The trail of the refugees was marked with corpses. Nor was the country to which they were going, impoverished by eleven years of war, in any state to receive this immigration. A country of four and a half million had to make room and provide a livelihood for more than one and a fifth million. The Greek Government had not even money for the first temporary housing and maintenance of the refugees. Again the Americans came to the rescue. During the first winter the American Red Cross supported 800,000 refugees.

It has been said that Nansen's plan for a permanent settlement in Greece did not meet with the approval of "practical politicians." Six months later they still insisted that the plan was madness, the refugees would have to be taken back to Asia Minor; but when a year had passed, Nansen's plan had been successfully carried out.

Before any attempt was made to put the final plan into action, an experiment was tried. Under the direction of Nansen's right hand man, Colonel Procter, ten thousand refugees were settled in Western Thrace in fifteen new villages, most of them as workers on the untilled land. Others started new industries such as carpet weaving, silk worm culture, and various other things. Within a year these refugees were self-supporting and no longer a burden to anyone.

If we can manage 10,000, we can manage a million in the same way, thought Nansen. There was a large amount of unused arable land within the expanded territory of Greece. The Greek Government granted the Migration Commission 500,000 hectares. To cultivate all this land required money. Nansen proposed that the League of Nations should assist the Greek Government by raising a loan. The work was begun under the direction of a commission with two members chosen by the League of Nations and two by the Greek Government responsible to the League of Nations control committee. The chairman of this committee was first Henry Morgenthau, former American Minister to Turkey. He was succeeded by P. Howland and C. B. Eddy.

Up to June 30, 1926, the commission had supplied eight million pounds and the Greek Government six million. The finances of the Greek State were stabilized by a loan of nine million pounds raised with the assistance of the League of Nations.

A million and a quarter refugees were settled in Greece, and half a million Turks were moved out of Greece on to Turkish soil. The intention was that the Turkish Government should take charge of them and place them on the farms vacated by the Greeks. The Turkish authorities have done this in their own way, and many of the refugee Turks have not yet been settled. But Turkey and not the League of Nations or Nansen is to blame for this.

All in all, it was a migration of almost two million people, the greatest known to history, and the result is, as Nansen prophesied, a new and greater Greece. The refugees carry on very intensive farming and gardening. They have given a new impetus to the cultivation of grapevines and tobacco and to the culture of silk worms. They have introduced a native industry, the manufacture of oriental rugs, which was not known in Greece before. Through their rents and taxes the refugees have become a source of wealth to the Greek State, and they are working industriously to pay back the loan which was put at their disposal by the League of Nations.

What seemed to be a calamity for the country has thus, through the help of the League of Nations, been transformed into an asset. And I have no doubt that Mr. T. F. Johnson,

Nansen's colleague for many years, the Assistant High Commissioner for Refugees, is quite correct in saying that the Greek refugees, once in direst need and now happy people in a thriving province, will not soon forget Nansen.

The day after Nansen's death word was received at a meeting of the Council of the League of Nations that the settlement in Macedonia of Greek refugees from Asia Minor was now completed and the administration taken over by the Greek Government. The Greek Minister, M. Michalarcopaulos, expressed the gratitude of the Greek people for the help Nansen had given them in the distressing period after the catastrophe at Smyrna.

NANSEN'S last rescue work was to save the unhappy remains of the Armenian race. The story of the prisoners of war and of the refugees represents a total of suffering which can hardly be described in words, but it does not compare with the Armenian tragedy and all its horrors. In the preface to his book *Armenia and the Near East,* Nansen says: "I hope that the facts themselves will speak from these pages to the conscience of Europe and America." Europe's policy as regards Armenia is in its bloodless passivity no less shameful than all the bloody massacres of the Turks.

The Council of the League of Nations had repeatedly discussed whether something could not be done for the Armenian refugees who were living in great destitution in various countries, and requested its High Commissioner, Fridtjof Nansen, to take up this case with the rest. Realizing the burden of responsibility that such an arduous task would involve, he declined, but was ultimately persuaded to try what he could do in co-operation with the International Labour Bureau. The Assembly of the League placed at their disposal a sum to defray their expenditures in making the necessary investigations and doing other preparatory work.

The representatives of the Armenian refugees had submitted to the Council of the League a project for transferring fifty thousand refugees to the Sardarabad desert in Armenia, which could be cultivated by means of irrigation. The cost was reckoned at one million pounds sterling. A commission was then formed of experts in irrigation and agriculture: Major Quisling was the Secretary of the commission, and Nansen was its head. This commission went to Armenia in 1925, and Nansen has given an account of their investigations and impressions in his book *Armenia and the Near East,* published in 1927.

In the preface Nansen thanks his kind and indefatigable colleagues for their efficient and self-sacrificing work, and for their invaluable collaboration. This is typical of the testimonials that Nansen's co-workers have always received from him; and where they have had an opportunity of speaking they have invariably been equally warm in their tributes to their leader's power to inspire his associates to do their best possible work.

Russia granted them permission to enter Armenia on two conditions: first, the commission must not come as representatives of the League of Nations and, in the second place, its investigations must be carried on in co-operation with a committee appointed by the Armenian Government. To these conditions Nansen agreed. The Armenian committee of engineers facilitated his work in every way, making the results of the investigations unexpectedly profitable. These results have been collected in a book published by the Secretariat at Geneva and entitled *A Scheme for the Settlement of Armenian Refugees. General Survey and Principal Documents,* Geneva, 1927.

Nansen's book gives a description of the country and also an historical account of the people, which I will recapitulate here. It is a severe arraignment of the Powers, especially of the Entente, and also of the League of Nations. In the German edition the accusation is already implicit in the title: *A Betrayed People.*

Armenia, in olden times a great and mighty nation, is now a shrunken remnant with a territory of 30,000 square kilometers and a population of one million.

Armenia is the cradle of mankind's earliest and most sacred story. Somewhere here lay the garden of Eden. Here Noah's dove flew out to reconnoitre and came back "in the evening" with the olive leaf. Here the second founder of the human race went forth from the ark on Ararat, 4300 meters above the present sea level, and planted vineyards. Here his intelligent and enterprising descendants created by their skill in irrigation a paradise from the lava soil in the warm tropical valleys. It was a pleasant place to dwell, and there in the land of Shinar they built the tower of Babel.

But this paradise was dangerously situated. The commerce of the world between East and West laid its caravan routes through the country, through the valleys and plains along the river Arax.

The migrations of people drew their bloody trails across the plains. Greedy neighbors and Great Powers, Persia, Turkey, and Russia, seeing the value of the land, cut off great slices. In the remnant of their country that was left to the Armenians, Turkish hordes have burned cities and villages, hewn down the people, destroyed the canals and irrigation system, and rendered large tracts desert again. It is men's misdeeds, it is war, not climatic changes that have laid waste these regions. "I feel sure that no one can study the story of this remarkable people without being profoundly moved by their tragic fate," says Nansen in the preface of his book.

In 1827 the Russians took from Persia the whole of the Armenian territory north of the river Arax. The delight of the Armenians at the promise of home rule was great but short-lived: a systematic Russification was begun. In Turkish Armenia, however, conditions were still worse. Turkey, having lost Greece, Serbia, Montenegro, and other countries, now dug her talons all the deeper into Armenia, and there was no limit to the extortion, pillaging, and cruelty that the Armenians had to suffer. Gladstone wrote, in 1876, an indignant protest against the misdeeds of the Turks. Turkey's rotten administration stank in the nostrils of the world, it was true, but disagreement as to the division of the spoils prevented concerted action. The Armenians would have fared better if the European Governments had never intervened. All the notes they sent with demands which they never once seriously tried to enforce simply irritated the Turks and incited them to still more sweeping atrocities against the troublesome Armenians. "This, in brief, is all that the statesmen and diplomats of Europe have done for Armenia," says Nansen. The aged Gladstone made a flaming speech against "the great criminal in the palace, the enthroned murderer," Abd-ul-Hamid, who listened attentively, and soon understood that things would not go further than words and paper. He could safely continue with his plan to "disarm" the Armenians.

The storm broke in the autumn of 1895. Armed mobs led by police massacred the disarmed Armenians in every town and village, while the regular troops kept order and saw that "the job" was properly done. The rivers of blood ended in July 1895 when 1200 Armenians were burnt alive in the cathedral at Urfa. In five or six months 9,000 were slain and many more perished from hunger and want. The Powers did nothing. In August 1896 the Sultan slaughtered 7,000 Armenians in Constantinople under the very eyes of the diplomatists. The ambassadors of the Powers sent a note.

Statesmen and diplomatists were tired of the eternal Armenian question which was causing public opinion in constantly widening circles to become disrespectfully critical of their shocking inactivity. The Peace Conference in Paris in 1900 and the International Socialist Conference there in 1902 adopted resolutions deploring the way in which Europe had neglected its obligations to Armenia, and recording the indignation of the civilized world. But that was all. Paper, only paper!

The Young Turk party which was fighting for "liberalism" and for "unity and progress" drove out Abd-ul-Hamid in 1908. He succeeded, by a military coup, in regaining power for a brief period which was nevertheless long enough for him to massacre 20,000 Armenians.

The program of the Young Turks was to establish a pan-Turkish empire. All non-Turks, and especially the Armenians, were to be suppressed, and the Young Turks planned much more methodically than the old régime. They had decided even before the World War to "thin out" the Christian population of Turkey. The Great Powers now took up the matter and two general inspectors were sent from disinterested countries to see that law and order were maintained in regard to the Armenians, but before they had reached their posts the World War broke out. Under the pretext of the War, the Young Turks decided "to liberate the Fatherland from the tyranny of this accursed race . . . to exterminate all Armenians living in Turkey, without permitting a single soul to escape. . . . The Government will give . . . the necessary directions as to the arrangements of the massacres."

Four thousand men were sent against Zeitun in Cilicia in 1915 and deported the whole Armenian population of about 20,000 people to the marshes and deserts. In Constantinople all the chief Armenians, teachers, writers, doctors, lawyers, editors, and priests, altogether nearly 600 people, were sent to Asia Minor. Eight of them returned, the remainder disappeared. Thus all who were capable of pleading the Armenians' cause were conveniently put out of the way.

Then, in June, 1915, the horrors began to which we know no parallel in history. From all the villages and towns of Cilicia, Anatolia, and Mesopotamia the Armenian Christians were driven forth on their death march. All they owned was confiscated by the Turks. The poor creatures were rounded up from the different cities and driven in long columns across the mountains into the Arabian desert. The idea was that those who were not killed outright should die of starvation.

"As soon as the columns had fairly started, the callous indifference of the guards turned into vicious brutality. The few men and elder lads were assembled, taken aside, and killed. The women, children, and old people were driven on, suffering agonies of hunger and thirst; the food, if there was any, was scanty and bad; those who could not keep up were flogged on till they collapsed, or were killed. Gradually the columns became smaller and smaller, as hunger, thirst, disease, and murder did their work. Young women and girls were raped or sold by auction in places where the Moslem population had assembled; 20 piastres was paid for a girl who had not been violated, 5 piastres for one who had been violated or for a widow, and children went for practically nothing. Often bands of *tyetas* and Kurds swooped down upon the columns, robbing, maltreating, murdering, and violating the women." A carefully planned torturing to death by starvation and violence, "a polite form of massacre"; the authorities saved their face by calling it "a necessary military measure!" Out of 18,000 expelled from Kharput and Sivas only 350 reached Aleppo, and out of 19,000 from Erzerum there were eleven survivors. Typhus raged among them. The corpses by the roadside poisoned the atmosphere.

In many places the Turkish authorities considered it unnecessary to resort to the subterfuge of these deportations and had the Armenians massacred in their own towns. Or another method was pursued: Armenians by the hundreds were sent down the Tigris by raft. When the rafts reached Mosul they were empty and the river was full of corpses and human limbs. Government troops butchered 25,000 women and children in the Kemekh gorge. The Armenian soldiers who had fought so bravely in the Turkish army that even Emir Pascha had publicly complimented them were taken behind the lines and shot by their Turkish comrades.

The Turkish Minister of the Interior telegraphed in September 1915 to the Police Office at Aleppo that an end was to be put to the existence of the Armenians "without paying any heed to feeling or conscience." In 1916 the work was completed. The concentration camps were emptied: 55,000 people who starved to death lie buried in one of them. Most of 60,000 deportees sent in 1915 to Deir ez-Zor on the Euphrates disappeared. Almost 19,000 perished on the way across the desert to Mosul, and 20,000 more sent to Deir ez-Zor in 1916 disappeared. The accounts of eye-witnesses are heart-rending.

When news of these events reached Europe in 1915, there was a perfect storm of indignation. It found vent in strong words and solemn promises, confirmed by Wilson, Lloyd George, and Clémenceau, that "when the cause of justice and liberty was won, the Armenians should receive full compensation in the form of their independence and freedom, provided they joined the Entente and sent their able-bodied men to fight." Armenian volunteers flocked to the colors and fought with magnificent bravery. Upwards of 200,000 gave their lives for the cause of the Allies.

After the Russian Revolution the Turks advanced on Russian Armenia to exterminate the Armenians there as well.

In May, 1918 Armenia proclaimed itself an independent republic—9,000 square kilometers with a population of 350,000. The Turks seized Baku and massacred almost 30,000 Armenians in three days. Upon the collapse of Turkey the Armenians recovered their country, but the Allies, who had promised them this country, sent no troops. As Nansen remarked, "There were, of course, no oil-fields in Anatolia." The Turks reconquered the country. Again the Armenians had been betrayed.

On January 19, 1920, the Supreme Council of the Peace Conference recognized the Armenian State and proposed that the League of Nations should protect it as a mandate. The League refused, stating that it had not the necessary means, military or financial, nor would any power accept the mandate.

By the Treaty of Sèvres in August 1920, Turkey recognized Armenia as a sovereign State, and Wilson defined the boundaries. Armenia received an area on the map embracing about 127,000 square kilometers. Unfortunately, however, the Allied Powers did not take any steps to secure to the Armenians this territory, and quietly allowed the Turks to occupy the Armenian territory again. They let the Armenians shed their blood in the Allied cause, and rewarded them with a worthless document. Erivan escaped the same fate by forming an alliance with Moscow. The Armenian Republic was reduced to 30,000 square kilometers with something less than a million inhabitants. In 1921 a federation of three Trans-Caucasian Soviet republics—Armenia, Georgia, and Azerbaijan—was formed in affiliation with Moscow. Now, "strange to say, the nations who failed to perform their obligations, who forgot all their promises, and did nothing to help the hard-pressed Armenians while there was still time to do so, have blamed them for accepting a soviet form of government in order to save their country and its people. This accusation is used as an excuse for doing nothing more; for these nations have lost interest in the Armenian people, as they lost interest in their own promises."

Then came the last grim act in the sombre tragedy of the Armenians, when in the fall of 1922 the Turks, under Mustapha Kemal, drove the Greeks out of Asia Minor. Thousands of Armenians were driven out at the same time. Stripped of everything they arrived in Greece, Bulgaria, Syria, and Russian Armenia.

In the persecutions of 1915 and 1916 the Turks had exterminated 1,000,000 of the 1,845,450 Armenians in Turkey, more than one-third of the whole Armenian people.

And what has the League of Nations done? Its first Assembly in 1920 resolved that something must be done "to put a stop to the terrible Armenian tragedy as soon as possible." At the next Assembly the necessity of giving the Armenians a "national home" (*foyer national*) was emphasized. This resolution was repeated at the third Assembly. At the Peace Conference at Lausanne in 1922 and 1923, Lord Curzon reiterated this demand and characterized the Armenian question as "one of the greatest scandals of the world." The Treaty of Lausanne was signed without containing a word about a home for the Armenians. In fact, this treaty was made just as though they had never existed.

In 1924 Mr. Stanley Baldwin, the leader of the British Conservative Party, and Mr. Asquith, the leader of the Liberal Party, sent a warm-hearted address to Mr. Ramsay MacDonald, then head of the Government, urging that Great Britain ought to give a large sum to help the Armenian refugees. There was no doubt, Nansen believed, that Mr. MacDonald and the Labor Party would gladly have done what was asked, but he was shortly afterwards defeated, and the Conservative Party, led by Mr. Stanley Baldwin, came into power. "Surely," says Nansen, "the time had come at last! But Mr. Baldwin's Government refused to do anything whatsoever for the Armenian nation or for the refugees. . . . In despair one can only ask what it all meant. Was it, in reality, nothing but a gesture—mere empty words with no serious intention behind them?"

"And the League of Nations—has it no feeling of responsibility either? By compelling its High Commissioner for Refugees, in spite of his repeated refusals, to take up the cause of the Armenian refugees, the League has almost certainly prevented others from organizing effective measures to help the Armenians; for it was assumed that the League of Nations would not espouse a cause of this nature without being able to deal with it satisfactorily. . . .

"Woe to the Armenians, that they were ever drawn into European politics! It would have been better for them if the name of Armenia had never been uttered by any European diplomatist. But the Armenian people have never abandoned hope; they have gone on bravely working, and waiting . . . waiting year after year. They are waiting still."

After Nansen with his committee of experts had travelled through Armenia in 1925 he proposed that the League of Nations furnish a loan of 19,000 pounds sterling to Armenia for the irrigation of the deserts, the rich soil of which would provide a home for 30,000 people. The Armenian Government, the

Soviet Government, and the State Bank in Russia offered guarantees. The plan was endorsed by all experts, but the opposition of the British Government made it impossible to secure the guarantee of the European Governments, and the loan could not be raised.

Nansen then proposed a smaller loan, of 300,000 pounds, to transport refugees and settle them on the land in Armenia, in hopes that the Armenian Government itself would undertake the irrigation. But the Entente declined.

The Armenians in Europe and America promised to raise 100,000 pounds. One wealthy Armenian offered to give the larger part of this sum to build a village which should bear his name, but the Bolshevik authorities would not agree to the plan, and the whole project fell through.

When Nansen returned home from Geneva that year he was profoundly cast down.

In Syria there are at present more than 100,000 Armenians who have been living in great misery, and still more have come in from Turkish Anatolia. The League of Nations is working in co-operation with the French Government and local French authorities to settle them on the land along the coast. There is a plan, too (in 1931), to settle refugees in the regions about the Euphrates, which was not regarded by Nansen as any final solution of the Armenian problem, since the refugees there are far away from their fatherland. They must be saved from starving to death, however, and there is no other way out except to help them to support themselves where they are.

When Nansen, disappointed, bitter, and indignant, resigned from his post as High Commissioner of the League of Nations, members sprang to their feet one after another, among them some of his opponents, and begged him to continue. Even his adversaries could perceive that the loss which the League of Nations would sustain in the estimation of humanity if he left could not be compensated for by any other man.

Nansen helped the many doubting adherents of the League

to have faith in it. They did not doubt him. He realized in his actions the idea which would justify the existence of the League. Their faith in him and in his faith had helped to keep the shares of the League of Nations up. The League had caused Nansen bitter disappointments, but he did not leave his post, he did not let fall his banner. For he believed, he must believe in the justness and force of the idea upon which the League of Nations was founded. He believed that if people and their leaders would determine to realize that idea, it offered a means of salvation. "If we do not succeed in reaching the goal along that road, then I see no way to salvation ... then I am afraid that the European civilization is no longer capable of development. It is really doomed to death."

With a faith that could move mountains, he again assumed the burden. Shortly before his death his position as High Commissioner of the League of Nations was extended for ten years.

In the course of time the dazzling exploits of the Greenland expedition and the *Fram* expedition will pale before Nansen's achievements in the last decade of his life. The ship on whose deck he stood, a saving pilot, is not like the *Fram* of the Polar Sea long since safe in port; she is, as long as men's minds are as they now are, in dangerous waters and uncertain weather. But is Nansen's spirit behind the eyes which from the commander's bridge are seeking the way and steering the ship? That is always the question. Nansen's thoughts and words, his spirit and deeds, will be like a hand on the wheel. There is hope in that.

His journey through Armenia was continued in the summer of 1925, through the Caucasus. This trip is described in his book *Through the Caucasus to the Volga,* which appeared in 1929. The object of the trip was to investigate whether there were vacant lands in the Caucasus for the Armenians, and shortly before his death he was able to sign an agreement for the settlement of 12,000 Armenian refugees there. This was a bright spot in his discouraging labors.

Nansen relates the following story in *Armenia and the Near*

East. The commission's automobile stopped beside a cotton field where some women were weeding. Nansen wanted to see how the work was done and walked across to them. "Then a curious thing happened: a handsome young woman got up, came to me, and gravely handed me a small cotton-plant. This done, without looking about her, she quietly returned to her place, and bending down, resumed her weeding without looking up again. It was a gesture of welcome in accordance with the custom of the country, very touching in its artless simplicity. I kept those modest leaves as a memento of Armenian womanhood."

And the Armenian women no doubt kept the memory of this tall, fair Northern man who had come to see Armenia and its betrayed people.

THE NOBEL PEACE PRIZE

THE SWEDISH inventor of dynamite, Alfred Nobel, established a fund, the income from which was to be used to confer prizes for outstanding work in science, literature, and the cause of peace. The Norwegian Storthing was given the honor of awarding the Peace Prize. The first award was made in 1905, half to Dunant, founder of the Red Cross, and half to Passy, who inaugurated the first French peace society.

The banquet room of the Nobel Hall in Oslo was filled on December 10, 1922, with a representative audience headed by the King and the Crown Prince. It was a very special event this time. The award of the Nobel Prize has probably never aroused greater enthusiasm throughout the whole world, and for Norway it was a particular satisfaction that the winner of the Nobel Prize this time was a Norwegian, Fridtjof Nansen.

He had just returned home to celebrate Christmas in Norway after the work of organizing the world's greatest migration of people. For two and a half years he had been occupied with one great international relief project after another: the repatriation of half a million prisoners of war, the settling of a million and a half Russian refugees, the maintenance of millions of victims of famine in Russia, the flight of a whole race from Asia Minor and Thrace—a work of such significance that the Nobel Committee wished to honor it with the award of the Peace Prize.

Professor Fredrik Stang, president of the Nobel Committee, described this work and the feelings with which it must fill us

when we try to realize what the tasks meant and how they had
been carried out. It was a stirring speech deeply charged with
emotion.

For the first time the Norwegian public heard a comprehensive and appreciative presentation of Nansen's relief work
during the years following the War, and it was sadly needed.
Only in isolated flashes had the Norwegian public received any
information about the stupendous work of the Norwegian
Samaritan out in the great world. The exploits and experiences
of a Norwegian pole-vaulter or a Norwegian boxer were more
closely reported and more eagerly followed from day to day;
their homecoming filled the wharfs and streets with cheering
multitudes. The news value of material differs. Nansen's own
saga has examples enough of this. The expedition across Greenland on ski and the expedition across polar regions on the
Fram brought the world to its feet, out into the streets in loud
jubilation.

Now when "the hero from the desolate snow-fields" came
home from his Samaritan labors holding a record in the service
of humanity, won in a struggle into which he threw all his
strength and risked his life, a struggle which saved millions of
human lives, the papers were silent, the streets empty and still.

But in silence the Genius of history carves a deed in deep
letters on her tablet. Not altogether in silence, however: the
great premium of the inventor of dynamite roused the public
with a jolt, the necessary jolt.

I quote from Professor Stang's speech:

". . . When we try to form a comprehensive view of all this
enormous work our imagination refuses to grasp it, as it does
figures of too great magnitude. One man starving, one man lying
like a forgotten wreck on a street-corner wasting away by inches
—that we can understand. We can feel that deeply enough for
the feeling to become sympathy. One refugee, a group of refugees if you will, with children and furniture in a wheelbarrow in
front of them—that we can comprehend. But before the spectacle

of millions of people scattered like wild creatures over the country, their homes ablaze behind them, emptiness before them in a future over which they have no control, our minds refuse to function. We simply cannot take it in. We can only repeat the figures we have been told. Local charity exercised towards fellow countrymen, towards sections of the country is within our range. We can conceive of that. But a work which sets as its goal the saving of millions from misery and death—that presents an objective so prodigious and such a swarming multiplicity of details that we give up in despair and allow our minds to rest.

"It will be the task of the future to assign this work its place in the history of the world. We who have lived contemporaneously with it can only add some reflections on it.

"What is it that has carried this work through? Has it been accomplished by the ordinary machinery of State? Were the feelings of the politicians and statesmen aroused so they found expression in achievement on such a grand scale? Ah, no. The source lies deeper. It is to the peoples themselves, to the deepest and broadest stratum, that the appeal has gone. We have seen an attempt to create a world opinion. The battle had to be waged against all the politicians. Minds and feelings had be guided over all the barriers with which States and classes and individuals hedge themselves in. Humanity had to be stirred down in those elemental depths of its being which no statecraft can alter.

"The deepest feelings of men are frequently invoked, and very often it is politics that call upon them. But the feelings to which they appeal most often are those which divide: national egotism, class feeling, suspicion, the lust for power. There are times when politics also appeal to the feeling that unites countries and classes, that binds mankind most closely together. But not often. The most significant factor in the work we have before us is, it seems to me, that it has delved deep into the primordial roots of human fellow-feeling which lie deeply buried in all of us, the feeling, namely, that the human race is one, however much it may split itself up into States and societies.

As Nansen says in one of his speeches, he wanted to enlist the love of one's neighbor in the service of his work. And he succeeded. The advance has not been rapid and the final goal has by no means been attained. The warm wave which shot upward from so deep within, so far below the surface, has struck ice and cold; but it has at least reached so far that the work it has borne has become an event in the history of mankind.

"In the front line of the whole drive we have a number of fighting men, each one effective in his place; organizations and individuals engaged in a battle of years to break way bit by bit through all the barriers which stand between the victims of misfortune and their salvation. And at the head of them a single man stands out in our minds. What a burden has rested upon his shoulders! How much has not his work demanded of organizing ability, energy, and initiative! What exercise of self-denying patience and of the great art of simplification it has exacted! And what has not the man come through who has seen Europe's distress at closest hand and with a feeling of responsibility for it!

"We see him among us to-day and many memories flow in on us. Back of him he has a life that all of us have, in imagination, lived with him.

"And what has perhaps made the strongest impression on all of us is how time after time he has been able to stake his life on an idea, on a theory, and to get others to follow him."

Stang recalled those expeditions and the memories of the man who set the *Fram* in the current he believed in—and it carried him through. "It is the same man that we see to-day. A submerged current which few have had faith in has again borne Nansen forward—the deep current of human sympathy underlying the layer of ice which surrounds States and individuals in the struggles of the day and the trials of life. He had faith in that current and through that faith his work has triumphed."

From Nansen's reply: "Professor Stang has said altogether too much, not for the work that has been done, but for my share in it.

"If this work is deserving of some recognition it is owing first and foremost to the help I have received from organizations and from individuals. First of all I wish to mention the League of Nations, then the International Committee for the Red Cross at Geneva, and the American Red Cross. Of other branches of the Red Cross I may mention particularly that of Sweden. I shall mention further the German Government organization which helped with the transport and the Soviet Government which transported the prisoners to the frontier. A number of private individuals have also given valuable assistance and of those who are working out in the field several have risked their lives. Of the five representatives we had in Moscow, three were smitten with spotted typhus; that gives some idea of how dangerous this disease is for Western Europeans.

"Now a few words about the work itself. It has been entirely a humanitarian work to alleviate the suffering resulting from the War, not to prevent war itself. The latter should, of course, be the object of a peace endeavor. The criticism has been levelled at the League of Nations that its work has been directed more towards the former than the latter object. But our work, too, has certainly a great importance in preventing war in the future, in that it tends to create a feeling of brotherhood and neighborly love. If we look about us in Europe we must agree that the state of affairs is appalling and far from promising for the future. The feelings upon which we seem mainly to rely are hatred, egotism, and suspicion between the classes of society and between the nations. The great War to end war—where are all the sounding phrases now? I believe that this War has shown more clearly than any previous war that war never leads to any good, not even for the victors. And yet there are those misguided persons who speak of the next war, although they must know that that war will bring ruination. It can mean nothing less than the downfall of Europe.

"We are on the road back to barbarism. Anyone who travels through Thrace and sees whole peoples on the highways with their property must have the feeling that we have gone back to the days of the great migrations. We have reached the place where we can calmly discuss such a thing as the extermination of a whole race. Whole communities are dying out in the Volga district. We must go back, not to barbarism, but to the old primitive Christian virtue, the feeling of brotherhood, precisely that which Alfred Nobel regarded as the heart of everything. What is needed now more than anything else is that self-sacrifice, that active humanitarianism, which can build up again what the War has torn down. The means of salvation are hard to find, but the thing which gives us hope is the League of Nations. Should the League fail, then everything is lost. But I do not believe it will fail. We must make every effort to strengthen the League of Nations. I believe it will have a great future. Through it we shall succeed in working more and more towards the United States of mankind.

"As I stand here to-day, I must confess that I had hoped now to be able to turn back to my scientific work, to all that has been accumulating. But I have a feeling that I have done so very little, and this great reward binds me fast to the work I have begun."

The Nobel Prize that year was 122,000 kroner. Nansen used part of it for the establishment of two large agricultural stations in Russia to instruct the peasants in the use of modern mechanized agriculture, and a part for the Greek refugees.

The Danish publisher, Christian Erichsen, gave Nansen a similar sum which was applied in the same proportions to the same objects. Mr. Erichsen, who donated his whole cash fortune to Nansen's relief work, did so in the hope that other wealthy men would follow his example, but this was not done. Aside from what was received from the various governments and from the Pope, who gave a million lire, it was from the ordinary ranks of people, indeed often out of the pittance of the poor, that help and sympathy came.

Nansen's acknowledgment proper of the Nobel Prize is

the speech he made a few days later on December 19, 1922, on
"Peace":

"In the Capitol at Rome, the marble statue of the Dying
Gaul has always seemed to me, in its simple pathos, one of the
most beautiful. He is lying, mortally wounded, on the field of
battle; his muscular body, inured to labor and warfare, has abandoned itself to fate. The shaggy head is bent, the strong neck
droops, the coarse, powerful, work-hardened hands, that so lately
wielded a sword, are now pressed against the ground in a last
attempt to support the failing body.

"He had been driven out to fight for strange unknown
gods, far from his own country, and so he met his doom, and lies
there silently bleeding to death. The fight rages round him,
but his ears no longer hear it; his eyes are dulled to outward
sights. Perhaps his last conscious thought is of the home of his
childhood, of the simple, happy life in his native land amidst
the forests of Gaul.

"That is how I see suffering humanity—the suffering peoples of Europe—bleeding to death on the battlefields at the close
of a conflict which, to a very large extent, was not their own.

"Lust of power, imperialism, militarism have run their
berserk-race across the world. Fields of ripened corn have been
trodden beneath iron-shod heels, the earth lies waste, society is
shaken to its very foundations. The nations bow their heads in
mute despair. The piercing battle-cry still echoes round them,
but they scarcely heed it now. Their eyes are searching for the
simple primitive elements of life, shut away in the Eden which
they have forfeited.

"The soul of the world is sick unto death, courage has
failed, ideals have grown dim, the desire to live is destroyed; the
far-off blue sky has been obscured by the fiery clouds of ob-
struction—faith in a coming dawn has almost vanished."

In this assembly where politicians and diplomats sat in rows
before him, he asked: "To whom shall we turn for a remedy? To
the politicians? True, their intentions are good, at least in many

cases; but it is plain that the world needs no more politics, no new political programs; it has had only too many of them already. The aim of politics has degenerated till they are little better than a struggle for supremacy.

"Can the diplomats help us? They mean well too, perhaps, but they are a barren race in these days, and have done humanity more harm than good of late." He reminded them of Oxenstierna's famous remark to his son: "If you only knew, my son, with how little wisdom the world is governed."

"The whole of Europe is a ball in the hands of unscrupulous speculators, political speculators, financial speculators— blockheads for the most part, men of inferior capacity who do not understand the trend of events. . . ."

The prevailing feeling among the nations was one of despair, of suspicion of everything and everybody. Without confidence there could be no peace, simply a continuation of war, without blood, but bloody enough.

Nansen had no faith in the politicians of the various countries. The only remedy lay in the co-operation and honest goodwill of the nations as a whole. But he believed in the League of Nations. He told what it had already done in the interests of peace by its mediation and settlement of the difficult controversies among the nations, of its relief work for prisoners of war and refugees. His faith in the League of Nations gave him "faith in the dawn."

*   *   *

In December 1926 Nansen again spoke at the presentation of the Peace Prize (for 1925 and 1926) to Dawes and the Locarno men, Briand, Chamberlain, and Stresemann.

Again he passed in review the state of the world and pointed to the League of Nations' part in it.

In 1923 the outlook had been dark, he said. Peace terms which were dictated by hatred and desire for revenge fostered still more hatred when the vanquished were unable to pay.

France occupied the Ruhr district, while a violent hatred of France spread among the German people, and this relation caused a disturbance in the whole economic life of Europe. There was talk of the "next war." Then came from America the idea of investigating scientifically Germany's capacity to pay. Dawes was made chairman of the committee. The Dawes plan of 1924 gave Germany the necessary relief, and the effect of this was felt at once in the economic life of Europe. Confidence was restored.

Another important step on the road to peace was the Geneva Protocol which had been adopted by the League of Nations in August 1924. It had definitely established for the first time that a war of aggression was a crime, that all international disputes should be settled by arbitration or in a court of law.

The Geneva Protocol had led up to the Locarno Conference of October 16, 1925. The Rhine Treaty which was concluded here eliminated the Rhine as a cause of friction, and arbitration agreements between Germany and each of the four countries, Belgium, France, Poland, and Czecho-Slovakia, pledged them to peaceful settlement of controversies.

"The Locarno agreements" said Nansen, "imply a complete reconstruction of European policy as it concerns the protagonists of the War and instill a new spirit into their mutual relations."

At the Locarno Conference the words "No more war!" had come from the lips of a statesman. It was not altruism that dictated these words, but necessity. "The War has taught us one lesson," said Briand, "namely that we are linked together by a common fate. If we sink we shall sink together; if we retrieve our fortunes it will not be by fighting with one another, but by co-operation."

On Germany's entry into the League of Nations the same year, it was again Briand who said: "No more war! ... Henceforth it will be the duty of the judge to see that law is observed. ... Away with rifles, machine-guns, and cannon. Clear the way for conciliation, arbitration, and peace!"

"No more war! That is the greatest movement of the age," said Nansen. More than anyone else he had seen the effects of war. For more than six years it had been his task to walk as a Good Samaritan in its hideous track. "War is the result of men's will. It is their own shame. With an intelligent political system it should be comparatively easy to make an end of war."

And the way to do so, he believed, was for the governments of Europe to throw themselves into the policy of the League of Nations.

He had a special word here for the small nations. The great States had so many things to consider that it was often difficult for their leaders to act on their own convictions. But the small nations and their leaders were less hampered; for them the unlimited policy of peace without any reserves was a more natural program. The small nations had great interest in the abolition of war.

The history of the League of Nations itself offers proof enough of what the representatives of small nations can accomplish in Geneva when they are firm and courageous. Of that the First Delegate of Norway was himself a good example.

AT GENEVA. THE NANSEN MEMORIAL FUND

FROM Geneva in September 1930 a Norwegian editor [1] writes: "He was missed at Lake Leman this year, in the Assembly hall, in the corridors, on the promenade. He was one of the sights of Geneva—the proudest after Mont Blanc!

"I used to meet him on the Quai Wilson at 8 o'clock in the morning, erect and vigorous after his cold morning tub. He was always the first man in the bath, the first man at his desk. The brim of his big grey hat tilted up in the sunlight. The other early birds turned to look at him—an athlete, his muscles firm as Hercules', better built than the Apollo Belvidere. When he waltzed round the ball-rooms of Geneva—and he was fond of dancing—he swept the small, swarthy diplomats from the floor like flies from the top of a table. His whole being emanated strength.

"He was missed in Geneva this year. His bust has been placed in the library of the Secretariat. When the leaders of the League of Nations during the first years finally get their pantheon, his strong features will shine forth from a place of honor. No other man has been given so many memorial addresses in Geneva—for his fearlessness, his frank humanity, his unwearying labor.

"There were politicians at Geneva who found Nansen annoying, but he won hearts. He was overwhelmingly popular. All the American women in the galleries of the Assembly hall in

[1] A. O. Normann in *Urd*.

NANSEN WITH THE WARDS OF THE NEAR EAST RELIEF IN ARMENIA

NANSEN AND LORD CECIL
AT GENEVA

CHANCELLOR LUTHER AND
NANSEN

Geneva murmured his name when he entered the hall. When he mounted the platform to speak he was greeted by loud applause.

"A master in getting his way by force of argument, by earnest persuasion and persistent effort, he was notably clumsy at that sharp, subtle, niggling game called politics.

"He was never taken quite seriously as a politician in Geneva. For this reason he was often rather exasperating to those who had greater sense for the value of the cards in the political shuffle, and hence people who otherwise esteemed and admired him were inclined to look down rather superciliously when he mixed in their game.

"Only through the limitations of a man does one approach to his intrinsic worth," says the appraising newspaper man. "He was no chieftain in Norway, he had no 'king's thought,' he did not belong to the great leaders. It is difficult to find consistency in his political views or plan in his career. His life is a series of detached episodes, single achievements, mighty tugs."

This qualified appreciation contains a glimmer of partial truth. Nansen himself thought it was hard to find consistency and plan in his life. The many-sidedness of his genius, his power to achieve and do battle in many and varied fields conveyed the impression to him and to others of "detached episodes."

What these achievements and struggles hid from the world was that Nansen was a scientist first and foremost and had no other wish than to be left undisturbed to devote his powers to scientific research. His research expeditions to the Arctic were in the eyes of the public brilliant sporting exploits. In reality they were the first great victories of the scientist in that field. Ocean research was the heart of the *Fram* expedition, and Nansen as oceanographer is in the closest harmony with Nansen as polar explorer. This scientific research was his regret and his longing during the many long interruptions filled with achievements and battles in other fields to which Norway and the world called him. We must not look for "consistency" here, but rather at the achievement itself. Man is not always able to follow his own plan: "We are but tools in the hands of greater powers; ours is not the choice," as Nansen said.

"They looked down on him when he mixed in their game." This may have been true. But now the point of view has shifted so considerably that contemplation is from below upward. Nansen said of himself: I am not a politician.

Of this non-politician Lord Robert Cecil says that Nansen was one of the few Scandinavian statesmen who had won a world reputation. And the historian Jacob Worm-Müller says: "From the point of view of foreign affairs, Nansen's death was the greatest calamity which could have befallen our country. . . . He was one of the few in the League of Nations who strove to realize Wilson's ideas." Björnson has defined the concept of politics as the highest form of altruism. Nansen's upright and dauntless figure will stand in the history of the League of Nations as a politician of this high type. Wherever there was anyone suffering misery or injustice, there he set to work. When the delegates met in Geneva in September, they used to say: "Let us hope that Nansen has not discovered another little nation since last time."

During the conflict between Italy and Greece in 1923, Italy suddenly occupied Corfu. It looked as though the other large nations in the Council of the League were afraid to intervene. Lord Robert Cecil could scarcely have succeeded in rousing his colleagues if Nansen had not been there.

Nansen made a speech attacking Italy so violently that the chairman ruled him out on a point of order. Such a thing had never before happened in this Assembly.

Then Nansen said: "Yes, now I shall stop; there was more that I should have said, but what I have said, I had to say." He bowed his head and went down.

Professor Gilbert Murray has described the scene: "When Nansen went up to the tribune to speak, he was ruled out of order on a technical point and had to be silent. Yet that unspoken speech, and the sight of that great figure which bowed its head and obeyed, carried a message which was not forgotten."

That the Corfu dispute found a happy solution was owing in no small measure to this one man's infectious courage. Philip Noel Baker puts it still more strongly: "Nansen again saved the League from destruction." It was Nansen who organized the opposition against Mussolini. Outside the Council it was he who stood by Cecil; it was he who mobilized the small nations and kept their ranks intact, who canvassed the other members of the Council, who encouraged both the delegations and the press.

Lord Robert Cecil in speaking of their acquaintance made at Geneva which "ripened into warm friendship on both sides" says: "We desired the same things, and we were prepared to collaborate in the same methods. . . . The fact that some of the greater Powers of the world were against him did not alter his judgment or his conduct in the least. . . . There was the great controversy over Corfu, when Nansen was a pillar round which the whole of the representatives of the countries assembled gathered in order to enforce what they believed to be right and justice."

Nansen was criticized, as the representative of one of the smallest States in the League of Nations, for involving his country so deeply. But Nansen was something more than the representative of Norway; he was the ambassador of humanity, the awakened conscience of Europe. He was himself a Great Power.

Germany's delegate, Count Bernstorff, puts an extremely high valuation upon Nansen's activity in Geneva. Nansen exerted himself to the utmost to have Germany admitted to the League of Nations. Bernstorff negotiated personally with Nansen regarding Germany's entry and Nansen facilitated it by his visit to the German Chancellor Marx, in 1924. He convinced him that Germany must no longer stand aloof; and from that moment Germany's attitude towards the League of Nations was changed.

Germany's entry into the League of Nations gave the League the worst shaking up it had ever experienced. The Assembly was convoked in special session, March 1926, for the consideration of this matter but was obliged to adjourn without any result.

Since Germany was to have a permanent seat in the Council, Spain and Poland also demanded permanent seats and were supported in this demand by France and England.

The Assembly stood outside and was quite powerless. The cause of the crisis was that the "Big Four" had control in the Council. They had the permanent seats, while the other seats went in rotation to the others. The States were, therefore, not on equal footing. France and England decided about the seats without respect to the Assembly. On the demands of Poland and Spain, England agreed to strike out the important resolution that a two-thirds majority in the Assembly could overthrow the Council and elect a new one. Holland, Sweden, and Norway united against this move, and it is particularly owing to Nansen's bold and fearless conduct that this resolution was again adopted and the sovereignty of the Assembly upheld in the new meeting in September. The Council could not be allowed to become a tilting ground for the mutual disputes of the various groups of powers. Nansen's daring speech of September 9 was received with demonstrative approval.

His greatest work in the service of the League of Nations was not done at Geneva, however, but in widely spread fields abroad, in Russia, in Greece, in Asia Minor, Armenia, and the Caucasus—altogether a gigantic work which has done more than that of any other single man to raise the prestige of the League of Nations.

As has already been mentioned, Nansen was shortly before his death appointed the League of Nations' High Commissioner for Refugees for another ten years. After his death the Commissariat was given his name: the Nansen International Office for Refugees.

In several countries expression had been given to the idea of erecting to Nansen a "living monument" as the Swedish writer, Fru Ann Margret Holmgren, called it in her proposal, a "Nansen Peace Fund" to be administered by the League of Nations for the advancement of peace and co-operation and for relief work in case of great disasters. This idea found response in wide circles.

On the first anniversary of Nansen's death, May 13, 1931, the League of Nations launched the following appeal:

Dr. Fridtjof Nansen acted for ten years as High Commissioner of the League of Nations, first for the repatriation of prisoners of war, and later for the protection and assistance of refugees. During the whole of that period, he gave his time and strength to the service of the League without reserve. By his unwearied labor, and thanks to his courage, his perseverance, and his organizing power, he repatriated nearly half a million prisoners of war belonging to more than thirty different nations, and helped to make tolerable the lot of over 1,250,000 Greek, 1,000,000 Russian, 300,000 Armenian and some tens of thousands of Assyrian, Assyro-Chaldean, Bulgarian and Turkish refugees.

In bringing about these results, Dr. Nansen not only supervised much of the day-to-day administration of his High Commission, but he made long and trying journeys in the service of the League. He travelled to almost every country in Europe, several times to Russia and to America: he made prolonged expeditions to Constantinople and to Greece after the events of 1922, and to the Armenian Republic of Erivan in 1925. He was thus compelled for long periods virtually to abandon other work, while his unceasing efforts did much to undermine his health and strength.

When Dr. Nansen died, his work for the League of Nations was unfinished. There remains a considerable number of refugees who, on social and economic, as well as on humanitarian grounds, need protection and assistance. The report of the Secretary-General of the League to the last Assembly shows that there are, in various European countries, in China and in Asia Minor, some 170,000 refugees unemployed though able to work, and over 60,000 aged infirm, war invalids, and infant refugees for whose welfare little or no provision exists. To complete the work, further funds are now required, for which the tenth Assembly of the League had authorized Dr. Nansen to appeal to the charitable public of the world. This appeal, which would have been issued by Dr. Nansen during the summer of 1930 but for his untimely death, contained a program under which, by the development of the constructive settlement measures applied by Dr. Nansen in the past, such as the making of advances for agricultural colonization, the finding of and transport to employment, the establishment of a re-adaptation training colony, and various other relief measures, the whole of the material part of the refugee problem could be liquidated finally by the end of 1939.

To make possible the satisfactory completion of the humanitarian part of the refugee work, the eleventh Assembly created, under its authority, the Nansen International Office for Refugees, with a Governing Body under the presidence of Dr. Max Huber, late President of the Permanent Court of International Justice, and consisting of representatives of Governments, of international relief organizations and of the refugees. The accounts of this office are audited by the League of Nations Auditor.

As we are convinced that Dr. Nansen's work for humanity ought, for every reason, to be finished, we, the signatories of this letter, have agreed to issue an appeal on his behalf. We have done so, both because of the inherent importance and public value of the work itself and because we believe that the completion of that work will be the only fitting memorial to a benefactor of humanity whose loss we so deeply deplore.

Dr. Nansen was a hero of peace, and we appeal with confidence to the peace-loving public of the civilized world to contribute to the Memorial Fund to enable the Nansen International Office for Refugees to finish the work which he began.

The appeal was signed by M. Aristide Briand, Minister for Foreign Affairs of the French Republic, the Rt. Hon. Viscount Cecil of Chelwood, the Rt. Hon. Arthur Henderson, Secretary of State for Foreign Affairs of Great Britain, Dr. Julius Curtius, Minister for Foreign Affairs of the German Reich, Signor Dino

Grandi, Minister for Foreign Affairs of the Kingdom of Italy, Dr. T. G. Masaryk, President of the Czecho-Slovakian Republic, M. E. Venizelos, President of the Council of Ministers of Greece, and Joh. Ludw. Mowinckel, former Prime Minister and Minister for Foreign Affairs of Norway.

The latest report from the League of Nations shows that there are still, in 1931, in Europe, Asia-Minor, and China, a quarter of a million refugees without employment and without any provision, and of these 60,000 are aged, infirm, and children in the bitterest need. Nansen had himself devised a plan which included loans for agricultural colonies, training of invalids, emigration, etc. It is for the fulfilment of this relief program that the League has established the Nansen International Bureau and is now launching a world-wide appeal for a Nansen Memorial Fund, a living monument which will carry the name of the Good Samaritan down through the generations as long as there is need and suffering and humanitarian feeling among mankind.

A few days after the issue of the appeal a letter was received by Minister Mowinckel from Fridtjof Nansen's brother, Mr. Alexander Nansen, announcing that a large sum which remained from the voluntary contributions that were put at Nansen's disposal to relieve want, among them the gift of the Danish publisher, Chr. Erichsen, and the Nobel Prize, would now be transferred to the Nansen Memorial Fund. A large amount of the money had been used in relief work as Nansen decided it was necessary, but money on deposit had borne interest the whole time, and there was a balance at Nansen's death of 250,000 kroner. It was the intention that this whole sum, principal as well as interest, should be devoted to the relief of refugees.

HOME AND DAILY LIFE

GODTHAAB, the home Nansen built at Svartebukta, Lysaker, in the early years of his married life, soon became too small. He therefore bought, in 1900, a stretch of wooded land from the old Fornebu estate in the hills above Lysaker. There he built the home Polhögda where he lived till his death.

Great red pines predominated among spruce and leafy trees, and in the thirty years that Nansen protected the forest the trees have not been thinned out or the undergrowth cleared. Along the path, when the growth became too dense, it would occasionally be hacked down with Nansen's curved knife. A spruce tree that was felled there last winter was so thick that almost the whole length of the blade of a big logging saw disappeared into it.

Polhögda is a large brick house. Fridtjof Nansen's Road, which leads up to it and far beyond, brings us to a gate on which the name Nansen is inscribed, and on between the great tall pines up to the court, a roomy courtyard, with no fence around it. The big pines form the bodyguard. The court extends beyond the house and ends abruptly at a forest clad crag. Through the tree tops we can look up to Erik Werenskiold's pleasant house.

Between court and garden there is neither line nor fence, nor yet between garden and woods. It is the forest that dominates here both at Polhögda and in the view—the purple range of hills in Bærum and Asker, with Kolsaas and Skaugumsaas and farther away the hills that surround Oslo Fjord. It is from the verandah on the other side of the house, the garden side, that we see this fine view. It is still better from the balcony on the second story, and best of all from the tower; from the flat roof of the tower we have a circular panorama—the fjord down to Dröbak, Nesodden with Amundsen's place Svartskog, Bunnefjord, Ekeberg with Grönvika, where Wergeland lived in his cabin and rowed his sweetheart across Björvika. And yonder lies the old fort Akershus under the walls of which Nansen used to go skating with Axel Paulsen, where the *Fram* listing heavily lay and waited one sullen St. John's day for a gasoline launch until it came speeding out from Svartebukta after a parting there! From the roof of the tower we see something of the city and of Grefsenaas and the ridges which hide the entrance into the land of Nansen's youth, the wooded mountains with the five streams, with cataracts and rapids and lochs and tarns. Some of the water from them reaches the fjord here in the Lysaker river.

Here from the roof he could look out across this kingdom of his. It was peculiarly his, right from the skerry opposite Godthaab where the bonfire of welcome to the *Fram* blazed one summer evening in 1896, to the mountain ridge in the north, the blue setting of the saga of a thousand boyhood memories of Nordmarka.

It is the forest that predominates. It gives protection and shelter to court and home and garden and at the same time offers freedom and space for foot and eye. But up here on the tower roof the fjord forms a more important element in the picture. Down on the fjord below the woods lay the *Veslemöy*, the famous Spitzbergen sailer. Sometimes Nansen used to work on board. There he had peace—no telephone, no door bells.

From the tower on June 7, 1910, he watched the *Fram* out on the fjord, starting off on the famous polar expedition with Roald Amundsen on the bridge. A bird of longing flew from the tower here after Amundsen had passed him, far off to the desolate snow-fields.

And on May 13, 1930, he himself took his last flight from the verandah below; the blossoming trees and the song of spring were the last things he saw and heard.

Polhögda was planned and designed by Nansen himself, a practical house and a beautiful home. The central room of the house is the great hall. The entrance from the court leads into this great hall which stretches across the whole width of the house, with windows and glass doors out towards the verandah, the garden, and the view. The hall is two stories high. The stairway leads up to a gallery surrounding the hall. The walls up there are covered with books and pictures. The bedrooms and guest rooms open off the gallery. Along the west side of the hall on the first floor are three of Nansen's studies chock-full from floor to ceiling of books and pictures; the tables are heaped with books and working materials. The guest rooms and living rooms are also pressed into service. The whole of this apparent chaos was catalogued and mapped in Nansen's mind. When he was ill and wanted books, he always knew exactly where the book stood: such and such a room and shelf, the eleventh book from the left. His fourth study, the holy of holies, was not here but in the tower. The way which leads to it is devious and passes finally through an attic crammed full of books, manuscripts, polar equipment, rolled maps, much-travelled trunks, and drawings. He had to work his way through all of this litter in order to reach his den. Here in "the tower," as this study is known, he preferred to be. Here he could arrange his work to suit himself. This was no reception room or office, but a work room and nothing else.

And if he raised his head from his desk, he could see the fjord and the purple hills. If he wished to have a wider and freer outlook, to stretch his legs and rest his brain a moment, it was only a few steps up the iron stairway to the tower roof. He used also to sit here sometimes with his work; he liked to bask in the sun.

On the mantel piece down in the hall there is a pen and

NANSEN'S HOME POLHÖGDA SEEN FROM THE AIR

FRU EVA NANSEN

NANSEN AND HIS GRAND-
DAUGHTER, EVA HÖJER

ink drawing, an illustration for a Christmas greeting from his son Odd, the architect: a desk heaped with papers; a candle emerging above the mountain of manuscripts throws its light on the only visible portion of the scribe, the mighty forehead of Fridtjof Nansen, which shines like a sphere above the heap. Around about the picture is the following inscription:

Der brænder et lys paa ditt arbeidsbord
det lyser over den ganske jord.[1]

On the east side of the hall, with a massive fire-place in the center of the wall, are two rooms, a living room and a dining room. The living room has a hand-painted tapestry by Erik Werenskiold—elks, grouse, brooks, and fir trees, but in spite of the motley contents the walls have a restful and subdued effect.

In this room hang Werenskiold's pictures of the young Nansen and of the historian Ernst Sars. Here in the hall several of our best painters are represented; but Nansen has not granted much wall space to his own artistic work here—just a couple of small polar sketches hung above the door to the living room. But up in his bedroom hang twelve or thirteen large drawings and water colors. On the gallery are two rather large portraits— Eva's paintings.

Polhögda is a real home, a place of work, where everything bears the stamp of its origin, and where the inanimate objects themselves conjure up the living man. Beside the fire-place in the hall he used to take his short rest after dinner while he enjoyed his coffee and a little chat. In this hall people from all the countries of the earth have met him. Many had something of importance to consult him about or wanted to unburden their hearts, and to such people he gave freely of his time, but in the later years of his life it became necessary to protect him against the curious who flocked there merely to see Nansen.

[1] There burns a light over thy work table,
It shines over the whole earth.

Even the social gatherings of his friends became rarer and rarer, as his work became more and more overwhelming.

In the beautiful surroundings of his home Nansen himself lived a life of rigid simplicity. At half past nine he came down to breakfast—a piece of toast with whey cheese, a plate of oatmeal porridge, which was always too big, and a glass of sour milk, which must never be lacking. Nor must a plate of sour milk with sugar and rusks ever fail to be served in his bedroom before he turned in.

During breakfast work began, first the newspapers, and then a stack of letters, so that the porridge was cold by the time its turn came round. At twelve he took a cup of weak tea and some biscuits. At 3.15 to the minute, dinner: two courses. He did not care for rich fare and preferred farinaceous foods. He did not rest after dinner, but took a cup of coffee with cakes immediately after. He liked cakes. His supper, at eight o'clock, consisted of toast and weak tea. He ate little and was no gourmand. At the old Valhalla feasts he would have got decidedly the worst of it. In this respect he was no true viking. He was very sparing in his use of spirits, but could enjoy a glass of wine in good company on a festive occasion, or a good Norwegian dram. Also a smoke.

After supper he continued with his work, in his later years when the burden became so heavy, often far into the night.

Up in his holy of holies, the tower room, he was not to be disturbed. The house telephone was not taken up except under dire necessity. It was only little Eva, Liv's daughter, who unhesitatingly ventured there: "Here I am with my sleigh, grandpa!" Then grandpa would come at once and he and Eva would start off.

Certainly grandpa needed more exercise and open air than he allowed himself in his later years. Vigorous exercise in the open air had always been his well-spring of health. To the woods, to the mountains he must go. During and after his hunting trips he was always in good condition and looked magnificently vigorous and strong; but in his later years there was often too little or none at all of necessary daily exercise—at most a hasty dash through the park. Out on the steps he would blow on his flute and his park companions would come, his three hunting dogs and the two big tabby cats with their tails in the air. But if the trip in the virgin forest were somewhat inadequate as exercise, it was perhaps, on the other hand, more than a little amusing; for dogs and cats in Nansen's company ceased to be dog and cat any longer.

Nansen was very conservative in his habits and did not easily forego an established custom. The enormous polar ski staff without disk, excellent on icy ground and among rocks, he used also in the loose forest snow. On a skiing trip between Christmas and New Year's just after his return from America in 1924, he set off on ski in deep snow with the thermometer between −30° and −40° C. His polar staff sank in up to the handle. From eight o'clock in the morning until eleven at night at one stretch, he wore himself out completely, but borrow a staff with a disk from one of his companions—no thank you!

He was equally attached to his old clothes and his old shoes. In the attic stood rows of well-worn shoes, finely polished twice a year. He always used the oldest pair. He had one luxurious and refined vice: he liked fine flannels of the best English quality, and they would be darned and darned. We remember how, in the hut on Franz Josef Land, he and Johansen sat by the hour in the sleeping bag and imagined entering a shop where fine soft flannels hung from walls and ceiling. At home at his work he preferred to wear old clothes. One day he upset the household by going out in a hideous old coat. The old serving maid hearing what had happened made the following true remark: "Nansen, he's an elegant figure of a man, he is, even if he goes in rags!"

Precision and a sense of order were outstanding traits in his character. He might be a bit careful and sparing with his pennies, a little Spartan perhaps in his concessions to the small, essential extravagances of life; but—and this was but little known —he would let his dollars go freely where they could serve a useful purpose or where there was a call on his warm heart. So generous were his grants that, although his income was quite considerable, he had a hard time to make ends meet.

In this connection it may be mentioned that he did a great deal of work without remuneration. For his enormous relief work, for example, within the League of Nations and without, through half a score years, he received no salary.

It is eminently fitting that Nansen's home Polhögda, so characteristic of him and full of memories of him, should become the property of the nation. Shortly after his death it was purchased from his heirs by a group of citizens headed by former Prime Minister Johan Ludwig Mowinckel, and donated to the University of Oslo, which has put it at the disposal of the Academy of Sciences. The donors have stipulated that it should not be kept merely as a museum, but be put to some practical use. Nansen's heirs have donated his scientific library.

THE FRIEND OF CHILDREN

IN THE English Channel, on the Isle of Wight, there is a school called Bembridge School which by virtue of its situation has the sea and ships constantly in its line of vision. Some of the boys of this school, with their head master, Mr. J. Howard Whitehouse, came on a little steamer to Oslo in April, 1928. With great care they unloaded an enormous case, mounted it on a motor truck, and drove off, the boys on top of the box. Out to Lysaker they drove, along Fridtjof Nansen's Road, a narrow, winding, peaceful way which meanders along among trees and villas up to Polhögda.

Eager, skilful, careful hands got busy at unpacking, and at the appointed time the boys' work was set up in the great hall in the middle of the house.

On the floor lay the skin of a polar bear with its huge paws spread out. If it had been able to see, it would have met a familiar scene: the arctic ice itself, the polar bear's own kingdom, where he had met Nansen and his fate many years before.

The inscription reads: "Model illustrating Dr. Fridtjof Nansen's journey Farthest North 1893-96 made by members of Bembridge School and presented to him with their homage. Bembridge, Isle of Wight, England, April 1928."

The model is a sort of relief map, six feet by four feet two inches, in an oak case with a glass cover. It reproduces the Arctic Ocean with the coasts and islands along the *Fram's* route and around the edge are models of the *Fram*, of the kayaks, of the

345

hut on Franz Joseph Land, of the last camping-ground, of the *Fram* in the pack-ice, and so on.

The work was begun as "an act of homage to one of the great heroes of the world in which we live" and the result represents the labor of "many happy hours."

Now they were eagerly awaiting their hero and finally he arrived. "I have never seen a more magnificent specimen of man," says Mr. Whitehouse in an address given two years later. "He was well over six feet high, and as he walked with that rapid step which was characteristic of him, the picture of energy and health, it was not hard to believe that we were in the presence of a viking, and it was true. For he had the viking's courage and spirit of adventure."

In a few heartfelt words Mr. Whitehouse conveyed the greetings of the school and presented the boys' gift, and the boys soon realized that they had touched Nansen's heart. He answered with a brief speech. It came right from his heart and it sank deep into the hearts of the boys. He then examined their work in detail, admiring how accurately everything had been done. He told them stories from the *Fram* expedition and described the tension that arose when she ceased to go forward and began to drift back. If this continued, it meant the negation of all their hopes, the destruction of all their plans. During those days of strain he again went through all his theories and the evidence which he thought proved their correctness. And as he did so he kept his faith that all would be well. There could be no failure now. What they had to do was to hold on. Soon he knew that he was right. The hostile winds were alone responsible for the strange backward movements of their ship. When these stopped the ship resumed her inexorable drift across the polar world.

Nansen was particularly interested in that part of the model which showed Franz Josef Land. He was especially pleased that the mountains on this land were shown snow-covered. For it was this snow which had prolonged his trials.

He had seen this land for some weeks without recognizing that it was land. He had taken the whiteness for the white light that is over the snow-fields and was unable to take accurate observations at this time because his watch was out of order. Then one day he saw two black spots where this line of a whiter color appeared and he realized that he was looking at rocks emerging from the snow-covered land. Thus his young listeners relived move by move the experiences connected with the things their hands had fashioned, and were enabled to feel more strongly the inspiration of Nansen's life and work.

The next day the boys received a letter from Nansen. It is addressed to the boys of Bembridge School and is one of the most treasured possessions in the archives of the school. Here it is:

Dear Mr. Whitehouse and my dear young friends:

It is difficult indeed to express the gratitude I feel, and to thank you as I should like to for this charming gift which you have built with your own hands and with your keen youthful interest, and then brought the long way to Norway and to Lysaker.

I am more touched than I can say by this admirable token of your sympathy and the interest you have taken in the work of our expedition in the *Fram*.

I must also express my admiration for the manner in which you have carried out your work and have stuck to it to the very end, and have finished it in every detail. And when it was finished you have yourselves taken the long journey to bring it to what you had decided to be its destination.

This is a remarkable proof of the right spirit in young people; an exquisite training for making men. It is only to be wished that there was much of it in the young generations. I do hope it will be the guiding spirit in the future life of all of you.

You are young, my friends; you have the life ahead of you with all its wonderful possibilities and adventure. I am sure that some day some of you may become great explorers in one field or other. We are all of us explorers in life whatever trail we follow.

But whether explorer or not, I have one advice to give you: stick to the work you begin in life, till the task is finished and finished well, whatever it may be. Go into it with your whole heart and your whole mind. Do not do things by halves, but carry your task through to the best of your ability; just as you have done this task; and be not satisfied before you have got the feeling that you cannot do it better. It is really remarkable how much you learn by doing a thing well. I am convinced that this is an important secret of real success in life, and it will give you the satisfactory feeling that you acquit yourselves like men; for we have come here, in this world, every one of us, to do our part and do it well.

It is men of that kind with the right stuff in them which the world now needs badly, and you, my young friends, will become some of them.

It is a difficult time you are living in, no doubt, and the world does not give you a bright outlook just now perhaps. But it is an interesting time, many important things are happening, and it is full of great problems for you to solve. It is you who have to create the future and make the world a better place to live in.

A thing of special importance is, I think, to do all we can to create a better understanding and more confidence between nations, and in that way a fuller co-operation between them.

You have in your young age come to this country. I hope you will have a pleasant time here, and will return home with nice recollections of old Norway and her people, and with the feeling that you have visited a kindred race. And I do hope that that feeling will last for life, and that you will as men do your share to strengthen the good relations between your great people and ours, as well as all other peoples, and thus help to create a solid foundation for really wholesome international relations and for a betterment of the world.

I once more thank you from all my heart for your great gift and for your coming here and for all the kind sympathy and interest you have shown me.

Believe me, my dear friends,

Your grateful friend,

FRIDTJOF NANSEN.

The same day Nansen paid the boys a visit at their hotel and presented each of them with one of his books in which he had written a kind inscription.

On their departure from Oslo Nansen was there to see them off and, says Whitehouse, never will they forget his noble figure as he stood on the quay waving them an affectionate farewell.

* * *

In Nansen's archives there are stacks of addresses of thanks, especially from Russia, from some of the many he helped. From the University in Kharkov there is a folio of leather, gold, and silk, thanking him for his aid to Russian scientists. There are folios with addresses from institutions and societies which he helped in their struggle against famine; and in the midst of all the large folios is hidden a page of note-paper written in pencil in large Russian letters from an eight-year-old expressing greetings and thanks.

And there is a score of letters from children in a foundlings' home in Bavaria. "For several weeks," writes the director of the home, "the children have been living with you and your work with an enthusiasm which could not be more beautiful or more pure." They are not thanking him for food and help, but for his stories from the polar expedition, especially the story of Nansen's and Johansen's ski trip to the north and their winter camp on Franz Josef Land. They reproduce such features as make a particular impression and illustrate them with drawings in the margin in red and blue crayon. One of them intends, when he is big, to go to Franz Josef Land and deal with the foxes that stole the thermometer from Nansen. He believes he will find it. When Nansen and Johansen go on their next north polar trip he would like awfully to be along to help them to explore a pole!

The children themselves hit upon the idea of writing to Nansen. Each letter is a piece of independent work and has been sent as it was. The children have taken the utmost pains and Nansen praises them in his reply for writing so nicely and for "the remarkably good understanding of the situations these boys have."

The director begs Nansen not to take it ill that the boys write so much about bear-hams and walrus meat and blubber. One pictures how Nansen and Johansen sit in the tent eating ham so that the bear's grease runs down over their chops. Another writes: "Ich wollte ich wäre dabei gewesen, mir ist manchmal das Wasser in dem Mund zusammengelaufen." The director notes that these children lived on thin soup and dried kohlrabi during the War years and that meat is still scarce at the institution. All are "terribly hit by the War." One boy's father was killed in the War; those of others are disabled, or were prisoners of war for many years, are insane, or have drifted into a life of crime. Starvation and disease, disruption and dissolution—and the children must take the consequences.

It pleased the great friend of children to learn that his exploit of twenty-eight years ago "mit Schlitten und Kajak" was the source of such great and pure delight to the war-marked children in Puckenhof.

* * *

Nansen who under his enormous burden of work could scarcely find time for his own family was, as all children who came near him knew, extraordinarily fond of children.

He had five children by his first marriage. His second marriage in 1919, with Fru Sigrun Munthe, née Sandberg, was childless. The four oldest children, two boys and two girls, grew up to be tall, strong, able men and women. The youngest, Aasmund, equally endowed by nature, was stricken by an insidious disease which turned to cerebral meningitis and caused his death in 1913 at the age of eleven. What the father's heart felt for the sick son is touchingly expressed in his diary. When, after Aasmund's death he seeks solitude out in the woods with his grief, Aasmund is with him. He hears him and sees him and talks with him. It is so hard to be reconciled to it that a nature so good as Aasmund's should not be allowed to live.

On New Year's morning 1913 he writes a letter to his closest friend, Moltke Moe, and the letter speaks eloquently enough of his friendly nature and his fatherly heart.

New Year's Morning, 1913.

Dear Moltke:

The first time I write this wonderful date must be to you to wish you a right prosperous and happy New Year and to thank you for your friendship and everything else in the old.

Things have not been going very well here of late. Aasmund's illness has proved to be cerebral meningitis and there is not much hope. Poor boy, he is touchingly good and gentle and patient although he has often had severe pains. Then when he is better for a while he is so sprightly and gay that I cannot realize that he will never be well again. This last week, since Christmas Eve, he has been so remarkably well that I have really begun to have a little hope and to feel more cheerful. At any rate he is fine just now and life seems lovely to him. I had to promise him to give you his best greetings and thank you for the books which have been such a delight to him. You should have seen how he jumped in bed for joy. He is so wonderfully good, this boy. He has been so gentle all his life that I cannot remember a naughty word from him. I cannot bear to lose him.

All the children were so grateful for what you sent—and I was no less so. I have read the ballads and your introduction. It was indeed a feast. I congratulate you with all my soul. I think it is a great work, small as it is and apparently so unpretentious. I hope that you may soon have peace to complete the whole work, but in the meantime I am hoping still more that you will not let too much of this year '13 pass by before you allow your face and your smile to shine in on us out here.

May I ask you to convey my New Year's greetings to your mother and sisters. With best regards,

Your friend,

FRIDTJOF.

From his diary for March 1, 1913:

"To-day at 1 p.m. Aasmund died quietly and gently as he

had lived. After the frequent attacks of pain earlier and the violent convulsions of the last few days, when he was unconscious, he became quiet this morning and then gradually calmer, with slower and slower breathing, until he glided imperceptibly away into the great silence. My sweet, lovable boy. You were always gentle and good. I have only fair and fond memories of you. So unspeakably gentle and kind were you that I have never known anyone like you. Your last thought was of what you would give your brothers and sisters when you were better again. Were you too kind and good to live? Oh beloved sweet boy of mine, I shall miss you sorely—beyond words."

And two years later on April 4, 1915, he writes: "A better and purer soul never lived. And then you died, died—had it only been I and you could have lived and shown the world what a good man is. . . ."

What he went through with his sick son and later lived over again in his memories of him left deep traces in his mind. His feeling was transformed into active sympathy. He literally gave his life to the great work of relief which formed the last and most beautiful chapter of it. The last picture in the hunger film of 1922 showed a child smiling and waving at somebody outside of the range of the film. That somebody was Fridtjof Nansen.

THE ARTIST

OLD SCHIERTZ, the painter in Bergen with whom Nansen used to study drawing, said in all seriousness: "Give up science and become an artist; that is what you are." He himself was in doubt about his career, whether it should be science or art. He chose to become the servant of science, and in recompense art became his servant.

Artistic ability gives the eye the deep power of vision. By word, line, and color the mood of a scene or an experience is caught—from the woods, from the mountain, from the sea, from the snow-fields; from solitudes and silences as well as from tense moments of action when all the pulses throb.

Nansen's deep feeling for nature and keen powers of observation are seen in the lyrical landscapes in his travel books, in the aquarelles from the country about Bergen and from the Arctic, and in the illustrations, drawings, and lithographs which he began to do in his later years with the help of the old photographs from the polar expedition. The mood in these pictures comes from the scenes within his own mind.

As he was already at home in the technique of photography and to some extent of typography—he could go into a printing-shop and show the printer how to mix the ink he wanted—he studied, in his later years with his usual thoroughness the technique of lithography.

During the Bergen years he illustrated his own scientific treatises; but it was a long time before he ventured to illustrate

353

his own books. He turned his sketch books over to the professional artists who illustrated his works. But *In Northern Mists* (1911), *Sporting Days in Wild Norway* (1916), and *Hunting and Adventure in the Arctic* (1924) are illustrated entirely by himself.

At Lysaker he lived in the inspiring neighborhood of Norway's greatest artists. His friend, Erik Werenskiold, en-

SEABIRDS

Drawing by Nansen

couraged him to draw on a larger scale. To Nansen this seemed pretentious, but Werenskiold convinced him that drawing on a larger scale was easier and more effective. Drawing gradually became a favorite form of recreation. If he were surprised late in the evening by the reproachful question, "Are you still working?" he would answer: "No, no, I am just drawing."

Werenskiold wanted him to exhibit, but he could not be prevailed upon to do so. Consequently the first exhibition of his work did not take place until after his death. This exhibition,

arranged by Werenskiold and Axel Revold, the painter,
Nansen's son-in-law, certainly came as a great surprise to the
public at large. His drawings were displayed in chronological
order—from the Bergen years, from the *Viking* expedition, from
the *Fram* expedition. One long wall was filled with the large
lithographs of his last years—self-portraits, pictures from hunting and skiing trips, and of the polar bear in his kingdom.

On reviewing one's impressions from this exhibition and
from the illustrations for his books, one is struck by the fact the
memories and moods from the Polar Sea, from the arena of
his youth up in the north, are subjects of which he was particularly fond. The moods of the polar regions have not been
effaced by the years. On the contrary, they condense into pic-
torial scenes which he must reproduce again and again until
monumental expression is attained. Look at the mighty polar
bear standing on an ice hummock roaring out across the desolate
wastes, or that picture of the polar night and the aurora borealis
in *In Northern Mists.* An ode in black and white to the poetry of
the Arctic, a basic harmony in Nansen's artist soul.

He was always very much interested in art and had an
understanding, too, of the modern movement. He was, for instance, one of the first to buy the paintings of Edvard Munch,
when that artist was still regarded as an innovator, and he
helped a number of artists. He did not play any musical instrument, but he loved music, especially Eva's songs. When he
looked at the aurora in the arctic sky he longed for creative
ability in music.

LAST DAYS AND DEATH

RIGHT up to the last year of his life Nansen remained singularly untouched by age and toil. Half a year before his death, when I last saw him, his figure and personality still bore the stamp of strength and vitality. Among the gifts laid on his cradle were a splendid physique and a richly endowed brain. An all-round and vigorous training of both had given him a peculiarly harmonious development, a rare unity and fusion of physical and intellectual powers, of strength, intelligence, will-power, and character.

To the last his mind was so fertile and rich in ideas that he would have needed the lifetime of a Methuselah to carry them out. Consequently the restricted span of years allotted to man had to be used all the more intensely.

At an age when most men's powers are slackening, he undertook a series of labors beside which the celebrated twelve of Hercules sink into insignificance. These labors in addition to all that he had already performed, undoubtedly overstepped the limits even of his gigantic strength. Added to the burden of the work itself came the impact on a sensitive nature of all the misery with which it brought him in touch. He felt the strain of the suffering particularly when he was forced to stand helpless before it, faced with all the folly, hatred, and cruelty which was frequently its cause. He wore himself out. He refused to allow himself sufficient rest or regular exercise, taking only a brief turn in his bit of primeval forest, his park, with his four-footed companions. When in his later years he managed on rare occasions to tear himself away and get out to the mountains, he would forget his years, forget that he was out of training, and exert himself in a way that was scarcely restful for a weak heart.

Of the last skiing trip to the mountains, Worm-Müller writes that Nansen was more tired than usual. He who always used to be far ahead now dropped so far behind his companions that they went back for him. They found Nansen standing quietly down in the grove beside a birch tree leaning on his staff. He did not say anything, but there was a resigned expression on his face. That was at New Year's in 1930. In February he became ill of phlebitis of the foot. A clot of blood in his lung almost caused his death.

Fridtjof Nansen recovered and gradually began to resume his work. On May 13 at noon he was sitting out on the verandah after his morning tea enjoying the sight of the blossoming trees in the garden below and chatting with his son Odd's wife. Suddenly his head fell forward on his breast. His daughter-in-law ran over to him and raised his head. He was dead.

On board the *Fram* he had written of death in his diary: "It will come one day vast and silent, opening the heavy portal of Nirvana, and you will be washed away on the sea of eternity."

If it were his wish that it should come so, death, vast and silent, that wish was fulfilled.

On Tuesday May 13 at 12.45 p.m. Fridtjof Nansen died.

The news of his death came like an unexpected bolt of lightning. Although people knew that he had been seriously ill, they were quite unprepared for his death. They could not believe that *he* was gone—he who was so strong, so indispensable.

Seldom or never has the sorrow of a nation been so much a sorrow of love. And it was more than a national grief. A whole world mourned.

His funeral took place on the Seventeenth of May, Norway's Constitution Day. On that day Nansen was to have made the speech of the occasion at Oslo as he had done twenty-five years before, when all minds were tense in the shadow of coming events, looking towards "the milk white light where a star will break forth," as Wergeland expressed it. In 1905 he addressed the greatest assembly of people the country had ever seen.

Constitution Day 1930 was consecrated not by his speech but by his life as a whole. Nansen's saga, a great and brilliant chapter in the saga of Norway herself. It glowed in all our hearts on that day, a saga with pictures that will never fade. . . .

We remember the old Norwegian in Australia who used occasionally to come down to the Nordmannslag Hall. He sat and stared at the wall of portraits; his eyes glided from one to another till they reached Nansen's. There they lingered a long time, and finally he said: "When we ordinary folk die, we shall be gone and forgotten, but he yonder, he can never die; for he will be remembered as long as there are human beings on the earth." He had followed Nansen's career from a distant corner of the world and had estimated his worth. He saw more clearly perhaps just on account of the distance.

For us here at home some distance of time will be required before we are able to measure the dimensions of the mountain to which we were so near. His death came upon us so suddenly that we are compelled to draw back in order to get a survey. We did not have here the perspective which the eye has of a man who is done with life. He was in the center of the current of life right here in our midst.

OUT ON the steps of the central hall of the University, between the columns, stood the coffin covered with the flag of Norway.

A sea of people, at least 100,000, filled the University square and the adjacent streets and squares. It was a touching sight to see the procession of children from all the schools of Oslo as they filed silently past the catafalque. All the usual music and

THE NANSEN PASS

THE FUNERAL PROCESSION

cheers were hushed, flags and banners were lowered, eyes sought and rested upon the flag-covered bier, as the steps of the children became slower and softer.

Exactly at 1 o'clock came the heavy salute from Akershus announcing two minutes silence. Every noise was stilled, automobiles and trolleys stopped, all pedestrians halted, all hats were removed and heads were bowed—only the song of the birds from Studenterlunden and the cooing of doves were heard through the silence.

The Philharmonic Orchestra opened the ceremony with Grieg's funeral march. Three official speakers followed. The Prime Minister, the last of the speakers, concluded his speech with Anders Hovden's beautiful poem: "My life with courage glad I gave."

Then the silence was broken by "Yes we love the land that towers," the national anthem, sung by the whole multitude— an impressive moment.

To the strains of Grieg's "I laid me down so late," the bier was placed on the carriage with the four black horses. An endless procession followed to Nansen's last resting place.

CHRONOLOGICAL TABLE

1861. October 10. Fridtjof Nansen born at Store Fröen in Vestre Aker.
1880. Matriculation examination.
1881. Senior matriculation. Student of zoology.
1882. March—July, on the sealer *Viking* to the Arctic.
       August, appointed curator at Bergen Museum.
1884. Ski trip from Voss to Christiania and back.
1886. Studied at the biological station at Naples.
1888. Dr. phil. May—September, Greenland expedition.
1888—89. Wintered in Greenland.
1889. Appointed curator in the Zootomical Institute at Christiania University.
       Married Eva Sars.
1893. June 24, departure of the *Fram*.
1895. March 14, dash for the Pole on ski. April 7, reached 86° 14'.
1896. June 17, meeting with Jackson.
       The Nansen Fund established.
1897. Professor of zoology at the University. Work on the scientific results of
       the *Fram* expedition. Lecture tours in Europe and America.
1900. First oceanic research expedition on the *Michael Sars*.
       Oceanographic conference in Stockholm.
       International committee on oceanography.
1905. Articles, speeches, and negotiations at home and abroad.
1906—08. Norway's Minister to England.
1907. Death of Fru Eva Nansen.
1908. Professor of oceanography.
1912. Scientific expedition to Spitzbergen.
1913. Trip through the Arctic Ocean to Siberia and by rail to Vladivostok.
1917. June, to May 1918. In Washington as head of the Commission negotiating
       the American Agreement.
1919. President of the Norwegian Union for the League of Nations.
       In Paris and London to discuss Norway's entry into the League of Nations.
       Attempt to procure food for Russia.
       Chosen as chairman of the permanent arbitration commission for the British
       Empire and the United States of America.
       Married Fru Sigrun Munthe, née Sandberg.
1920. Norwegian delegate to the League of Nations.
       April. Entrusted by the League of Nations with the repatriation of war
       prisoners.
1921. June. Entrusted by the League of Nations with the care of Russian refugees.
       The Nansen passport.
       August. Relief work for the starving Russians.
1922. February. Lecture tours in Europe and America to collect means for the
       relief work in Russia.
       September. Relief work for Greek and Armenian refugees.
       December. The Nobel Peace Prize.
1923. The Corfu affair in the League of Nations.
1923—24. Trip through the United States and Canada as representative of the World's
       Alliance for International Friendship through the Churches, and as High
       Commissioner of the League of Nations for the economic reconstruction of
       Greece.
1924. Work for the admission of Germany to the League of Nations.
       President of Aëro Arctic.
1925. Leader of a commission to Armenia and the Caucasus.

1926. Lord Rector of St. Andrew's University in Scotland.
1928. Trip to America on behalf of the Armenians.
1929. Lectured in America on "Why the Arctic Calls Me Again"; preparation for the *Graf Zeppelin* expedition.
Chairman in the council for the Chr. Michelsen Institute.
1930. May 13. Fridtjof Nansen died.
May 17. His funeral.

BOOKS, TREATISES, AND SELECTED ARTICLES BY FRIDTJOF NANSEN

1884. Skisse av et isfjell under kysten af Öst-Grönland. *Nyt magasin for naturvidenskab.*
Langs Grönlands Östkyt. *Geogr. Tidsskrift* (Danish).
En skitur fra Voss til Kristiania og tilbake. *Aftenposten*, Oslo.
1885. Bidrag til myzoostomernes anatomi og histologi. Bergen Museum.
1886. Forelöbig meddelelse om undersögelser over centralnervesystemets histologiske bygning hos ascidierne samt hos Myxine glutinosa.—Bergen Museum.
The structure and combination of the histological elements of the central nervous system. Bergen Museum.
1887. Nerveelementer, deres struktur og sammenheng i centralnervesystemet. (Doctoral thesis) Nordisk medicinsk Arkiv.
Om hvirveldyrenes tredje öie, panneöiet. *Naturen.*
Om drivisen, dens dannelse og transport. *Naturen.*
Den zoologiske station i Neapel. *Naturen.*
Protandric Hermafrodite amongst the vertebrates. Bergen Museum.
Lavtstaaende dyrs og planters naturhistorie.
1888. Grönlands indlandsis. *Naturen.*
Grönlands indbyggere. *Naturen.*
1890. Paa ski over Grönland. En skildring af den norske Grönlands-ekspedition 1888-89. Ill. H. Aschehoug & Co.
Plan til en ny polarekspedition. *Naturen.*
1891. Eskimoliv. Ill. af Otto Sinding. H. Aschehoug & Co.
Fra Grönlandsfærden. Det norske geogr. selskabs aarbog.
1892. Om den kommende Nordpolsekspedition og dens udrustning.
Wissenschaftliche Ergebnisse von dr. Nansens Durchquerung von Grönland 1888. Von Prof. H. Mohn und Dr. Fr. Nansen. *Petermanns Mitteilungen*, Gotha.
1893. Dr. Fr. Nansens polarekspedition. *Kringsjaa.*
Fra barneaarene. *Illustreret Tidende for Börn.*
How can the North Polar region be crossed? *World Magazine.*
1894. On the development and structure of the Whale. Part 1. On the development of the Delphin by Gustav Guldberg and Fridtjof Nansen. Bergen Museum.
1897. Fram over Polhavet. Den norske polarfærd 1893-96. Med et tillæg af Otto Sverdrup. I/II 1897. H. Aschehoug & Co.
1900. Karakter og idealitet. In *Om opdragelse og undervisning*, by Hulda Garborg and others.
1901. Some oceanogr. Results of the Expedition with the *Michael Sars.* Headed by dr. J. Hjort in the summer 1900. Preliminary Report by Fr. Nansen.
1900. The Norwegian North Polar Expedition 1893-96. Scientific results ed. by Fridtjof Nansen. Vol. I/IV. Kra. 1900-06. (J. Dybwad.) Oceanography of the North Polar Basin, 1902.
1902. On hydrometers and the surface tension of liquids.
1904. Was ist Todwasser? (Discussion between H. Mejer and Fr. Nansen.)
1905. Die Ursachen der Meeresströmungen. *Petermanns Mitteilungen.*
Bathymetrical Features of the North Polar Sea, with a discussion of the

continental Shelves and the Previous Oscillations of the Shore-line.
Review—From the American Geologist.
Hvad nu? *Samtiden.*
Veien. *Verdens Gang*, Feb. 12.
Mænd. *Verdens Gang*, Feb. 15.
Mot. *Verdens Gang*, Feb. 18.
Letsindighet. *Verdens Gang*, Sept. 24.
Vilje. *Verdens Gang*, March 2.
Unionssagen. *Verdens Gang*, March 26.
    Times—London, March 26.
    Le Temps—Paris, March 26.
    Kölnische Zeitung, March 26.
Norge og foreningen med Sverige. 7. Juni. Jacob Dybwad, translated into English, German and French.
Hvad vi vil. *Verdens Gang*, Sept. 24.
Heltemot. *Verdens Gang*, Oct. 6.
Svar til Sven Hedin. *Verdens Gang*, Oct. 13.

1906. Northern Waters: Captain Roald Amundsen's oceanographic observations in the Arctic Seas in 1901, with a discussion of the origin of the bottom-waters of the Northern Seas. Kra. Videnskabsselskabet.

1907. On North Polar Problems. *The Geogr. Journal.* London.

1908. Videnskab og moral. Speech upon becoming president of the Social and Political Education League in London. *Samtiden.*

1909. I dagens spörsmaal. Form—ikke indhold. Indflyttere. Sprog. Artiums-stil i "Landsmaal." Reprints from *Verdens Gang* (Narvesen).

1910. Foredrag over Vinland, med diskusjon. Oversikt over Videnskapsselskapets möter.

1910–11. Nord I Tåkeheimen. Utforskningen av jordens nordlige strök i tidlige tider. Illustr. Jacob Dybwad.

1911. Norsemen in America. *The Geogr. Journal.* London.

1912. The race for the South Pole. *Scribner's Magazine*, New York.
Das Bodenwasser und die Abkühlung des Meeres. *Internationale Revue der gesamten Hydrographie.*
Die Entdeckung Amerikas durch die Nordmänner. Reprint from *Zeitschrift der Gesellschaft fur Erdkunde.* Berlin.
De oceanografiske undersökelser gjort med Fram i Nordatlanteren 1910 og Sydatlanteren 1911. Av Bj. Helland-Hansen og Fridtjof Nansen.
Særtrykk av R. Amundsen: Sydpolen.

1914. Fjellhilder: löse dagboksblade. Norge 1814-1914, b. 2. Cammermeyers Forlag.
Gjennem Sibirien. Illustr. Jacob Dybwad.

1915. För det blir forsent. Jacob Dybwad.
Spitsbergen Waters. Oceanographic observations during the cruise of the "Veslemöy" to Spitsbergen in 1912. Videnskapsselskapet.

1916. Friluftsliv. Blade av dagboken. Jacob Dybwad.
Temperaturschwankungen des nordatlantischen Oceans und in der Atmosphäre av B. Helland-Hansen og Fr. Nansen. Videnskapsselskapet, Kristania.

1917. Nordens stilling og opgaver under og efter krigen. *Samtiden.*
The Food Situation of Norway. The Annals of the American Academy of Political and Social Science. Philadelphia.

1918. Dyrk ditt land! *Norsk Landmandsblad.*
Lecture in oceanic and atmospheric temperatures and their relation to changes in the sun's activity. Report: Washington Academy of Sciences.

1918–19. Amerikansk idealisme. *Atlantis.*

1919. Oprop til beste for Wien og Tysk-Österrike. *Tidens Tegn.*
Nasjonenes Forbund og forsvaret. Vår hær.
Vekslinger i solens virksombet og i jordens klima. *Teknisk Ukeblad.*

1920. Spitsbergens opdagelse. *Naturen.*
Rob. Edv. Peary. *Naturen.*
En ferd til Spitsbergen. Billeder og karter av forfatteren. Jacob Dybwad.
The strandflat and isostasy. With 170 illustr. Videnskabsselskapet.

1921. Tale i Genf 30. Sept. Utenrikspolitikken.
Das frühere Klima Spitsbergens. *Die Umschau.* Frankfurt am Main.
1922. Hjelp til de hungrende i Russland. Foredrag holdt i Europas storbyer. *Politiken.* Copenhagen.
Friluftsliv. En tale til ungdommen. *Kra. Turistforeningens Årbok.*
Næstekjærlighet. *Samtiden.*
Om Russland. *Politiken.*
1923. Russland og freden. Illustr. Jacob Dybwad.
Russland og freden. 12 artikler i *Tidens Tegn.*
1923. Flyktninger. *Politiken.*
International Co-operation the only Way. *Christian Work.*
Russia 1923. *The New Republic.*
Europe and the hope of Peace. An estimate of Europe's need and an appreciation of America's help. *Our Work.*
Fred. Tale i Nobel Instituttet. *Samtiden.*
1924. On the France-Germany Situation. *The Cosmopolitan Student,* Syracuse.
Tilstande i Europa og Folkenes Forbund. Tale. *Politiken.*
Grönlandssaken. *Politiken.*
Blant sel og björn. Min förste ishavsferd. Billeder og karter av forfatteren. Jacob Dybwad.
1925. Nordboerne i Grönland. *Politiken.*
Fedrelandslaget. Tale. Fedrelandslagets Forlag. Oslo.
Det armenske folk. *Tidens Tegn.*
Utforskning av de ukjente arktiske strök. *Tidens Tegn. Arktis.*
The oceanogr. problems of the still unknown Arctic regions. *American Geogr. Society.*
Klima-vekslinger i Nordens historie. Videnskabsselskapet.
1926. Nationalisme og Voldgiftsaftaler. *Politiken.*
Eventyrlyst. Tale holdt som rektor ved St. Andrews Universitet 3. Nov. Jacob Dybwad.
Klimavekslinger i historisk og postglacial tid. Videnskaps-Akademiet.
1927. Die Wissenschaftliche Notwendigkeit arktischer Forschung. *Petermanns Mitteilungen.*
Eventyrlyst.—Ingen krig mere! To taler. Jacob Dybwad.
Gjennem Armenia. Illustr. Jacob Dybwad.
1928. På ski over Grönland. Omarbeidet utg. og illustr. H. Aschehoug & Co.
The earth's crust, its surface-forms and isostatic adjustment. Videnskaps-Akademiet.
Vorschlag für ein Telt aus Segeltuch mit Schneepackung für Polarstation. *Arktis.* Gotha.
Science and purpose of life. *Hibbert Journal.* Boston.
Minnetale over Amundsen. *Norsk geogr. Tidsskrift.*
Det nordiske samarbeide. *Norden.*
Die Gleichgewichtbewegungen der Erdkruste und die Oberflächen der Kontinente. Forschungen und Fortschritte. Berlin.
Et nytt Norge. Tale. Fedrelandslagets Forlag.
1929. Rescuing millions of war victims. *Current History.* New York.
Gjennem Kaukasus til Volga. Illustr. Jacob Dybwad.
What I believe. *Forum,* New York.
Ved årsskiftet. *Politiken.*
Arbeidet for krigsfanger og flyktninger. "Folkeforbundets förste ti-år," published by the Danish Foreign Department, Copenhagen.
1930. Over Grönland og Polhavet. Minneutgave I-II. Fram over Polhavet. Förste del. Illustr. H. Aschehoug & Co.
Nansen's speeches in the Assembly of the League of Nations are found in Actes de la 1.—l'Ome Assemblée 1920-29. Séances plénieres et séances des commissions (Geneve Service des publications de la Société des Nations).
Discussions on Armenia to 1926 are in Plan de l'éstablissement des Réfugies Arméniens. Exposé general et documents principaux. Publications de la S. d. N. Questions sociales 1927 IV, I.
Til Mauds menn. Tale. *Norge II.*

ENGLISH TRANSLATIONS
(WORKS ORIGINALLY PUBLISHED IN ENGLISH ARE FOUND IN
THE PRECEDING LIST)

1890. The First Crossing of Greenland. London, Longmans. 2 vols.
1893. Eskimo Life. London, Longmans.
1897. Farthest North. New York, Harper. 2 vols.
1905. Norway and the Union with Sweden. London, New York, Macmillan.
1911. In Northern Mists. New York, Stokes. 2 vols.
1914. Through Siberia, the Land of the Future. New York, Stokes.
1920. Temperature variations in the north Atlantic Ocean and in the atmosphere, introductory studies on the cause of climatological variations, by Björn Helland-Hansen and Fridtjof Nansen. City of Washington, Smithsonian Institution. (Smithsonian miscellaneous collections, v. 70, no. 4.)
1923. Russia and Peace. London, G. Allen & Unwin.
1925. Hunting and Adventure in the Arctic. New York, Duffield & Co.
Sporting Days in Wild Norway; pages from my Diary. London, T. Butterworth.
1927. Adventure, and Other Papers. London, L. & V. Woolf.
1928. Armenia and the Near East. London, G. Allen & Unwin.
1931. Through the Caucasus to the Volga. New York, W. W. Norton.

BIBLIOGRAPHY

Fr. Hammerich: Hans Nansen. Copenhagen 1858.
Louis Bobé: Hans Nansen's Efterslægt. Copenhagen.
Brögger and Rolfsen: Fridtjof Nansen 1861-93. 1896.
Jacob B. Bull: Fridtjof Nansen. 1897.
Fridtjof Nansen. Written to commemorate his homecoming in 1896.
Ann Margret Holmgren: Fridtjof Nansen, I-II. Stockholm 1922.
Jens Marinius Jensen: Fridtjof Nansen. 1926.
J. H. Whitehouse: Fridtjof Nansen. An Homage. 1930.
Fritz Wartenweiler: Fridtjof Nansen. Zürich 1930.
Elsa Brändström: Bland krigsfanger i Ryssland och Sibirien 1914-1928.
Ernst Didring: Sveriges Hjälp till Krigsfång arna 1915-19.
Tidsskrift for Det danske Röde Kors 1922 and 1923.
Det Norske Stortings Nobelkomite: Redegjörelse for Nobels fredspris. 1922.
Morgenbladet 1922, December 11: (Fredsprisutdelingen).
Hjälp Russland. Published by Centr. Hjälpkomite. Stockholm 1922.
The American-Scandinavian Review. 1928, 1931.
Dansk Tidsskrift for Folkeoplysning. 1927, 1931.
Geogr. Aarbok (Swedish), 1930.
Svenska Dagbladet, July 15, 1931.
Urd. 1930.
Norsk Kirkeblad, 1930.
Kirke og Kultur, 1930.
Skiforeningens aarbok, 1930.
Christiania Skiklubbs Julilæumsbok. 1877-1920.
B. A. Nissen's and S. C. Hammer's books about events in 1905.
Worm-Müller: 1905.—Samtiden, 1931.
Nordens Aarbok, 1930: Bj. Helland-Hansen: Fridtjof Nansen.
Memorial address by Björn Helland-Hansen in the Academy of Sciences.
Samtiden, 1930: Articles by E. Werenskiold, Ph. N. Baker, S. Torup, Knud Rasmussen, Emil Smith.
Newspaper cuttings of the University and the Whaling Museum, 1930.
Archives of the Department of Foreign Affairs in the League of Nations office.

Folkeforbundet första Ti-aar. Det danske Utenriks-departement.
Reports of the League of Nations on relief work.

THE FOLLOWING WERE ALSO USED AS SOURCES:

Nansen's books, treatises, articles, and lectures.
Nansen's archives regarding relief work.
Manuscripts of lectures in oceanography.
Nansen's diaries from 1905. Other diaries.

INDEX

COMMITTEE ON PUBLICATIONS